The Unraveling of Scientism

The Unraveling of Scientism

*American Philosophy at
the End of the Twentieth Century*

Joseph Margolis

Cornell University Press

Ithaca and London

First published 2003 by Cornell University Press

Printed in the United States of America

Library of Congress Cataloging-in-Publication Data

Margolis, Joseph
    The unraveling of scientism : American philosophy at the end of the twentieth century / Joseph Margolis.
        p.   cm.
Includes bibliographical references (p.   ) and index.
    ISBN 0-8014-4152-8
    1. Analysis (Philosophy)—United States—History—20th century.
2. Philosophy, American—20th century.   I. Title.
    B944.A53M27 2003
    191—dc21

                                            2003005453

Cornell University Press strives to use environmentally responsible suppliers and materials to the fullest extent possible in the publishing of its books. Such materials include vegetable-based, low-VOC inks and acid-free papers that are recycled, totally chlorine-free, or partly composed of nonwood fibers. For further information, visit our website at www.cornellpress.cornell.edu.

Cloth printing   10 9 8 7 6 5 4 3 2 1

for the pleasure of asking and answering

Contents

Preface

I recall attending an annual meeting of the American something-or-other society for the study of the classical world ("in all respects") sometime in the middle '60s, in Cincinnati, Ohio. The University of Cincinnati had a first-rate classics department. My friend, Hamish Cameron, a colleague at the University and a member of the department, thought it would amuse me to see how things were done. We found ourselves at one point in a largish conference room ready for cocktails. It seemed as if everyone could have taken a seat in an easy chair in that one room. Cameron began to identify some of the luminaries. "Do you remember that debate?" he asked. I don't really remember the precise topic, but it must have been related to an up-to-date version of the Quarrel-between-the-Ancients-and-the-Moderns. He then defined two "positions" which seemed to collect two great legions of academics pitted heroically against one another over what might have been an age. "Well, the first is the opinion of that man over there"—pointing him out—"and the other is the view of that man"—now pointing to the other end of the room. Suddenly the scale of the sort of debates one only reads about quickly shrank to their actual size. I started thinking that even Plato's *Dialogues* were really based only on chance remarks in fortuitous conversations on a very small number of occasions. Cameron had identified the editors of two learned journals, who pursued their personal harangue in the pages of their own properties.

The philosophical academy is not quite so small, I admit; but it *is* still rather on the small side, if you compare it with other university disciplines. For example, it takes three or four very large hotels, in the largest cities, to house the meetings of the American Psychological Association, whereas the professional philosophers tend to fit nicely into one moderately sized hotel even in the smaller cities. The United States itself is an immensely large country that has supported a professoriat (in philosophy) that runs into the thousands. Nevertheless, when you read the leading disputes, or reports and analyses of what they are said to have accomplished, which seem to engage the attention of the entire guild, you cannot help noticing that a very small handful of figures dominate the entire discourse—they appear to be everywhere—possibly stitching together the general drift of all the conversations we might collect in a way not terribly different from the way the figure we know as Socrates unifies the *Dialogues*. One needs some such mechanism to catch the unity of the changing fashions of debate, especially where the issues are somewhat abstruse and often threatened by an uncertain logic. That is what I have sought to define in *The Unraveling of Scientism*.

American philosophy achieved its best standing and greatest influence only in the second half of the twentieth century. It was hardly more than a minor, respectable presence in Eurocentric philosophy in the first half of the century, largely through the reception of the classic pragmatists—chiefly, when all is said and done, as a result of John Dewey's enormous energy and productivity. Charles Peirce was undoubtedly a greater figure and William James was plainly more magnetic. But Peirce was all but unknown, and James was disinclined to be systematic in his philosophy. There would have been no well-formed movement known as pragmatism were it not for Dewey's indefatigable labors.

That's not unimportant to my story, because, in the second half of the last century, American philosophy divides oppositionally along the lines of pragmatism and what we now call analytic philosophy. The same cast of characters dominates the narratives of both movements but with very different weightings. As far as pragmatism goes, as that has come to be understood, the leading pragmatists of the "second wave" (self-styled and flawed) are surely Richard Rorty and Hilary Putnam; but you cannot understand what happened from the 1970s to the end of the century and what the resurgence of pragmatism meant (in the period in question) without examining the relationship between Rorty and Putnam and the leading American analysts, Donald Davidson and W. V. Quine. For related reasons, the altered energies of American analytic philosophy, after mid-century, came to be dominated by Quine's large presence and, increasingly, though also more quarrelsomely, by Davidson's more cautious efforts. You cannot really penetrate what their work signifies without at least reviewing *their* reception by the latter-day "pragmatists" Rorty and Putnam and the late resurgence of new versions of the scientistic reading of the philosophy of science.

I concede that it is something of a distortion to advance the idea that the entire fifty years of the end-of-century and a bit of the twenty-first should be occupied primarily with the work of no more than four men. And although I myself don't think it's true, I also don't think anyone could give a rounded sense of the significance of what was accomplished (in the period, which has just been made part of the past) if one didn't feature just these four philosophers. Certainly, they are hardly figures of equal standing. Quine is assuredly the most important, viewed in terms of the permanence of his contribution. I have no doubt that his paper "Two Dogmas of Empiricism" (1951), together with *Word and Object* (1960), will influence the technical treatment of strategic topics long after the other three settle into footnotes. But even Quine's fortunes come under severe fire in the period in question, and it remains to be said what of permanent importance Quine finally contributed. The entire span of American philosophy in any sense close to contemporary taste hardly goes back before the end of the Civil War. So it is worth noting that it might not unfairly be claimed to have reached its zenith among the most salient Eurocentric currents only in the second half of the twentieth century. All the more reason to ask how compelling its best work really is.

I sensed the importance of writing a manageable sketch of both pragmatism and analytic philosophy (for the period in question) sometime during the last five years of the last century. It's risky, of course, to report in a detailed way on one's own time even if, as Hegel believed, philosophy, like art and history, is the expression of an age remembered in its own time. The validity of such a tale normally requires a much greater temporal distance. Though I think much of its detail and interest would have been lost if the sketch had waited politely for another generation to pass.

In any event, the original plan took the form of two separate studies: the first, *Pragmatism Reinvented*, appeared earlier (2002); the second, *The Unraveling of Scientism* (2003), now joins the first, which colors and is colored by the other. I don't know of any similarly sustained attempt, and I admit that, in offering my assessment, I am hardly a disinterested party. But then, philosophy is a partisan matter, which the recent history of American philosophy amply bears out. I would say that "objectivity" is a function of an ongoing contest between informed partisans. Here we are not very far from what Cameron noted in the conference we visited. But of course this doesn't mean that we cannot distinguish between good and bad arguments. Nevertheless, it does suggest that the effort is not as easy as it may seem.

I felt the need, I should add, to work quite quickly, to catch all the important philosophical beads on a reliable string before they were scattered like the exceptional ephemera that they really are. I felt the need particularly in writing about the "second wave" of pragmatism—about Rorty's and Putnam's papers. But it proved impossible as well to make sense of Davidson's continuation of, and reaction to, Quine's new leadership among the American "analysts" without capturing the sense in which Davidson played a muted role in the seemingly independent quarrels between Rorty and Putnam. That very qualification could not have been reliably identified without demonstrating just how Davidson's own philosophical program really counts Quine as its principal target, despite the fact that it seems at first to be so very close to Quine's project.

You can imagine how complicated the final story would have to be, hostage as it was to the peculiar transience of all the philosophical turns of the period. Davidson tries to steer Quine in his direction, but Quine resists; Quine engages the important scientisms of the first half of the century (distantly, it's true), but Davidson hardly discusses them at all; Davidson and Rorty never find more than uncertain common ground (which Rorty makes much more of than Davidson), though you cannot finally say just who is cannibalizing whom; Putnam is closest to Carnap's original concerns and those of the early strands of the philosophy of science, but American analytic philosophy increasingly marginalizes its original questions without abandoning or legitimating its insistent scientism; Rorty attempts to characterize Quine as a postmodernist of sorts, but Quine publicly demurs. The entire tale demands a careful reckoning. Yet that reckoning could not have been attempted, so soon after the event, without relying on a sense of a very small number of very small conversations overheard by an entire continent—as well as abroad. Through it all, one begins to hear American voices speculating about the prospects of ending their isolation, of forming alliances with Europe.

Now that I've completed the labor, I venture to say—in a friendly way—that the record of the last half-century is, philosophically, largely a record of the dawning exhaustion of an impressive vision (scientism) and the incompletely developed, still somewhat inchoate, possibilities of a promising alternative philosophy (pragmatism). The strength of the latter lies, I think, in being closer to the corrective lessons of the post-Kantian and post-Hegelian world that never lost sight of the inescapable strategy by which to escape the paradoxes of pre-Kantian philosophy. The analytic tradition has, of course, a longer and more brilliant record. But, truth to tell, it has never managed to overcome the nagging *aporiai* of what is now read as Cartesianism.

My sense is that only the combined talents of the pragmatist and analyst could possibly make a reasonably complete American philosopher and that only such a figure would be comfortable enough to reestablish communications with the important work of the continental European world or promote discussions with the Asian world. The exhaustion I speak of is, surely, also Eurocentric, as much British as continental. I'll make no prophecies of what our century may now expect. Except to say that perceived exhaustion is not a bad thing to spot when it is really there. For then, reasonable philosophers, like reasonable politicians, will try to think more carefully of the now-global setting of their future labors.

I must, before I begin, thank Ruth Brooks for her usual skill and reliability in putting my manuscripts in good order; also, Roger Haydon at Cornell University Press, whom I count a friend and reliable adviser; finally, an anonymous reader for the Press who gave me some very good suggestions about improving the book.

J.M.

Philadelphia
July 2002

Acknowledgments

All of the chapters previously commissioned for publication or presentation as lectures have undergone changes to some extent, some to a considerable extent. "Anticipation of a Final Reckoning" was first published in *Facta Philosophica*, vol. 4, no. 1 (2002), pp. 51–66. "Materialism by Less than Adequate Means" was first presented as the Marx W. Wartofsky Lecture (2001) at the City University of New York, New York City; a shortened version was also presented at the Academy of Sciences in Moscow, Russia, Spring 2000. It has appeared, in a Russian translation, in *Voprosi Filosofii* (2002) and, in English, in *Idealistic Studies* 32, no. 3 (2002): 1–19. "Incommensurability Modestly Recovered" was first presented in a conference, "Incommunsurability (and Related Matters)," at the University of Hannover, Hannover, Germany, Summer 1999. "Restoring the Bond between Realism and Truth" and "The Unraveling of Scientism" have previously appeared only as part of the Spanish translation of the full text of *The Unraveling of Scientism* (Oviedo: Nobel Ediciones, 2002).

The Unraveling of Scientism

First Word
Anticipation of a Final Reckoning

I

American philosophy passed through two distinct depressions by the middle of the twentieth century. Both were reversed by the 1970s. And both recoveries have been sustained through the beginning of the new century. One of the declines was almost total, an eclipse of interest in the classic pragmatists by the 1940s and early 1950s, completing a strong first phase of nearly eighty years. The other turn-down was centered in the apparent failure of the grand systems of analytic philosophy formulated largely through (or even before) the first third of the last century by figures like Gottlob Frege, Bertrand Russell, Ludwig Wittgenstein, and Rudolf Carnap. Both declines may well have been fueled by social events somewhat distant from professional concerns: the end of World War II for instance, the lengthening Cold War, the revival of normal life following the War itself. Even the unprecedented success of the so-called (American) G.I. Bill (for the state-supported education of veterans), which profoundly altered the composition of the faculty and students of the American university world, surely affected the perception of our philosophical options.

In any case, both pragmatism and analytic philosophy rallied, regained their stride, however differently, in a startlingly short time. Almost without anticipation, pragmatism revived in the 1970s as a result largely of a running quarrel between Richard Rorty and Hilary Putnam, though it remains widely disputed as to whether what is now associated with Rorty's name is indeed rightly regarded as a revival of pragmatism.[1] The grand systems of analytic philosophy faded well before pragmatism did. The atomisms and the extensionalist materialisms of Russell, the positivists, the unity of science program all simply collapsed as a result of internal weaknesses that could not be satisfactorily patched or papered over. They were, it seems, precocious in vision, deficient in resources, and damned by basic errors that all who cared could see. Logicism's failure sealed the fate of Frege's and Russell's programs; and the insuperable difficulties of the theory of meaning and meaningfulness sealed the fate of positivism. Pragmatism suddenly seemed outmoded, and early analytic philosophy was filled with well-deserved self-doubt—that is, until each acquired a new voice and a new champion.

Certainly, the great analytic systems overreached themselves. The unity movement could never actually demonstrate the unity of science, whether by methodology or internal relations among the laws of nature or the conceptual adequacy of materialism itself; and, according to the clichéd verdict, the positivists could never show the meaningfulness of their own account of meaning. The failure of the pragmatists was much less interesting, except perhaps for the brute fact of failure within the American heartland. Certainly, pragmatism's near-demise did not depend on its being led astray by its technical proficiency. For the pragmatists hardly deigned, in the last moments of their heyday, to master the skills the analysts had made so much of. Frankly, they were outclassed even when their arguments and questions were palpably better than their rivals'. The analysts were obliged to face their own transparent mistakes; the pragmatists could only acknowledge their dwindling relevance—let us be frank, their inertia.

Rorty, we may say, obliged the revivified pragmatists—the movement he himself revived—to attend to the fresh work of the post-Quinean analysts, even though *their* best work and *his* postmodernist provocations could hardly have been reconciled with the best work of the original pragmatists. By contrast, W. V. Quine, who was largely responsible for reorienting American analytic philosophy in the 50s and 60s, explicitly opposed, or turned away from, the fatal topics of the earlier British and Continental masters.

Rorty's best effort amounted to reacquainting the pragmatists with the best work of their own analytic contemporaries. Quine's contribution was always more substantive and more far-reaching: preeminently, *(a)* in the exposé of the analytic/synthetic dogma in Quine's deservedly admired "Two Dogmas" paper (1951)—in effect, completely dismantling the centerpiece of Carnap's philosophy (or so it seemed[2]); but also *(b)* in the dismissal of the would-be subtleties of the positivist theory of meaning in favor of a commonsense semantics (obfuscated, perhaps deliberately, by a behaviorist overlay of pretended precision) that cleverly entrenched the extensionalist objectives Quine openly shared with his predecessors; *(c)* in the easy acceptance of logicism's failure; *(d)* in his opposition to any foundationalist assumptions; *(e)* in the replacement of any specific empiricist scruple regarding the theory of meaning or evidence by programmatic rehearsals of the extensionalist and materialist conception of science; *(f)* by a tolerant pluralism (even a relativism)—really a constructivism—regarding alternative ontologies and epistemologies, so long as they could be extensionally regimented by way of that marvelous (but baffling) trick of the "indeterminacy of translation" thesis of *Word and Object* (1960);[3] and *(g)* in the utterly relaxed refusal to treat as particularly significant the preference for either the material or semantic mode of analysis over the other, beyond the fact of ensuring that choice itself. In all these matters, Quine was bent on recovering what could be saved of positivism from the positivists themselves that might be thought to derive from his own informal sketches of the formal resources of a first-order logic.

In this way, Quine breathed new life into American analytic philosophy—and, ineluctably, into analytic philosophy worldwide. Succeeding there, he became the indisputable don of the second half of the century. The grand visions of the earlier analysts morphed into leaner programs, whether or not led by Quine's own example. The newer enthusiasts turned to piecemeal trials cast more often than not as semantic inquiries, though you cannot suppose that the very different work favored by figures like P. F. Strawson, J. L. Austin, Michael Dummett, Donald Davidson, and Jerry Fodor actually shared a common understanding of what "semantic" inquiry signified. The work of all these figures was infected by what Rorty dubbed "the linguistic turn" of the 1950s, which, on his own account, was responsible as well for the sudden decline in interest in pragmatism's first wave.[4]

Quine regularizes our reading of Russell's *Principia* and Frege's initiatives, our reading of the work of the Continental logicians of his younger days (the Germans, the Austrians, the Poles, the Dutch), the reading of the first skilled uses of a formalized idiom fitted to the problems of science and the philosophy of science, even the pioneer work of the closest pragmatists Charles Sanders Peirce and C. I. Lewis. Quine constructs a notably simple and straightforward picture of extensionalist reduction applied to ordinary perception and behavior and enlarged to include, without strain, the technical work of mathematics and the physical sciences. Quite literally, Quine makes the near-unity of Eurocentric logic accessible to the American academy. His great gift lay with his ability to make the analytic nerve of scientism as matter-of-fact as you please; so that, now, at the start of the new century, we cannot fail to notice a surge of fresh interest in the recovery of the same kind of grand systems (now, much altered) that originally opened the twentieth century—for instance, along Darwinian, Chomskyan, and computationalist lines. To my ear, these recent "systems," beginning already in the 60s, sound "post-Quinean," though Quine himself was never (could never have been) a party to any of them. (He had had apparently his fill with the defeated visions of Carnap and Russell.)

It would not be far from the mark to say that the more recent "system-atizers" (the Darwinians and the others) are quite literally committed to the ultimate validity of a "closed universe" read entirely along scientistic lines: that is, read exceptionlessly in extensionalist and materialist terms. You cannot find a comparable commitment in Quine's own work, though Quine shares the same conviction. Quine rarely ventures beyond such carefully worded pronouncements as in this well-known remark: "If we are limning the true and ultimate structure of reality, the canonical scheme for us is the austere scheme that knows no quotation but direct quotation and no propositional attitudes but only the physical constitution and behavior of organisms."[5]

That is Quine's conviction, all right, but it is always offered formulaically. Quine is too much of a "pragmatist" (by his own lights) to place much confidence (or labor) at the disposal of any assured analytic strategy confident about how actually to "limn the true and ultimate structure of reality" in the detailed gauge favored at the start of the century or through the early decades, as in the work of such diverse figures as Pierre Duhem, Henri Poincaré, Hans Reichenbach, and Karl Popper. Our shifting interests and the deep informality with which we fix the meanings of whatever is said—plus, of course, the implacable lesson of the "Two Dogmas" paper—make it more than unlikely that Quine could ever have followed the example of such zealous figures as Daniel Dennett, Paul Churchland, Noam Chomsky, Jerry Fodor, all of whom have returned (in their different ways) to one or another confident full-blown form of scientism. Quine worked primarily by analyzing very shrewdly selected specimen puzzles. He clearly prefers the light guidance of the "true" canon for describing thought and reality over the misguided labor of building toward the final system of the world. There's too much indeterminacy, for Quine, too little in the way of principled fixities, for assurances of the second sort.

It is for this reason that a newer breed of analyst, writing close to the end of the last century and moving on into the new, has turned to Wilfrid Sellars for an alternative inspiration: not Chomsky or Fodor to be sure, who favor a deviant scientism of their own, one of a distinctly Platonist and Cartesian persuasion (though not dualistic) that cannot be reconciled with either Quine's or Sellars's vision and is distinctly less global in its pretensions. Certainly Dennett, Churchland, and Rorty, at the very least, would count as part of the newer breed, since they are essentially eliminativists of Sellars's stripe—Rorty, rather more equivocally than the others, possibly inconsistently as well, since, despite the equivocations, he is responsible for training a new cohort of Sellarsian "pragmatists," preeminently, Robert

Brandom.[6] The "Sellarsian" pragmatists of Rorty's sort never return (nor does Sellars) to the detailed work of the various scientisms of the first half of the century. Indeed, late-century enthusiasts like Dennett and Churchland are remarkably vague about the fresh arguments they mean to provide—in order to restore confidence in one or another full-blown scientism. That is what I mean by the "Quinean" economies that infect the reductionist and eliminativist rigor of the scientisms of the end of the century. Sellars, let be it noted, has no confidence in the philosophical promise of the neurophysiology of the brain.

If you compare the following notorious statement of Sellars's eliminativist vision with what I have just cited from Quine, you begin to see the fresh appeal of the salient forms of recent scientism: "According to the view I am proposing" Sellars says, "correspondence rules would appear in the material mode as statements to the effect that the objects of the observational framework *do not really exist—there really are no such things.* They envisage the *abandonment* of a sense and its denotation."[7] Both Quine and Sellars oppose any foundationalism of the empiricist sort—just compare *Word and Object* with "Empiricism and the Philosophy of Mind." Quine relies on ordinary empirical resources, whereas Sellars rejects (perhaps inconsistently) any such reliance as utterly misguided. In this sense, they cannot possibly share the same sort of scientism. Not only that, but Sellars cannot be made over into a pragmatist of any sort (as Rorty and Brandom pretend to do[8]) except by deliberate deformation—which I'm bound to say both are willing to embrace.

Nevertheless, late analytic philosophy is largely a struggle, within its own terms, between the programmatic and the systematic. Both strands adhere to the canon of materialism and extensionalism. But the first (*per* Quine) relies on interpretive interventions of a distinctly pragmatist cast that cannot be overcome; whereas the second (*per* Sellars) believes that we are now in a position to force a permanent gain on the final theory of reality (that joins the resources of philosophy and science). It is a further irony that Carnap had already favored a programmatic turn, moving, so it may have seemed to Quine himself, in Quine's new direction. It remained only for Quine to capture the loyalties of American analysts at midcentury, which of course he did by dint of his treatment of the analytic/synthetic issue.

II

I leave the peccadillos aside in order to get clear about the principal contest. The point of essential interest remains the parsing of "scientism" itself. (I use the term in an unqualifiedly derogatory sense; we shall have to see whether its application is justified.) Eliminativism is, of course, the most extreme form of scientism that we know: it signifies, as Sellars says, the "abandonment" of our commonsense idiom, "the manifest image," as he calls it, *in favor of* the idiom and orientation of Science ("the scientific image").[9] Scientism, therefore, is hardly meant to be confined to a skepticism about commonsense discourse; it signifies, rather, the assurance of a deeper and more reliable access to ultimate reality. That is the connecting theme to the naive reductionism Carnap once favored early in his positivist career.[10] You cannot find its match in Quine or, say, in the alternative "positivism" of a theorist like Pierre Duhem, from whom Quine draws a "holist" scruple noticeably more labile than anything Duhem's methodology would ever favor.[11] Quine's holism is surely incompatible with Sellars's curious characterization, *meditations hegeliennes*, regarding his own "Empiricism and the Philosophy of Mind."[12] At best, that juxtaposition betrays the unresolved equivocation of Sellars's own convictions, which, for example, Dennett and Churchland on the one side and Brandom and Rorty on the other have exploited in very different ways.

In this delicately balanced sense, it makes sense to collect Sellars, the early Carnap, the Tractarian Wittgenstein, Dennett and Churchland as wedded to one or another form of scientism, though not to one another's particular thesis. "Scientism" signifies the assured possession of a privileged methodology or mode of perception, or even the assured validity of a metaphysics deemed ineluctable or overwhelmingly favored by the self-appointed champions of "Science" even in the face of insufficient evidence or substantive doubt or their proclaimed opposition to cognitive privilege or Cartesian foundations.[13]

Quine certainly favors a form of scientism, but he also insists on a pared-down evidentiary scruple and a constructivist view of "ontic commitment."[14] He is entirely candid about his personal conviction, but he never affirms—in the way of a first or last principle—anything as extreme as Sellars's dictum. Theorists like Chomsky and Fodor favor a deviant version of scientism, for they insist, in a way that cannot rightly count as a ramified argument, that there simply is no reasonable alternative to an innatist science of language or thought.[15] Yet they relent under fire: their claims prove to be a piece of serious rhetoric offered in the service of a heartfelt bias, at best the promise of an argument, not more than that.

In the case of the others mentioned, we find ourselves much closer to the voices of certainty regarding the way the world really is—no matter what objections may arise! One recent partisan of this kind announces without the least compunction: "the [virtually] universally held position in science today is the view that all things are physical things and nothing else."[16] What our author means is that resistance is futile, possibly illiterate, certainly professionally imprudent.

The truth is, very little has changed in the twentieth century. The strongest analytic voices of the first half of the century made their way rather slowly against an entrenched and unconvinced professional protectorate, though rapidly enough among the recruits of a new generation. Pragmatism, itself the first distinct American movement to be taken seriously in the Eurocentric world, counts as the most natural English-language opponent of those original forms of scientism. Now revived, however eccentrically, pragmatism's second wave appears (sometimes equivocally) to be the natural opponent of the correspondingly refurbished scientisms of our end-of-century. The contest between the pragmatists and the analysts, implicit at first in John Dewey's prime, was obliged to focus more and more pointedly—in terms of the opposed claims of Hilary Putnam and Richard Rorty (as self-described pragmatists)—on the central question of how "naturalism" should be understood. That is the essential pivot on which *any* rapprochement between Anglo-American and continental philosophy must rely.

Those more loyal to the older pragmatist calling, but not Rorty—if I may characterize matters thus—favor a generous, comparatively bland reading of "naturalism" that is meant to preclude very little more than the supernatural, or "transcendent," or what is privileged in an *a priori* way or are no more than fictional resources mistakenly read as real. But there was also an edge to these demurrers that was already suspicious of reductionism and eliminativism and any "regimented" extensionalism. By the time we arrive at Rorty and Putnam's quarrel, it proves fair to say that "classic" pragmatism's opposition to the "analytic" forms of naturalism has acquired a specific animus against what (in very different ways) Quine and Davidson advanced as their respective forms of "naturalizing."[17]

Now, at the end of the twentieth century and the beginning of the twenty-first, that same contest has been internalized within analytic philosophy itself, largely centered on the prospects of certain extreme "scientisms" but hardly very differently motivated than those local quarrels (between pragmatists and analysts) as to whether "naturalizing" was a suitable reading of the best claims of a milder naturalism. Apart from personal convictions, Quine, Davidson, and even Rorty (as a deft though not entirely reliable advocate of Davidson over Quine[18]) defined naturalizing in terms of the supposed adequacy of one or another form of materialism together with its extensionalist "semantics." However unevenly distributed, these two themes have been the constant topics of the entire century of Anglo-American analytic philosophy. In that sense, "naturalizing" is a local American form of "scientism," originally inspired by Quine and "made" as rigorous as possible (somewhat against Quine) by Davidson. Doubts about the sustained work of each must be read, therefore, as doubts about the ulterior prospects of a whole array of scientisms that run from the informal to the formal, from the open ended to the closed, from the programmatic to the detailed, from the autobiographical to the constative and methodological, from the piecemeal to the systematic, and from the canonical to the deviant.

The entire century of Anglo-American analytic philosophy has evolved within an extraordinarily small orbit. To be sure, it has never lost its attraction; but it has also never toppled the conceptual visions that oppose it. Where, for example, first-person reports of mental states (as viewed, say, by Thomas Nagel or John Searle) are rightly thought to be unacceptably dualistic (by the extreme materialists), consciousness itself seems to be worrisomely intractable to the scientistic strategies that oppose the dualists. When, therefore, a clever theorist like Daniel Dennett (abetted by Rorty, it should be said, though not relevantly, on Dennett's own conviction[19]) proposes to axe or marginalize "first-person" reports of the "mental" in favor of "third-person" reports—somehow in the name of Science— fair-minded readers have never found the argument to be compelling and have even doubted the bare coherence of any such maneuver.[20] The counterargument, common ground shared by pragmatism and various strains of continental philosophy, though analyzed in very different, often opposed, ways, refuses to confine our "mental life" to some inner theater of the mind. The analysts who rightly oppose the "inner theater" merely substitute one untenable strand of Cartesianism for another.

Surely, it must be admitted, very little of mental and cultural life has ever yielded ground in such a way that anyone could claim to see how close we are to confirming scientism's final goals. Scientism has always been a banner, not an argument. As we shall see, late twentieth-century philosophy has made no difference in this regard, though it has indeed refined certain technical distinctions that clearly enrich analysis, yet without bringing it any nearer to its goal. I believe we are no closer to vindicating scientism today than we were during the best work of the first half of the last century. There is no compelling evidence that we are inching closer.

We *are* gaining ground, but what we seem to be learning concerns the depth of our own puzzlement, which is gripped by the profoundest stalemate of the entire philosophical undertaking. Not only that, but the bare fact shows that we must support both sides of the *agon* if we are to advance at all and that stalemate is a kind of victory for both sides, though hardly for the same reasons or with the same consequences.

Furthermore, the sheer coherence of opposing visions of mind, culture, history, and language presupposes the viability of incommensurable epistemologies, to say the very least. That comes as a surprise. For, if the viability of introspective reports is conceded, despite the fact that such reports cannot be commensurably matched by third-person behavioral or physical descriptions, then incommensurabilism must be an essential part of the ultimate *agon* itself; and if that is so, then the sanguine scientisms that we know so well cannot possibly have come to terms with the full challenge that confronts them. The prospect menaces the analytic brotherhood. For if you admit its force, you see that it will inevitably extend to relativism, historicism, constructivism, and similar deviant options. And if that is so and if the *agon* is pursued wherever it leads, then it will be difficult to deny that analytic philosophy is itself something of an arbitrary restriction within the full range of play that concerns Eurocentric philosophy.

You see, therefore, how the contest deepens without ever approaching resolution. What remains so arresting about it is the near-certainty that the largest of its opposing visions are separately coherent, capable of fitting the full range of our unrestricted speculations, if not the strongest partisan loyalties one can imagine, and endlessly inventive and (seemingly) never finally defeated. There is, nevertheless, one extraordinary advantage still in the hands of the opponents of scientism, namely, that they and not its champions can always proceed *faute de mieux*. All they need collect are the mounting puzzles that the scientistic visions seem unable to break through. The visions themselves, however, are also never finally defeated by any such means: the objections are turned to advantage, rather like the objections posed by negative theology in the hands of true believers.

Put more sympathetically, eliminativists like Sellars and Churchland are likely to explain—they do explain, in fact—that our commonsense views ("the manifest image," "the folk-theoretic" perspective) have been entrenched for thousands of years. The contest is, therefore, an unequal one (for extraneous reasons) and confirms how radically our thinking must be changed if the final goals of "science" (such as they are) are ever to be rightly tested. Paul Feyerabend, speaking on behalf of an exceptionless materialism (which he simplifies as the doctrine "that the only entities existing in the world are atoms, aggregates of atoms and that the only properties and relations are the properties of, and the relations between, such aggregates") offers a skillful defense of the following plea: "It took a considerable time for ordinary English to reach its present stage of complexity and sophistication.

The materialistic philosopher must be given at least as much time. As a matter of fact he will need more time as he intends to develop a language which is fully testable, which gives a coherent account of the most familiar facts about human beings as well as of thousands more recondite facts which have been unearthed by the physiologists."[21] I grant the point but judge the argument to be weak, because it appeals to something like the "principle" of the equal distribution of ignorance and something like the principle of fair play. It is not an argument focused on any substantive question.

III

My own impression is that the contest has been greatly polarized in recent decades by the availability of relatively new models of well-developed genetic, linguistic, computational, and informational resources—and even of their combination. It's entirely possible, of course, that there will in time be still more powerful resources to add—the specific neurophysiology of the brain, for instance. But my guess is that it would only deepen the stalemate we already know. So we may be close to the limit of the range of fundamental new options open to the scientistic treatment of mind and culture. In that event, prolonged stalemate is likely to be seen as a victory of sorts for one's opponents. There's no need, however, to hurry to that conclusion. The better labor is to collect the sense in which scientistic visions cannot, as we now understand matters, expect to gain significant ground on the most strategic questions. Still, if there is a noticeable shift in emphasis between the scientisms of the first half of the 20th century and those of the second (leading into the 21st century), it is surely due to a new confidence about the possibility of a frontal analysis of the materials afforded by psychology, language, and culture. That is the promise of the new Darwinism, Chomskyan linguistics, the information sciences, and allied disciplines. It yields a sense of the full play of the final contest, if not that contest itself. Remarkably little has changed in the space of a hundred years.

Here, we must remind ourselves that modern philosophy up to the start of the twentieth century got its largest lessons from two distinct sources. The focus of the first spans the great inquiries of Descartes and Kant; it isolated the paradoxes of any realism that would legitimate objective knowledge in spite of having disjoined cognizing subjects from cognized world at the very point of issuing truth-claims, or disjoined epistemology and metaphysics—or, more pointedly, it did so despite having failed to grasp that there must be a reasoned ground on which the cognizable structure of the "independent" world remains accessible to human inquirers, without invoking the *deus ex machina* of facultative or *a priori* privilege.

Given the conditions of such failure, realism, whether within the classic interval that Descartes and Kant define, or recapitulated (in however dampened or obscure a way) as in much of twentieth-century Anglo-American philosophy, may fairly be called "Cartesian." Read as a viable epistemology, realism *is* the master theme of the whole of modern philosophy. The questions raised by scientism, therefore, fall within the same narrative. Broadly speaking, scientism *is* Cartesianism by way of the materialisms and extensionalisms by which it seeks to gain its goal. The term is admittedly pejorative—as, I'm afraid, it must be. For the history of the century confirms the charge, and the argument that follows I judge to justify the verdict. Scientism remains the most salient vision of the whole of analytic philosophy, which is no closer now to being vindicated than it was a hundred years ago. In fact, given the new emphasis on the analysis of mind, language, and culture, we are clearer now than ever before on just how difficult are the challenges to its intended success. The gathering strength of the new sciences also contributes to a firmer grasp of its inherent problems.

The other decisive period of modern philosophy, the "post-Kantian" (it includes Kant once more), spans the efforts of Kant and Hegel to overcome the Cartesian *aporiai*. It succeeds—preeminently in Hegel's *Phenomenology*—in that we find in Kant, Fichte, and Hegel, the serial development of the essential theme of a recuperated realism that no movement has successfully dislodged since the beginning of the nineteenth century. I hasten to add that *this* achievement is often ignored, profoundly obscured by the purple grandiosities of post-Kantian philosophical prose. But we must learn to separate the saving lesson from its printed page. In a way, scientism is the best witness of the good sense of that reminder. It is an extraordinary fact that at the very start of twentieth-century analytic philosophy the two philosophers who were to launch English-language analysis against the prevailing "Hegelian" currents, Bertrand Russell and G. E. Moore, had (it seems) actually embraced (before 1898) some form of (British) Idealism, as "Idealism" had devolved from its putative Kantian and Hegelian sources—notably, in accord with the views of T. H. Green and F. H. Bradley. In effect, the second classic period of modern philosophy is still the prescient source of the principal objections to twentieth-century scientism. There's the cunning of history for you.

The master currents of British Idealism feature at least the following views (views not uniformly shared by all who may be labeled Idealists): (1) "the existence of an eternal self-consciousness, in which all human minds 'partake'—where the sense of this last word remains, in the end, obscure" (Green);[22] (2) that the doctrine just mentioned "is not part of the subject-matter of empirical psychology" (hence not "psychologistic" in the way of any empiricist epistemology—say, Hume's or Mill's);[23] and (3) "all [human] thought, all judgment, is in the end inadequate to reality [though, indeed, some judgments are 'correct' and some 'incorrect' in the human way—without being able to capture or even approach comprehending] reality as a single, all-embracing experience revealed to us [somehow], perhaps in transcendent and ineffable moments" (Bradley).[24]

The doctrines of the Idealists begin to form in the post-Kantian interval in which, as I suggest, the stalemate or defeat of twentieth-century scientism also begins to collect. Hence the trick is to separate the two, since Idealism in its characteristic form—as in doctrines 1 to 3 —can hardly be expected to pass muster now. The fact remains that the rejection of the three doctrines still leaves us with the constructivist lesson that Kant and Hegel first begin to analyze, which no satisfactory realism since that time has ever successfully evaded. That is the essential difference, for instance, between late Cartesianism—as in twentieth-century scientism—and, say, pragmatism. And it is a difference that is hardly local to American philosophy.

Here we must bear in mind that the classic pragmatists were also infected by Idealist doctrines drawn from the post-Kantians (Peirce—from Kant and Schelling chiefly; Dewey—from Green and other British Idealists, by way of his teacher and eventual colleague, George Morris).[25] Dewey himself interpreted Hegel (in the "right wing" way) as committed to an "Absolute" Mind or *Geist*, although Hegel is really an opponent of the "transcendent" and "transcendental" reading.[26] The important point is that Dewey, the quintessential pragmatist by most accounts (a very different figure from Peirce and James), made a grand effort—from the time of the Carus Lectures collected as *Experience and Nature* (1925, 1928) to the end of his life—to eliminate from his philosophy any vestigial effect of the untenable Idealist sort I've just tallied, which of course did mark his early work profoundly.

In this sense, Dewey and Russell converge somewhat, though by very different means: Dewey, as a pragmatist (and post-Hegelian) opponent of the Idealists, the Cartesians, as well as the Russellians. You see, therefore, how legible and straightforward the narrative line is that runs from Descartes to the beginning of the twenty-first century. Dewey does indeed cleave to the effective Hegelian argument that "finally" defeats the Cartesians, simplified along Darwinian lines. Dewey, of course, does not actually defeat the scientistic company, though he more than reminds us of precisely how that defeat may be gained. The irony is that it is a theme salvaged and transformed *from* the Idealist movement that Russell and Moore thought they had rooted out.

All this defines the busy life of twentieth-century Anglo-American philosophy, particularly in the second half of the century as it edges into the new millennium. The principal theme, I would say, remains realism in a sense reasonably close to what was intended in the mingling of epistemology and metaphysics from Descartes to Kant, adjusted through the master discovery of Kant and the post-Kantians— a sense the analytic tradition found impossible to distinguish from idealism, which of course it abhors. The analyst's complaint, however, rests entirely on the old mistake (known to everyone) of defining metaphysics in Descartes's way, even though such efforts were known to lead to insuperable paradoxes that could only be avoided by adopting one version or another of the correction offered in Hegel's *Phenomenology,* whether read back into Kant or not and (of course) whether improved upon or not in the way of analyzing historicity and collective societal life.

For the truth is that Hegel introduces the theme of history and cultural evolution into the debate about cognition in an inexpungeable way, although he does not quite explicitly develop his idea along specifically historicist and collective lines. That is, he does not press history in terms of the artifactual formation of human conceptual and cognizing resources by way of internalizing the evolving collective tradition of particular societies. That is a theme that may owe more to Marx (as a Hegelian) than to Hegel himself, to Nietzsche, to Dilthey, to Heidegger, to the early Frankfurt Critical school, to Gadamer, to Foucault—rereading Hegel in more radical ways that lead the theory of science in a direction inimical to what, against the mounting evidence, is still preferred by scientism. It is a more than incipient theme in Hegel; it is no more than incipient in Dewey. But it needs to be addressed in a robust way by contemporary philosophers, whether pragmatists or analysts. It is the gathering theme of the central argument against the scientists, the seemingly final fruit of Hegel's best post-Kantian critique: that is, acknowledgment of the public nature of mind and culture.

The plain fact is that the continental European tradition never lost sight of the issue. Now armed at the end of the twentieth century with mounting evidence of scientism's having failed to answer the doubts that confront all its inventions—its having stonewalled on the realist issue, its doctrinaire resistance to the Hegelian and post-Hegelian accounts of realism, and especially its refusal to admit the viability and reasonableness of a constructivist and historicist reading of science and practical life—we may have run out of deceptions by which to prolong scientism's hegemony.

Transcendental Idealism, Kant's remarkable solution of the problem of knowledge in realist terms—too early to have benefitted from his own successors—is an opportunistic and dark doctrine, partly because it *is* an idealism that cannot be read in naturalistic terms, partly because it confuses matters by conjoining constructivism and idealism, partly because it failed (in Kant's hands) to offset Cartesianism, and partly because it encouraged subsequent Kantian-oriented contributions—notably those advanced by Schelling, Charles Peirce, and T. H. Green—to persist in postulating an intelligibilizing Mind in nature.

A similar tendency must be admitted, of course, in the more Hegelian-oriented efforts of Edward Caird, George Morris, and the early John Dewey. But Dewey, unlike Peirce, worked, even toward the end of his life, to rid his analysis of "experience" of any taint of the Overmind. Put in the simplest terms, Kant's transcendentalism was initially not an epistemology at all but a metaphysics of necessary invariants masquerading as an epistemology (affecting human minds from above) that therefore constrained the "facultative" resources of human reason and experience along the lines of an improved Cartesianism. Certain post-Kantians cleave to that larger Mind in nature (which cannot then be captured naturalistically), which the post-Hegelians (from Marx to Nietzsche to Dewey to Foucault) have always been bent on exorcising.

Kantian transcendentalism yields to an increasingly historicized constructivism (Hegel's remarkable insight) wherever necessitites *de re* and *de cogitatione* come to be challenged. Indeed, the stabilities and regularities of our conceptual resources tend to be viewed as the upshot (at least in part) of acquiring a first language and a home culture. Hence, the transcendental subject proves to be a place-marker for a historicized account of conceptual and cognitive regularity. But to yield along these lines, in the post-Hegelian world—whether, say, in the direction of Dewey, Kuhn, and Feyerabend or in the direction of Nietzsche and Foucault—cannot fail to put scientism on the defensive without threatening the purpose of the philosophy of science.

Still, even if you admit the good sense of all this, you must see that the "refusal" (at least implicit) on the part of the analysts to acknowledge the inseparability of epistemology and metaphysics, which *is* Kant's true discovery, is not so much the advocacy of idealism as the persistence of Cartesian realism—at least as that has worked itself out in English-language philosophy. The charge applies with equal force, though for very different reasons, to the views, for example, of Michael Devitt, Michael Dummett, Donald Davidson, and John McDowell.[27] In each you will find the same fatal disjunction, however seemingly qualified.

The American opponents of this line of thinking derive from Hegel or a Hegelianized Kant, though not officially, not directly, and not always perspicuously. The three most important opponents of latter-day Cartesianism in the United States I make out to be John Dewey, Thomas Kuhn, and Hilary Putnam, though they are hardly collected in this way and though all three are effectively retired by the analysts.

Hands down, Dewey is the most coherent and successful of the three—is still the most successful when viewed against the best labors of recent scientisms. I would go so far as to say that Dewey's *Experience and Nature* remains, in its general lines, the best sketch by far of any American model of realism. It is not, it must be said, entirely free of the vestigial influence of its origins, and it is not as crisp as it should be. But it addresses head on, with a fresh invention, all the essential aporetic embarrassments of the Cartesian and Kantian worlds, and it solves them in a convincing way that, in my opinion, ensures pragmatism's continuing contribution. No other American formulation can claim to have done as well (which you may find unlikely).[28] Putnam turns his back rather courageously against the positivists and unity of science program he so much admired in his early work, as well as against the conventional realists of his day, though his own realism failed, by his own reckoning.

Kuhn was really the most daring and original of the three, in spite of the plain fact that he was unable to formulate his doctrine in a coherent way.[29] He—and Paul Feyerabend—were responsible, almost single-handedly, for a detailed body of pioneer evidence of the profoundly historicized nature of scientific thought, of radical discontinuities in the very conception of scientific inquiry, and (consequently) of the ineliminable threat of relativism and incommensurabilism at the very heart of the analysis of objective knowledge.[30]

The record shows that Kuhn and Feyerabend have been effectively eliminated from mainstream analytic debates in the philosophy of science, and the irony is that the great question of history's constitutive role in the formation and transformation of our cognizing powers is now largely ignored with their eclipse—which, we may suspect, conforms with the gathering recovery (among the analysts) of both Cartesianism and scientism.

Seen this way, the whole of modern philosophy has remained remarkably constant in its commitment, in its evolving interest in the concerns that occupy Descartes's original inquiries and Kant's reformulations of Descartes's questions. The puzzles and the solutions that have nagged the tradition from its inception are, by now, as clear as they are ever likely to be. They were effectively sketched in the interval spanning the late eighteenth century and the beginning of the nineteenth; and, although it would be fair to say that the resolutions offered in the second half of the twentieth century benefitted clearly from two centuries of close testing and matched efforts at precise improvement, many of the most influential Anglo-American formulations approaching the new century are plainly open to a charge of recycling defeated arguments or venturing even weaker ones.

In any event, I daresay, there has been no acknowledged innovation of incontestable originality produced in the last few decades of the twentieth century in analytic quarters that has transformed (or is likely to transform) the terms of the contest regarding realism and scientism that would lead us to expect a more decisive resolution than the previous century managed to provide. The most inventive and promising essays I have seen—not always the "best" or the most rigorous or even the most "analytic"—suggest that the seeds of important change are already before us waiting to be gathered. Here, if "analytic philosophy" may be construed more broadly than is usual, I would say the greatest promise of the last half-century (or more) rests with the lessons of Quine's "Two Dogmas," Wittgenstein's *Philosophical Investigations,* Kuhn's *Structure,* and Dewey's *Experience and Nature.* I am open to correction here, but I see no convincing replacements.

Analytic philosophy's best energies and insights have been stalemated (however deepened) by its seemingly single-minded career drawn from convictions that have changed very little over nearly four hundred years. On a completely unsympathetic reading, the history of twentieth-century analytic philosophy is the history of that perseveration at its most zealous, risky, and fateful—*and* retrograde. Viewed more congenially, analytic philosophy has been engaged in testing, in the most uncompromising way imaginable, the limits of every conceivable form of scientism. The entire philosophical community hangs on its results even where it pretends to ignore them. For if scientism—or the strong forms of "naturalizing" or the post-post-Kantian "Cartesianisms" of our time—could reasonably claim to have changed the balance of the classic contest "permanently" in its own favor, the ethos of the Eurocentric world might well, in time, be completely changed. And if not, if its best options appeared to be approaching exhaustion (which I believe is true), then once again the world might be very differently perceived.

We cannot prophesy with confidence here. It's entirely possible that the new century's history will simply confirm that our perfectly respectable stalemate will not have been bettered. It's quite true that we cannot now see a way to change the terms of the debate we've inherited. But, of course, that's the trouble with fresh intuitions that we have yet to invent. I've mentioned my own best clues about what might move us in a new direction. If they fail to catch fire, we may be obliged to return again and again to dissect the limitations of the past until we happen on a more suitable substitute. But we have been made to realize—by recent political events if not (or not yet) by philosophy—how fragile is the vision of the relatively constant order of our conceptual space.

Reflecting on all this and anticipating the argument that follows, I would say that American analytic philosophy has always focused on providing an adequate and convincing form of realism fitted to the needs of the natural sciences. But in the second half of the twentieth century, it has favored a close study of the semantics of materialism and extensionalism often detached from the substantive challenges posed by the actual work of the physical sciences that had dominated Eurocentric analytic philosophy in the first half of the century. Symptomatically, you cannot find in Quine and Davidson, for instance, any sustained discussion of the special problems posed by the sciences, of a gauge that compares with the work of the Vienna Circle or Hans Reichenbach or Carl Hempel—or, indeed, Kuhn and Feyerabend, or the early Putnam, or younger figures like Michael Friedman bent on recovering Carnap's contribution (only partly against Quine), or of course the more recent programs of the neo-Darwinians and the computationalists. What that suggests is a division of interest and labor within analytic philosophy itself.

It has always seemed a reasonable idea to distinguish between the doctrinal themes that have dominated analytic philosophy and the admirable forms of conceptual rigor that could be fitted to a wider swath of issues than the ones it has always preferred. We are now actually at a point where it seems no longer foolish to suggest that, if scientism is spent (as I believe it is, though it obviously survives), it hardly follows that analytic philosophy need be spent as well.

Many will wish to consider whether the philosophy of science may have taken a wrong turn in following analytic philosophy's own "turn" in the second half of the twentieth century, and others will be tempted by the failure of scientism itself to ask whether philosophy of science is best served by an unyielding stand on materialism and extensionalism. For if the latter programs are as problematic as I claim they are, then it may be that Quine's "turn" is really a halfway house toward dismantling even the more recent reductionisms and eliminativisms that seem to have favored something close to Quine's own scruple. After all, there is already an obvious distance between fitting extensionalism to the analysis of causal laws (say) and fitting it to natural language in general. The pivotal issue remains (as it always has) the public standing of the mental.

The record signifies, in effect, that the entire century has spent its best energies pursuing the question of an adequate philosophy of science by way of a failed scientism, if not also the questions of semantics and epistemology and the philosophy of mind by way of certain extreme forms of materialism and extensionalism that have served scientism so badly, but that are now detached from the corrective details of the empirical sciences themselves. To see matters this way is to put the prospects of analytic philosophy in a light very different from its usual presentation. There is, after all, no essential connection between its characteristic discipline and its doctrinal preferences. For instance, would the "analytic" discovery of the irreducibility of complexities of natural-language discourse be a contradiction in terms? Surely not! But if that is true, then there is absolutely no reason why analytic philosophy should not apply its skills in collaboration with Eurocentric, pragmatist, or Asian philosophies that it usually shuns. I'll say no more about that. But if you see that much, assuming the validity of the argument that follows, there will be a lot that will have to be said about the meaning of an entire century's labor and the prospects for the present century.

1

Materialism by Less than Adequate Means

I

I begin with some fragments of a familiar kind taken from a recent popular account of what may be the most prominent Darwinian conception of the mind current in the academic lists, which I won't name for the moment:

> Our physical organs [our author affirms] owe their complex design to the information in the human genome, and so, I believe, do our mental organs. . . . Yes, every part of human intelligence involves culture and learning. But learning is not a surrounding gas or force field, and it does not happen by magic. It is made possible by innate machinery designed to do the learning. The claim that there are several innate modules is a claim that there are several innate learning machines, each of which learns according to a particular logic. . . . Our organs of computation [our minds] are a product of natural selection. The biologist Richard Dawkins called natural selection the Blind Watchmaker; in the case of the mind, we can call it the Blind Programmer . . . [for] the brain is destined to be an organ of computation. . . . Every part of the body from the toenails to the cerebral cortex takes on its particular shape and substance when its cells respond to some kind of information in the neighborhood that unlocks a different part of the genetic program.[1]

I won't say this is unconditionally false, though it is certainly indemonstrable at present, and most of it is probably false and generally misleading. For instance, there is almost nothing our author provides to explain what he means by "information," and what he suggests hardly favors any single determinate notion of information as that concept is used in a variety of disciplines. Furthermore, if the various patterns of "learning" our author assigns to "innate learning machines" cannot be shown to yield to computational analysis, and if we cannot show that learning must be computational in some appropriately strong sense of "must," the entire conjecture will collapse of its own weight.

Our author pretty well subscribes to Richard Dawkins's "selfish gene" theory, but not to the "meme" theory, which he takes Dawkins to have introduced more in the way of an instructional tool than as a serious biological hypothesis. (I return to the "meme" shortly.) He qualifies his own allegiance in the approved way, as far as canonical genetics is concerned— I'll add a few lines to confirm this—but his remarks are characteristically thin on the contested issues: "There have been [he says] no discoveries of a gene for civility, language, memory, motor control, intelligence, or other complete mental systems, and there probably won't ever be. . . . Complex mental organs, like complex physical organs, surely are built by complex genetic recipes, with many genes cooperating in as yet unfathomable ways."[2] You see the slippery combination of the words "surely" and "as yet unfathomable." The implication is that the explanation is genic but not perhaps according to the rule "one gene, one enzyme" or "one gene, one organ." There are, it must be admitted, confirmed cases in which the defective mutations of a single gene are thought responsible for distinct diseases, like Tay-Sachs and Huntington's Chorea. But it seems more probable that a strategic defect of such a sort might have consequences that are unlikely to be overridden than that the whole of the ontogenetic development of the human organism can be accounted for in terms of genetic information alone.

There's no question that the doctrine just sampled is very much an "in" view; furthermore, though I believe it to be mistaken in a number of important ways, all rather shadowy, perhaps, I cannot offer a knockdown argument to make the case. I cannot show that a coherent computationalism is empirically impossible. To put the issue as temperately as I can, I would say there are at least two grand contests involving opposed theories here— one regarding the biology of evolution and development, the other regarding the philosophical standing of the mind/body problem and (I would add) the culture/nature problem. Both are very close to the heart of current disputes about our best conceptual options—on which our author takes a line that is much more sanguine about materialism, the extensionalist analysis of human language and thought, the adequacy of a computational model of the mind, and, in general, a bottom-up or compositional account (a "modular" account) of biological, psychological, and cultural phenomena, than most of us believe can be evidentiarily defended at the present time. But I concede straight off that I see no formal paradox or incoherence or self-contradiction in merely thinking that the analysis of the human mind might proceed fruitfully along materialist and extensionalist lines. In short, I still think the mind doesn't work that way—that is, on any grounds known to me—but I cannot say that it's impossible in the modal sense many are tempted to invoke.

Our author says in summary that "the proper label for the study of the mind informed by computers is not Artificial Intelligence but Natural Computation."[3] Very neat but hardly enough. For the minimal explanation offered regarding the analysis of natural language yields little more than the following:

> According to the computational theory of mind, . . . information is embodied in symbols: a collection of physical marks that correlate with the state of the world as it is captured in [familiar English sentences intended to be used to speak about some actual state of affairs]. These symbols cannot be English words and sentences, notwithstanding the popular misconception that we think in our mother tongue. . . . [S]entences in a spoken language like English or Japanese are designed for vocal communication between impatient, intelligent social beings . . . but they are not needed inside a single head where information can be transmitted directly by thick bundles of neurons. So the statements in a knowledge system are not sentences in English but rather inscriptions in a richer language of thought, "mentalese."[4]

It is more than doubtful that anyone has worked out a straightforward connection between any robustly semantic conception of information (associated with English or Japanese, say) and either the information of a genetic "recipe" (1) or the mathematical treatment of the degradation of information (otherwise semantically unanalyzed) transmitted through any physical conduit[5] (2) or the information imputed to a computer programmed by some set of abstract algorithms (3) or a neurophysiological system functioning in any computational way (4). In any case, neuronal language or communication, even if admitted, never surfaces in an epistemically explicit form among speaking humans. These very different ideas are not infrequently conflated or confused with one another, as if they were known to be no more than variant expressions of one and the same thing. They are not variants in this sense, however. Some have no semantic or intentional content at all, and for any that might claim such content there is no known "correlation" or supervenience between neuronal sequences and semantic import or, indeed, between such sequences and beliefs or actions. Our author apparently believes his formula resolves the mind/body problem or shows us how to resolve it.

I disagree—both because there is nothing to support the strategy beyond enthusiasm, and because there are conceptual challenges that are not satisfactorily taken up, without which the matter cannot be resolved.

II

Let me take advantage of this provocation to press in an unguarded way in two directions: in one, to suggest difficulties for the short account I've cited—which I take to capture a central theme in the ethos of contemporary philosophies of mind; in the other, to acknowledge my own motivation in beginning this way. The theory I've sampled (I hope you'll regard it as a specimen of a widely supported view) means to integrate a reductive materialism applied everywhere in the world: a strong Darwinian account of the evolution of the mind, an extensionalist analysis of the mind's contents computationally modeled, a preference for bottom-up, compositional, "modular" analyses of complex physical and biological structures and complex physical and biological forms of functioning, and a reductionistic treatment, cast in biological and informational terms, of whatever manifests itself at the level of human thought, language, and culture. Quite a grand package.

But we are in treacherous waters here. Whatever I personally believe or am prepared to affirm on the questions before us, I admit straight out that we are almost always at a very primitive first pass in such reckonings. Reviewing what our author says, I draw your attention to certain doctrines implicated in what I have so far cited, as not having been effectively supported anywhere or by anyone, which nevertheless dominate the fashions of the field. There is, however, reason to believe that a very different conceptual orientation may well be required—all of which is complicated by confidently joining the work of one or another strong science with some problematic philosophical conjectures.

Straight off, I cannot agree that it is only a "popular misconception" that claims that we think in our mother tongue! I hold rather that—paradigmatically—we do utter and identify our thoughts linguistically, though not in any correspondentist way and not in any sense that is impervious to alternative analysis.

Thinking is an activity we engage in deliberately; and where we do, we do so linguistically or (as I would add) "lingually" (as in composing at the piano or choreographing a dance, which presupposes linguistic competence but is not itself an exercise of speech). Also, when we report what we "must" have been thinking but are not actually aware of it, we report its would-be content linguistically—by anthropomorphizing (as I would say), though we are never aware of what, according to any neurophysiological or information-processing theory of thinking, we must be thinking or must have thought in the way of reportable content. In any case, at the human level (which is paradigmatic even for nonlanguaged animals), there is no known way to identify determinate thoughts except as enlanguaged or as linguistically identified. In this sense, the idea of a "language of thought" (Jerry Fodor's proposal, which Chomsky questions) cannot, as we now understand matters, be empirically examined in any way independent of languaged thought. It remains a conceptual possibility of course, but it cannot provide any evidence entirely independent of the *model* of natural-language discourse.

This is not a small quibble. What it emphasizes at the very least is the logical and methodological priority of the epistemological data of speaking and thinking in the familiar, conscious, culturally informed and enlanguaged, reportorial way that we all master from infancy, over whatever any theory that eschews first-person reports alleges is the real structure and content of our mental life. I don't think it's possible to show that the would-be replacement could never make sense. But I see no viable, empirical reason for thinking that such replacements would not always be parasitic simulations or paraphrases of what was already accessible to our "folk" abilities.

I am skeptical of any strong invariances where the "folk" features of the mind are concerned—where, even for internalist or innatist grammarians (even for Noam Chomsky, for instance), we must rely, in some measure, on our intuitions regarding language and experience—that is, where the would-be invariances are either phenomenologically abstracted or imposed from a privileged vantage. The thesis we are examining threatens to be circular or to suppress an obvious cultural and empirical dependence. I don't believe, for instance, that Herbert Feigl's "cerebroscope" (which matches thoughts and neurophysiological firings) would make any difference here, and I think Paul Churchland's total replacement of "folk-psychological" priorities would forever run the risk (which Churchland nowhere resolves) that it never explains how we exceed a mere simulation of human abilities (such as face-recognition) or how we should construe an anthropomorphized extension of the folk paradigm itself as applied to machine skills that humans recognize in terms of exceeding their own in certain benign ways.[6] Can this limitation be overcome? I don't believe it can, but I haven't explained why, and so I shall come back to that. In any case, count this item (1) in an open ended tally I am beginning to lay out. Call it, for convenience, the paradigm argument: the folk-model as the paradigm of the human mind.

Let me add item (2) at once, namely, that "mentalese," which is somehow processed by our neurons (and that our author has perhaps Darwinized from Jerry Fodor), is conceptually dependent on the folk paradigm itself, unless it can be shown (or shown to be reasonable) that natural languages harbor an underlying algorithmic structure that we are normally unaware of, possibly even an algorithmic process attributable to Darwinian selection (a thesis Fodor would oppose). I put this in a careful way—to counteract the easy charge that I am simply repeating something like Roger Penrose's notorious mistake (if indeed it was a mistake); or that I am taking unfair advantage of a concession Noam Chomsky makes in an earlier defense of his former view of deep grammar (which, incidentally, goes utterly contrary to the innatism of our unnamed author).

I would say, on the first count, that Daniel Dennett was entirely justified in objecting, against Penrose's objection to a Darwinian account of the mind, which (for both Dennett and our author) must be algorithmic, that

> if the mind is an algorithm (contrary to Penrose's claim), surely it is not an algorithm that is recognizable to, or accessible to, those whose minds it creates. It is, in Penrose's terms, unknowable. As a product of biological design processes (both genetic and individual), it is almost certainly one of those algorithms that are somewhere or other in the vast [that is, finite but "very-much-more-than-astronomically" large] space of interesting algorithms, full of typographical errors or "bugs," but good enough to bet your life on—so far. Penrose sees this as a "far-fetched" possibility, but if that is all he can say against it, he has not yet come to grips with the best version of "strong AI."[7]

You may have noticed the ease with which Dennett treats his would-be algorithms as, at one and the same time, incarnate as the actual genetic information of Darwinian selection and as the abstract programs of a hypothetically embodied computer. There is no logical reason why this linkage could not obtain, but it is a very extreme guess that neither empirical biology nor the analysis of thought and language can yet confirm. Fair play requires acknowledging this fact. Moreover, the algorithms alleged are of course taken to be formulable in extensionalist terms, though it turns out that the English or Japanese sentences on which the argument rests are not known to yield to such translation. Hence, the bare conjecture does not yet advance the reductionist cause at all. It tells us no more than what we wish to establish. Nevertheless, in Dennett's hands, the very absence of any convincing exemplar seems to render the computational conjecture well-nigh invulnerable to evidentiary challenge!

Penrose may have faltered, but he may have had something important to recover. The substantive issue is somewhat of a stalemate. Certainly, at the level of replicating DNA, synthesizing amino acids and proteins, a strong argument can be made for determinate algorithmic processes cast in terms of genic selection; but there is much in the recent literature of genetic (or genomic) processing—in both evolution and individual development at higher organismic levels—that begins to challenge the adequacy of the assured central role of particulate genes on which the algorithmic conception has historically depended. In itself, this need not disallow the algorithmic model, but it suggests that the classic conception—Dawkins's and Dennett's model, however carefully qualified—may have been a very good idealization at a moment of biological history that reached its zenith about the time of François Jacob's and Jacques Monod's work leading to the operon theory.[8]

There are bound to be serious qualifications of any algorithmic determinism applied at higher organismic levels and in individual development. We simply don't know that the construction or synthesis of an organism is algorithmic or controlled by determinate genes. Not knowing that, we are unclear about the principled division between the genotypic and the phenotypic and, because of that, about the difference intended (here) between a metaphoric vision and a literal hypothesis. In any case, we don't know the answer wherever human language and human culture are involved; and we cannot really say that the neo-Darwinian line of reduction holds the best cards. There are other possibilities.

The early efforts of the sociobiologists were seriously defective because, for instance, they neglected to make a close analysis of what the reduction of culture would require.[9] But that seems just as true of Dennett's and Dawkins's proposals, which are further qualified by the pointed admission that memes, though postulated to be physical particulates themselves, are not expected to embody genetic recipes. I see this as an elaborate dance step, moving sideways, that signifies that Darwinism has not really brought us closer to the vindication of any strong form of philosophical materialism—in short, reductionism.

On the second count, you will remember, our author (who is in fact none other than Steven Pinker, the well-known theorist of mind and language) maintains that the brain is an "organ of computation," implying that the mind (the brain's mode of functioning) proceeds algorithmically. I am quite prepared to argue that a good case can be made against the algorithmic reading of natural language discourse (or its "generation" by whatever means), even if there are sentences that can be generated algorithmically. In fact, I claim that natural language is not essentially algorithmic at all; nor is culture or enlanguaged thought; also, the encultured mind is not demonstrably limited to the functioning of the brain (though it obviously involves the brain and body in an essential way). Even the evolution and development of biological organisms are not demonstrably algorithmic in all significant respects, for instance, wherever proto-cultural or cultural regularities have influenced the course of evolution—preeminently, in the emergence of language itself.

Count all that item (3) of my intended tally. For the moment, I will confine myself to some candid remarks of Chomsky's that bear on the issue of whether language is algorithmic and what to understand by our viewing the analysis of mind and language and culture as part of the natural world— hence fair game for the natural sciences and yet not (for that reason alone) bound to proceed algorithmically. I admit that it would be implausible to deny that the development of our general linguistic capacity was decisively facilitated by genetic factors; although it remains (for all that) an open question whether the determinate structure of actual languages is also explained entirely in selectionist terms—hence in a strictly algorithmic way (according to the neo-Darwinian canon). Or, for that matter, algorithmic without being Darwinian, as Dawkins appears to admit. If language is a hybrid achievement, uniting distinct biological and culturally acquired aptitudes (as I believe), then reductionism is bound to prove false.

III

It would be very hard to find a more forthright formulation of the neo-Darwinian doctrine than the version Daniel Dennett advances. But it is also hard to find any compelling evidence, scientific or philosophical, brought to the table by Dennett, that could possibly confirm his thesis apart from his firm assertion of what Darwinism finally means (which opposes what Darwin himself believed).[10] Darwin may have been mistaken, and Dennett may be right. But the only evidence Dennett offers is a tendentious reading of philosophical "naturalism" or "science" (not anything one actually finds confirmed in the "natural world"). Here, Dennett claims, without visible support, that mind, language, and culture must be explained essentially in terms of Darwinian selection—hence algorithmically!

Here is Dennett's candid formulation:

> [This] is Darwin's dangerous idea: the algorithmic level is the level that best accounts for the speed of the antelope, the wing of the eagle, the shape of the orchid, the diversity of species, and all the other occasions for wonder in the world of nature. It is hard to believe that something as mindless and mechanical as an algorithm could pro-

duce such wonderful things. . . . An impersonal, unreflective, ro-
botic, mindless little bit of molecular machinery is the ultimate basis
of all the agency and hence meaning, and hence consciousness in the
universe.[11]

You will have to judge this for yourself. What Dennett says here is remarkably close to the "mechanical" philosophies Descartes originally opposed
nearly four hundred years ago.

The minimal clue to correctly grasping the difference between Dennett's
and Chomsky's views on Darwinism and on the Darwinian account of
language—which, then, begins to redefine our own scientific options—
rests with the fact that Dennett advocates bringing science into line with a
prior metaphysical commitment, largely based on Quine's "naturalizing,"
which constrains all explanation within the biosphere along neo-Darwinian lines.[12] For his part, Chomsky professes to be open in principle to whatever alternatives of inquiry and explanation the study of mind and language
may require. "Outside of narrow domains," he says by way of Descartes's resistance to the then-current mechanistic explanations of the mind, "naturalistic inquiry has proven shallow or hopeless, and perhaps always will,
perhaps for reasons having to do with our cognitive nature."[13] Chomsky
thinks of the complex functioning of language as relatively autonomous and
built up along modular lines. He therefore resists large Darwinian conclusions, without yet opposing the relevance of natural selection.

I am not, however, concerned to vindicate Chomskyan linguistics over
Dennett's neo-Darwinian intuitions, except to acknowledge that the testing
of any empirical theory about one or another part of the world is ultimately
inseparable from the testing of the conception of how such testing should
proceed. Count that item (4) of my tally. I see no reason to think that scientific methods are not themselves in some fair sense empirically tested. For
all we know, both Chomsky and Dennett are profoundly mistaken. If you
concede the point, you see why it is that recent challenges to the primacy and
adequacy of genic selectionism, the model Dawkins and Dennett pretty well
share, begin to suggest the productive possibility that there may be a quite
diverse family of explanatory models that are best fitted to different parts
of the biosphere. For both general and technical reasons, a strong algorithmic realism may be conceptually premature. The quick way to settle the
matter would be to show that the algorithmic generation of biological and
cultural structures and modes of functioning cannot but be necessary in the
strongest possible sense. But neither Dennett nor Chomsky—nor anyone
else—knows how to make that argument compelling.

I agree with Chomsky's warning that, in spite of the fact that mind and language "belong" to the biological world, it's unlikely that their complex processes can be convincingly described and explained in exclusively or chiefly selectionist terms, or by algorithmic means. Frankly, it seems preposterous to claim that the bare appeal to "scientific method" could ever decide whether (say) first-person reports of sensation, memory, intention, belief, or experience could or ought to be displaced in principle by third-person reports alone, or assigned a disadvantageous standing in the scientific lists, or coherently abandoned. And yet that too is a consequence of Dennett's argument.[14] I would be less than candid if I did not say straight out that the claim seems flatly incoherent. Think for instance of the strategic fact that discerning pain is often, in the same context, viewed as a sensation as well as a form of nociception, or the fact that an experienced hypnotherapist can train a hemophiliac to control bleeding under dental surgery, and at both capillary and deeper levels that are correctly monitored through introspective responses during trance.

It is a very reasonable conjecture that first-person reports and avowals of mental states are part of natural-language discourse, are (as part of public discourse) semantically inseparable from third-person discourse, and are therefore open to empirical testing in some ineliminable measure. But if so, then Dennett's strategy in disjoining third-person discourse from first-person discourse must prove self-impoverishing for at least three compelling reasons: first, because it couldn't possibly be true that "Science" required the disjunction claimed; second, because the mental is not private but actually public; and, third, because the conceptual linkage between first- and third-person discourse would undermine the would-be informational contribution of third-person discourse itself (bearing on the "mental") wherever separated from the routine use of first-person discourse. Even a purely behavioral or functional vocabulary purporting to capture the "mental" presupposes the fluency of the idiom it claims to replace. Think of the dubious standing of a purely behaviorist reading of a person's intentions or the effect on the discrimination of hues of a merely behavioral treatment of perception (*à la* Skinner or Quine) separated from first-person phenomenal avowals.

By contrast, I find Chomsky's approach to mind and language—especially in *New Horizons in the Study of Language and Mind*—remarkably sensible, refreshing, untendentious, and considerably more skillfully managed than the usual doctrinaire views of what philosophers believe science requires. (Chomsky has his own profound prejudices, of course, which I find I cannot accept.) "Let us understand the term 'naturalism' [Chomsky suggests] without metaphysical connotations: a 'naturalistic approach' to the mind investigates mental aspects of the world as we do any other, seeking to construct intelligible explanatory theories, with the hope of eventual integration with the 'core' natural sciences. . . . Internalist naturalistic inquiry [Chomsky's approach to mind and language] seeks to understand the internal states of an organism."[15] Fine. That is the essential reason Chomsky opposes externalist views of language (Dennett's, say) or externalist views of visual perception (David Marr's, say).

Nevertheless, I believe Chomsky is mistaken about grammar for reasons that are not altogether distant from the reasons that appear to invalidate Dawkins's and Dennett's "universal Darwinism"—though I hasten to add that Chomsky is wholly opposed to universal Darwinism. I think it is simply not clear that, in spite of having made an excellent suggestion about the openness of science, Chomsky actually follows his own advice. Innatism seems to be as opportunistic as universal Darwinism. So, too, is the theory that we are clear about what it is to be a science—anywhere. The considerations that ultimately undercut Dennett's and Dawkins's view undercut Chomsky's rationalism as well, though that may not be easily perceived. The issue is close to the nerve of the brief I am beginning to formulate. Both Dennett and Chomsky, I would say, are not careful enough about the epistemic data and are in fact distinctly suspicious of relying on empirical data.

Dawkins realized that the neo-Darwinian thesis he advocated, which is a great improvement (if that is the right word) over E. O. Wilson's "New Synthesis"—sociobiology—relieved of the infelicities of the latter,[16] could not succeed unless it could complete at least two tasks: one, to prepare a selectionist account of evolution and development that specified the genomic contribution to social behavior and mental competence up to the level of Homo sapiens; the other, to invent a physically realized supplement to an essentially algorithmic reading of the first that ranged, by non-genetic means (though congruently and algorithmically in its own way) over the whole of the cultural world of humans. That, of course, is precisely what now falls within the intended scope of Darwinized psychology and sociology. (Witness Pinker.) The first project is pretty well what Dawkins means by "the selfish gene"; the second accords with his replacement of the seemingly disastrous doctrine of the "culturgen" by his own equally conjectural account of the "meme," itself clearly divorced from genotypic function.

There are two sorts of reductionism that are involved here: one concerns the reductive explanation of phenotypic cultural traits by genic selectionism (an idea more strenuous and more restricted than that of the culturgen[17]); the other concerns the extensionalist, hence particulate, hence potentially algorithmic, analysis of cultural phenomena themselves. The idea is coherent. But the supporting arguments are all front-loaded, both in the sense that neo-Darwinism is reasonably secure in whatever way it can be extended piecemeal from the synthesis of proteins, and in the sense that the reductionists and eliminativists who concede the limitations of a purely genetic account of human culture come already armed with convictions that are no worse off than they would have been before the Darwinian economies were added to their arsenal. The trick is to hold fast to the principal ways of challenging reductionism that remain essentially unaffected by Darwinian enthusiasms.

I think this agrees with the general lines along which Chomsky raises compelling doubts about reductionism and eliminationism—whether, say, championed by Dennett or attacked by Thomas Nagel or Colin McGinn (from very different perches, of course). Except that I mean to be more hospitable than Chomsky to the philosophical quarrels, though I freely admit that Chomsky makes an excellent case against conflating scientific and philosophical concerns in any easy way. It falls out at once that Chomsky is an opponent of the new Darwinism (which is either strongly reductionist or eliminativist in intent). Also, Chomsky's central corrective is agreeably straightforward. About the usual scientific inquiries—whether, say, cosmology or judging the intention with which another person does what he apparently does—Chomsky takes note of the question of the origins of the modes of human understanding (which introduces innatism) and the analysis and explanation of the phenomena to which our understanding is applied. Chomsky believes this strengthens innatism's actual prospects, but I believe this will require a close reconciliation with irreducible cultural sources. Here is what Chomsky says:

> The answers, insofar as they are accessible to human intelligence, will be framed in terms appropriate to the problems at hand, with little concern for the intellectual apparatus of the folk sciences, and no expectation that constructs and principles that are developed will receive direct expression in terms of more "fundamental" branches of science, even if the unification problem has been solved. . . . There seems to be no coherent doctrine of materialism and metaphysical naturalism, no issue of eliminativism, no mind-body problem.[18]

What Chomsky means, scanning the opinions of discussants like Quine, Dennett, Nagel, McGinn, Tyler Burge, John Searle, and others, is simply that all of them too casually pronounce reductionism to affirm just what (whatever) science takes the world to be like! Chomsky's very neat point is that the history of the physical sciences tends not to proceed reductively, in the sense that reductionism typically addresses very local theories, for example, with regard to "the problem of reducing electricity and magnetism to mechanics, unsolvable [as such, Chomsky says,] and overcome [only] by the [strange] assumption that fields are real physical things; [or] the problem of reducing chemistry to the world of hard particles in motion, energy, and electromagnetic waves, only overcome with the introduction of even weirder hypotheses about the nature of the physical world." "In each of these cases," Chomsky concludes, "unification was achieved and the problem resolved not by reduction, but by quite different forms of accommodation."[19]

I am persuaded that Chomsky is probably right in this. But I doubt that is enough to justify disjoining the work of the physical sciences and the data and intuitions of the "folk sciences" or the questions posed by reductionism and the mind/body problem or, indeed, our ignoring the reasons for affirming that theoretical inquiry itself rests on the practical adequacy of our deepest conjectures. The "folk" sciences play an evidentiary role in the so-called "fundamental" sciences. Call that item (5) of my developing tally. I mean, there is a kind of noticeable difficulty in merely dismissing the ubiquitous data of our "folk" sensibilities (because, let's say, they are intentional or reliant on first-person avowals). If they are not beyond attack or revision, they cannot be dismissed (as in Richard Rorty's case) as a mere façon de parler[20]; and they cannot be dismissed on the presumption that Science can make no room for first-person introspection or intentional content (as in Daniel Dennett's case) on the grounds of being incapable of reconciliation with the constraints of objectivity.[21] Any argument that rests on "Science" or "objectivity" is patently self-serving. No doubt such scruples will affect what we may ultimately expect from the vaunted objectivity of science itself.

IV

It's in this same spirit that Chomsky calls attention to Thomas Nagel's summary of his own account of a "Language Acquisition Device [LAD] by which a child learns the grammar of a natural language by the minimal samples of the language it encounters." Nagel insists that Chomsky's theory introduces a "psychological mechanism" as opposed to a "physical mechanism" (which idiom [the latter] Chomsky favors), because, on Nagel's view, physical mechanisms are essentially incapable of accounting for consciousness. Here you can see how philosophical prejudice invades scientific inquiry.[22] Nevertheless, Chomsky cannot really claim that his own innatism is confirmed (say, against Quine's empirically lax intuition) by the evidence (which

Chomsky has always emphasized) that "association and conditioning have little to do with language acquisition or use."[23] It probably shows that certain theories of learning and inductive inference are not tenable in the language case (Skinnerian and Quinean behaviorism, say), but it hardly shows that Chomsky's own sort of innatism is valid or will prove as promising as new conceptions of learning that may be as difficult to formulate now as the conception of consciousness itself. Chomsky's line of attack on conditioning, for example, could only go through if his own theory were itself empirically confirmed, even though it is not confirmed and probably will never be.

Chomsky now identifies his own account (in his recent, seemingly very radical pronouncement) as a "bold hypothesis," not yet a "specific theory," which then retreats from explicit invariances at the level of deep grammar ("principles") at the same time it recommends that there must be such principles underlying the contingent and variable "features" of all natural languages (the executive "parameters" of different languages imposed by factors "external" to the "language faculty" itself). Chomsky now maintains:

> A plausible assumption today [holds] that the principles of language
> are fixed and innate, and that variation is restricted [largely in terms
> of the contingencies of the acquisition of natural languages]. Each
> language, then, is (virtually) determined by a choice of values for
> lexical parameters. . . . These ideas constitute a radical departure
> from a rich tradition of some 2,500 years. If correct, they show not
> only that languages are cast in very much the same mold, with a near
> invariant computational procedure and only restricted lexical varia-
> tion, but also that there are no rules or constructions in anything
> like the traditional sense, which are carried over to early generative
> grammar: no rules for formation of relative clauses in English, for
> example.[24]

It is not at all clear, let me say—as temperately as I can—whether or why the evidence that has always been collected against Chomsky's view of deep grammar would not still count effectively against his current willingness to treat deep grammar as itself profoundly contingent and in some way externally triggered. It could for instance show the implausibility of not adopting a hybrid account of initial language acquisition, one that admitted the distinct (but co-functioning) resources of biology and emergent culture at a level that bridges deep structures of some kind and the empirical features of natural discourse. You must bear in mind that the plausibility of Chomsky's innatism had always—previously—rested on the compelling skill with which Chomsky assembled promising approximations to (anticipated) universal grammatical rules that had not been previously noticed. Now, it turns out, the regularities of the various natural languages are somehow assured, without supporting evidence, from a prior conviction regarding the near-necessity of innatism itself. That is a stunning and risky change of strategy, to say the least. I believe it actually threatens the very plausibility of linguistic innatism.

Chomsky has previously worried about specific grammatical invariances, not narrowly construed in evolutionary terms (but not actually inhospitable to evolutionary preconditions), as in reviewing, much earlier, the need to revise his so-called Standard Theory (advanced in *Aspects of the Theory of Syntax*[25]) against the allure of generative semantics and even more extreme alternatives. The Standard Theory had originally held (mistakenly, Chomsky would now concede) that "it was the deep structure of language that completely determined its semantic interpretation." Others, notably Ray Jackendoff (whom Chomsky singles out for special mention in his earlier reflections—I myself simply don't know the full history), provided grounds that led to the replacement of the Standard Theory by the so-called Extended Standard Theory, according to which it was admitted that "surface structure played a much more important role in semantic interpretation than had been supposed" (for instance, as Chomsky conceded, with regard to the relative position of negation and quantification within a sentence).[26] Here you can see the threat that Chomsky means to counter.

This, of course, was meant to be a benign revision that would not put the underlying innatism at serious risk. But, encouraged by the concession, the so-called "generative semanticists" effectively joined what was viewed as deep structure and what as semantic representation at the surface of language. Chomsky responded earlier, in a well-known interview:

The situation grew even worse—if that is possible—when generative semanticists began to incorporate nonlinguistic factors into grammar: beliefs, attitudes, etc. That amounts to a rejection of the initial idealization to language, as an object of study. A priori, such a move cannot be ruled out, but it must be empirically motivated. If it proves to be correct, I would conclude that language is a chaos that is not worth studying—but personally I do not believe that any evidence or substantive arguments have been brought forward in favor of such a hypothesis. Note that the question is not whether belief or attitudes, and so on, play a role in linguistic behavior or linguistic judgments. Of course they do, no one has ever doubted that. The question is whether distinct cognitive structures can be admitted, which interact in the real use of language and linguistic judgments, the grammatical system being one of these.[27]

Chomsky's own radical reversal raises the question whether, if the now-unknown innate structures he posits, which are alleged to operate at a deeper level than do the structures of what he had earlier identified as generative grammars (now, seemingly contingent, not rule-governed in any invariant way), need segregate (or can legitimate the segregation of) linguistic and non-linguistic elements (beliefs, say), as Chomsky had once thought when he was battling the generative semanticists.

In fact, if Chomsky conceded the point, he would at one stroke have weakened the argument for linguistic innatism and retreated to the prospects of an innatist theory of thought, which seems even more problematic. Thus, if linguistic structures are, in part, a function of historical forces, for instance, of a sustained, differentially effective interaction between Czech-speaking communities and politically, economically, and culturally dominant German-speaking communities over centuries—which is said to have resulted in the acquisition, by the Czech language, of certain German grammatical constructions acquired at different rates and with different degrees of penetration—then grammatical innatism will be seen to be much more vulnerable than has usually been conceded. That would certainly constitute a serious challenge to Chomsky's new innatism.

There are indeed empirical studies of language that defeat any simple model of conserving underlying grammatical structures said to be free of the influence of belief, attitudes, history, and the like. These concern the formation and modification of pidgins and creoles under conditions of continuing change where grammatical structure clearly is affected quickly, opportunistically, often by seemingly arbitrary deformations of discourse patterns (across apparent borrowings). Peter Mühlhäusler, a specialist on Polynesian and Melanesian pidgins and creoles, draws conclusions from diachronic (or historical) linguistic studies of changes that are often quite rapid and continually vulnerable to further such changes that go decidedly contrary to the strong universalizing feature intended by Chomsky's earlier "language acquisition device": for instance, that "[transformational generative grammar is], strictly speaking, not suited to explaining the formation of pidgins, but only creole formation"; that "adults retain the capacity to restructure and drastically change linguistic systems"; that, for creoles formed from stable or expanded pidgins, "little carry-over of substratum influence [that is, from the sources of the pidgin] can be expected in the formative years of a creole, because little was encountered in the models"; that, in fact, "what seems to be discourse usage [in one area: that is, a semantically or pragmatically qualified pattern] may have become a syntactic rule [elsewhere]."[28]

In general, Mühlhäusler and other historical linguists, speaking chiefly of pidgins and creolizing, emphasize rapid diachronic change, the mixing of language sources in "non-mechanical" ways (Mühlhäusler suggests the loose metaphor of chemical transformation), the weak presence of substratum grammars, the deformation of phonetic borrowings leading to unrecognizability from presumed source to pidgin, the dynamics of pidgin regularization internal to pidgin societies, sui generis patterns not matched among strong grammaticalized languages, characteristically nonuniversalizable grammatical features, and the like. All of this suggests the strong ineliminability of cultural and historical processes that cannot be reduced in either the Darwinian or the transformational grammarian's way that (on Chomsky's say-so) would lead to a "chaos" but clearly need not do so. Linguistic modularism is clearly threatened by these considerations.

The truth of the matter is that neither Chomsky nor we are at all clear about the possibility of forms of very rapid societal and linguistic learning among infants that might accommodate the grammatical regularities of the languages Chomsky features, without yet relying on "deep grammar" (as constituting the so-called "language faculty") distinguished from innate prelinguistic recognitional capacities of a deeper sort.

It is easy to see that, despite important differences, close studies of genetic processes may well dislodge the universalized model of the particulate gene and, accordingly, the reductive treatment of culture and language. The Chomskyan model is subtler but more elusive. For, on Chomsky's current view, there are invariant grammatical (or perhaps deeper than grammatical) universals, but they need not be specified beyond being implied in the disjunctive universalities (if indeed there are such universalities) relative to one natural language or another. The study of pidgins and early stages of creolizing draws attention to the historical dimension of a living language (which Chomsky almost never examines) and, accordingly, the reasonable interpenetration of grammatical, semantic, and such "nonlinguistic" factors as "belief and attitudes" which, if granted, would undermine Chomsky's boldest and most recent speculation.

If you grant innate prelinguistic learning capacities to be sufficient for rapidly learning a first language but subject to being modified and overridden by emerging forms of cultural learning not adequately captured by familiar inductive processes, and if you admit the counter-considerations of the generative semanticists and the historical linguists, you will have driven Chomsky's recent notion of the "language faculty" and parametric "switches" back to the vulnerabilities of deep grammar itself.

I may as well add: if you concede the point I might have pressed earlier in this discussion (regarding the "lingual"), then Chomsky's strong distinction (perhaps even a disjunction) between the use of language and learning specific aptitudes for action or acquiring beliefs may be seriously challenged. That is what I had in mind in speaking of the fact that choreographing a ballet presupposes linguistic fluency even if it is not itself specifically "linguistic": hence, language is itself lingual and may not be capable of being analyzed, properly, without attending to lingual, contextual, and intentional circumstances. I find that as reasonable a conjecture as any.

Chomsky regards the language faculty as an "initial [biological] state" functioning modularly, though in accord with other parts of the brain (or "mind/brain"), that is "fixed by genetic endowment" and thus not functionally describable in terms of acquired beliefs or acquired concepts.[29] But if we emphasize the characteristic contingency and limited importance (according to Chomsky himself) of the "features" of actual languages (including their grammars), the lack of comparably fixed genetically determined "principles," the importance of the historical features of natural languages, lessons drawn from the study of pidgins, the ability of the generative semanticists to accommodate the same evidence that Chomsky provides, Chomsky's own assumptions about innate concepts and beliefs, and the general difficulty of applying genetic distinctions to the intentional complexities of concepts and beliefs (which Chomsky acknowledges), we must concede that we are very far from the innatist model Chomsky advances, though we cannot deny the profound (still unexplained) relevance of the famous "poverty of the stimulus" argument and the formal consistency of the entire model.

If we cannot deny the force of the innatist thesis, we may be inclined to doubt overly robust linguistic claims of the innatist sort. These include modularized disjunctions between an innate language faculty relevant to concepts, grammars, and beliefs (in some sense) that are either part of our "initial" biological state or part of "the systems that grow naturally in the mind, beyond the instantiation of initial endowment as [what Chomsky calls] I-language (perhaps also I-belief and related systems)" and whatever else is said to be contributed by natural acquisition growing up in a society possessing a natural language.

Chomsky clearly believes that much of what belongs to what he calls I-language and I-belief (innate, individual, genetically determined, meant to replace "deep grammar" systematically) is "unlearned and universal."[30] But this is very difficult to grasp in any familiar way (unless platonistically), considering that, as Neil Smith confirms, "if [say] two people are equidistant from the [external] surface [of a house], one inside and one outside, [then since] only the one outside can be described as 'near' the house," we are encouraged to conclude that "even very young children seem to know such facts, suggesting that the knowledge is in some sense antecedently available to the organism": in short, innate or innately developed from what is initially innate.[31]

That is very difficult to accept and really is a desperate stretch. Its analysis is confessedly puzzling; yet, Chomsky's thesis also seems untestable, finally, resting as it does much too heavily on the "poverty of the stimulus" argument. Chomsky may well have secured his essential doctrine by insulating it from the usual challenges, but an unconvinced reader may also conclude that he has yielded considerable ground to his principal critics.

v

Broadly speaking, there are at least three large lessons that may be drawn from the foregoing analysis regarding materialism's prospects, that is, the prospects of reductionism and eliminativism. The first is that if the scientific gains of neo-Darwinism and transformational grammar (what Chomsky now characterizes as a constructive biology of the "language faculty") count as the most promising attempts to test the adequacy of a materialist account of mind and culture, then we must conclude that the current state of these sciences yields next to nothing toward strengthening materialism's prospects. Genetic studies appear to have had almost no bearing on the conceptual analysis of the hard-core features of the distinctive mental and cultural life of humans. Lumsden and Wilson, for instance admit that, "in human behavior, the genes do not specify social behavior." Yet they insist on "gene-culture coevolution," which is both more and less sanguine than the minimal thesis that "social behaviors are shaped by natural selection."[32] This is pretty well the limited thesis of the sociobiologist's "culturgen," which presumes fixed rules of epigenetic development but cannot really supply such rules, and avoids claiming that they are themselves genetically determined.

Dawkins makes much the same concession regarding the essentially nongenetic nature of so-called "memic" processes, but he also touches on the possibility that the transmissional powers of cultural processes may go contrary to the selectionist trajectory of the selfish gene itself. That is an absolutely decisive concession. For one thing, Dawkins admits that Darwinism "is too big a theory to be confined to the narrow context of the gene"; he is anticipating in part the disanalogies between meme and gene; for another, he admits that "once this new [so-called memic] evolution begins, it will in no necessary sense be subservient to the old [genic evolution]." Moreover, in what is the ultimate concession for a Darwinian, he admits that "a cultural trait may have evolved in the way that it has, simply because it is advantageous to itself."[33] In a word, the entire play of culture is not explicable in Darwinian terms and may well go contrary to the general thrust of Darwinian fitness. That is, cultural fitness may have only a minimal congruity, on any scale, with the biology of genetics and may actually oppose it, viably. Indeed, this is an extraordinary concession!

Dawkins regards the meme as a physical (non-genic) "replicator," though he nowhere shows that it must be such and admits the fact. What we see is that the Darwinians and the Chomskyans prepare the ground for a materialism of one or another sort, but show no reason to disbelieve that a better answer might merely acknowledge the materialist ground on which the mental and cultural life of humans depends. They then go on to propose a sui generis form of (non-dualistic) emergence based on the emergence of language itself and open to whatever other forms of evolution language makes possible: forms of emergence that are not reducible in purely materialist terms, for instance, the development of the forms of Western painting. Nothing so far drawn from either neo-Darwinian or Chomskyan sources disallows such a possibility—which, based on the evidence, is at least as strong as the reductionisms that have relied on them.

Chomsky, as we have seen, is not a reductionist of the usual sort, though he is an extremely subtle materialist—if, that is, his admiration for Descartes and the Cartesians may count as materialism. In any case, where Dawkins (like Dennett) is a reductionist, Chomsky is what may be called an "ampliative materialist," meaning that he opposes reductionism along the lines already supplied, but believes that the meaning of the "physical" is itself always ampliatively defined (as per his own examples from the history of science) by what the evolution of physics, chemistry, and biology inventively posit ("fields of force," for instance) in resolving the salient cruces of normal science itself. But if so, then in principle Chomsky's materialism is entirely hospitable to what would be anti-reductionist in the recent neo-Darwinian sense!

Here, of course, we must remind ourselves that what in philosophical circles counts as materialism that is in any sense congruent with reductionism, even if not completely reductionistic, requires (1) an analysis of candidate phenomena adequately rendered in some canonical way in physical terms that (2) behave in a thoroughly extensionalist way as well (subject, for example, to the usual constraints of a first-order logic). Chomsky is not a reductionist by reference to condition (1) because he takes the history of science to proceed ampliatively rather than reductively; but he is a materialist nonetheless, because he means to enlarge the meaning of the "physical" in thoroughly extensionalist ways that are in accord with condition (2). Hence, both the Darwinian and the Chomskyan are drawn to the prospects of computationality (or, less restrictedly, extensionality) in perfecting their respective materialisms. But that is to define the problem, not yet to solve it. The Darwinians have never really come to grips with the intensional complications of language, culture, and history, whereas the Chomskyans have, but only by way of an enormously nervy and risky conjecture.

Let me bring some closure to the argument by citing a few telling specimen remarks. On the side of the Darwinians, Henry Plotkin, a self-styled "evolutionary psychologist," offers the following pronouncement in a well-respected recent book:

> Ontological reductionism is now virtually the universally held position in science. This is the view that all things are physical things and nothing else. Take a living creature, any living creature, and it comprises only physical processes and mechanisms. There is no mysterious, ineffable, undefinable, untouchable or unmeasurable force or property of life beyond a very complex organization of chemicals which is described by the laws of chemistry and physics. . . . The mind is the workings of the brain, and the connectivity of billions of individual brain cells is of a complexity probably greater than any other known thing, bar one. [Plotkin means, here, to single out culture as more complex than the human brain: that is, "the collection of human brains and their psychological processes that make up human culture, which is defined here as shared knowledge and beliefs."] Nonetheless, no matter how complex that connectivity, the mind and the brain are just chemistry and physics. There are simply no dualist psychologists in existence—nobody thinks that what psychologists study is some kind of immaterial spirit.[34]

Plotkin, who is certainly a well-informed discussant, has somehow misled himself into thinking that the conceptual difficulties posed by language and culture for reductionists would be completely resolved if we rejected dualism. I trust it will be enough to say that Plotkin's opinion is very widespread; for example, it is certainly shared by Dawkins, Dennett, and Pinker.[35] But if so, then all four have completely misunderstood the plain sense in which Franz Brentano's distinction between the mental and the physical,

if rightly understood, fixes the contemporary focus of the problem of reductionism, despite the fact that Brentano's own formulation is hardly more
than the barest beginning of what the pertinent data would support and
require.That aside, Brentano's distinction is not dualistic at all, in my esti-
mation.[36] That begins to confirm the sense in which contemporary neo-
Darwinian philosophers have simply never come to the essential problems,
which have to do (and have always had to do) with the prospects of extensionalist (characteristically, externalist, supervenientist, or similar) analyses
of the mental and the cultural. At the present time, there is no promising,
thoroughly extensionalist model of language, mind, history, or culture that
could be fitted to any known materialism in a way that would either preserve the "folk" description and explanation of the relevant data or would
support a strong replacement (eschewing folk conceptions) that would still
satisfy our predictive, technological, and explanatory concerns.

Chomsky's "ampliative" reading of the physical obviates at a stroke anything like Plotkin's error. This is why Chomsky does not recognize the mind/
body problem as a serious philosophical problem. He can afford to discount
it because, though he has neutralized the challenge of what I identified a moment ago as reductionism's condition (1), he requires, a priori, a thoroughgoing extensionalism in any "scientific" account of mind or language; hence,
no other options need apply. I believe this seriously qualifies his intended
open-minded review of what the data may require.

Chomsky's new theory is genuinely breathtaking. Here is a slim version
of it:

> We can think of the initial state of the faculty of language [innate,
> biologically determined] as a fixed network connected to a switch
> box: the network is constituted of the principles of language, while
> the switches are the options to be determined by experience. When
> the switches are set one way, we have Swahili; when they are set an-
> other way, we have Japanese. Each possible human language is iden-
> tified as a particular setting of the switches—a setting of parameters,
> in technical terminology. If the research program succeeds, we
> should be able literally to deduce Swahili from one choice of set-
> tings, Japanese from another, and so on through the languages that
> humans can acquire. They are, in effect, computationally generated,
> that is, thoroughly extensionalist. The empirical conditions of lan-
> guage acquisition require that the switches can be set on the basis of
> the very limited information that is available to the child. Notice that
> small changes in switch settings can lead to great apparent variety in

output, as the effects proliferate through the system. These are the general properties of language that any genuine theory must capture somehow.[37]

But suppose the child's learning is not negligibly small; suppose the child has learned enough prelinguistically to make what appears to be empirically negligible not negligible at all; suppose, that is, along the lines of Chomsky's worst worries, that grammar is not separable from semantics, pragmatic interests, beliefs, and history. The entire gamble on his extreme innatism would instantly fail, though all of Chomsky's splendid empirical work would stand (in a duly altered form). Chomsky himself observes that "the conclusions tentatively reached are unlikely to stand in their present form; and, needless to say, one can have no certainty that the whole approach is on the right track."[38] Just so.

But then, the fate of the innatism of the would-be "principles" rests entirely on the fixed, language-local, exceptionless, extensionalist uniformities of the would-be "parameters" by which all natural languages are predictably distinguished from one another. We will have risked a great deal for what may well be a most unlikely gain—if, for instance, the historical linguists and generative semanticists can go their own way more convincingly (with respect to the empirical evidence) than Chomsky can.

Imagine, for instance, that human languages are not all of one kind, though they can be learned from the vantage of any natural language; imagine, further, that it is not possible to learn a first language in its normally fluent way without living among apt speakers and that that is because linguistic fluency entails lingual fluency; imagine, again, that there is no principled modularity that separates the innate structures of human language from the historical contingencies of our apparent fluency and that this is due to the fact that any would-be deep structure is always hostage to the social forces that change and even deform the regularities on which our fluency depends.

My sense is that we are still at square one, but wiser.

2

Incommensurability Modestly Recovered

I

The single most important fact about incommensurability is how blandly it is ignored and casually denied.[1] I mean ultimately of course Thomas Kuhn's immensely troubling challenge to conventional conceptions of scientific method and rationality, which may be regarded as a natural extension of the ancient puzzle posed by the Pythagorean theorem. Kuhn's famous challenge, which seems to have upset the author himself, makes no sense apart from the very modern notion of the historicity of our explanatory concepts and the conditions of knowledge. If you scan the entire range of current English-language philosophy, hard-core analytic philosophy or something less decisive, you will find that incommensurability is conceptually well-nigh invisible. At the risk of a bad joke, I would say that it's a little like racial prejudice viewed through the eye of a satisfied liberal: it does not exist because it would be incompatible with our legal assurance of equal opportunity— "which no one can deny." But that means, of course, that incommensurability is essentially a political or ideological problem for the dominant currents of recent American philosophy. Or, better, it needs to be analyzed as if it were (if its proper challenge is to be grasped at all).

The question is a conceptual one, but the trick is to help those who can't even see what must be seen, to get their proper bearings. For you realize that the familiar, much-trafficked philosophical terrain still harbors mysterious practices—right under our nose. The best philosophies are often occupied with making the obvious obvious.

The latter-day saints of incommensurability—or, better, incommensurabilism—are, of course, Thomas Kuhn and Paul Feyerabend. Both were intuitively gifted, but neither was politically adept in the required academic way. Kuhn was deficient in dialectical skills and was even temperamentally opposed to his own argument; and Feyerabend was, finally, too antic to care about making his argument effective. The result was that both were outflanked, though they made their case in an arresting way. It's been officially written off, you realize, most famously by Donald Davidson, and so cunningly that no one now admits the blind sight of our polite denials. There's my charge, at least.

Incommensurabilism is still worth recovering, except that if the charge is valid, then much of recent canonical philosophy may have victimized itself, may have failed to perceive the profound distortion of its sincerest practice. Seen that way, our usual inquiries cannot be trusted to mean what they are said to mean: we shall need all sorts of indirection to see what we are asked to see. I warn you, therefore, that we cannot expect to rely on the corrective power of instant intuition, though it remains true enough that we must finally fall back to something like intuition. In the last analysis, things either fall into place happily or they do not—or so we say!

Start, then, with an oblique clue. Hilary Putnam, who yields to no one in his contempt for relativism and incommensurabilism, asserts unblinkingly: "as soon as one tries to state relativism as a *position* it collapses into inconsistency or into solipsism (or perhaps solipsism with a 'we' instead of an 'I'). The thought that everything we believe is, at best, only 'true in our language game' isn't even a coherent thought: is the very existence of our language then only 'true in our language game'?"[2]

This is a very slippery line of reasoning, hardly hospitable to Kuhn's and Feyerabend's reasoning. (I admit that incommensurabilism is a form of relativism, but not if relativism is construed in Putnam's way.) Putnam sides with the argument brought, in Plato's *Theaetetus*, against Protagoras; for Putnam holds that relativists and incommensurabilists are either solipsists "with a 'we'" or solipsists "with an 'I'"—where, that is, the latter formula is assigned Protagoras, though the former might be Putnam's preferred description of Protagoras as well.

I grant the force of the imputed charge, though not the charge itself brought against either Kuhn or Protagoras: I agree entirely with Putnam—and with Plato, *if* Plato did believe that what he dramatized in the dialogue was the best reading of Protagoras's position (which I do not accept). I agree that, thus construed, relativism and incommensurabilism would be hopelessly inconsistent and incoherent. Fine. But you cannot fail to remark that the divergence, or incompatibility, or even the incommensurability of the beliefs and convictions of different individuals and different societies *does not entail* that those who differ thus subscribe to the "relationalist" formula (Socrates's, in the *Theaetetus*, Putnam's, in the passage cited) construed either as a solipsism "with an 'I'" or "a 'we,'" the formula, that is, that holds that "true means 'true-for-x'" (where "x" is either an individual or a society).[3] Putnam has gained his point in a peculiarly spare way: he simply admits no obligation to examine other possibilities.

"Solipsism with a 'we'" is not even a true solipsism, of course, though it is a fatal mistake for societies that interact with one another (and are aware that they do). Bear in mind that there is no known language for which there are no apt bilinguals. Nevertheless, the mistake may be no more than a naive conviction. "Solipsism with a 'we'" rises to the level of deep incoherence only if it is a deliberate philosophical presumption on which an entire body of would-be truths is thought to depend. We are not driven to any such premise. It was indeed Evans-Pritchard's famous and fatal premise offered in his account of the Azande, which, memorably, Peter Winch undertook to examine closely.[4] It was also the presumption of Ranke's very different but comparably incoherent historicism.[5]

Curiously, Putnam overlooks the possibility that judgments and truth-claims may diverge, may be incompatible, may even be incommensurable, without the opposed parties ever being committed to divergent, incompatible, or incommensurable accounts of truth, *or* ever committed to the relationalist theory of truth in any form.[6] All we need admit is that to have an *adequate* theory of truth does not entail our having adequate criteria of truth (adequate criteria for the application of truth-values). Certainly, the correspondence theory of truth is still invoked, though almost never with the hope of specifying its adequate criteria. Here, we normally fall back to distinguishing carefully between "truth" and assignable "truth-values." The matter is altogether different in theorizing about knowledge.

It is not in the least clear that Putnam ever admits the relativist or incommensurabilist possibility. It would of course go contrary to the spirit of his *Grenzbegriff*, or limit-concept, mentioned only once at the very close of his best-known book, *Reason, Truth and History*, which suggests that he does not allow for any such possibility.[7] He offers only this unguarded (and unexplained) dictum—in the context of airing relativism's prospects: "The very fact that we speak of our different conceptions as different conceptions of *rationality* posits a *Grenzbegriff*, a limit-concept of the ideal truth."[8]

But there is no known compelling argument to the effect that subscribing to "different conceptions of rationality" (or truth) *entails* the incomparability or unintelligibility of such conceptions. Putnam never addresses the problem, which bids fair to undermine his entire argument—both his realism and his pluralism. It also undermines, as we shall see, Donald Davidson's extraordinarily influential charge against Kuhn and Feyerabend, which, thus far at least, converges with Putnam's pronouncement. For Davidson is the acknowledged architect of the widespread judgment that incommensurabilism is and must be utterly incoherent—utterly beyond redemption. And yet, of course, there is nothing intrinsically incoherent about a contest between incompatible or incommensurable doctrines. If true, then incommensurabil*ism* may prove viable after all; and if it is, then its coherence will expose a very deep mistake in our present dismissal of Kuhn and Feyerabend. There's a premise missing—and ignored.

Please notice that, in my putting the matter this way, the fate of incommensurabilism (and relativism) cannot be made to depend on Putnam's flawed analysis of relativism or Davidson's flawed analysis of incommensurabilism, or (for that matter) on Kuhn's or Feyerabend's flawed analyses of particular episodes in the history of science. All that is needed are reasonable specimens or proposals of what to count as relativist or incommensurabilist options. My aim here is to draw attention to neglected conceptual possibilities that cannot rightly be ignored, if the usual realist options be admitted. The reason, obviously, is that we cannot segregate the options in question by any satisfactory criterial rule so that the threat of relativism and incommensurabilism (or historicism and constructivism) can be kept from sight until the central cases are disposed of in the approved canonical way. No. The point is that the threat of the deviant options bleeds into the fate of the central cases themselves. *That* is what should trouble us.

Putnam's formulaic "solipsism-with-a 'we'" is, in effect, a clever summary of Davidson's more ramified attack on Kuhn's and Feyerabend's incommensurabilism—the nerve of Davidson's well-known essay, "On the Very Idea of a Conceptual Scheme."[9] Putnam offers the same charge in a Wittgensteinian idiom that he invents for the purpose, which, once again, betrays the inexplicable blind spot already remarked. Glossing Wittgenstein, he says very neatly: "To say something is true in a language game is to stand outside of the language game and make a comment: that is not what it is to play a language game."[10] Of course, he's right—*on* the reading he advances. But it's hardly true that "*to* say something is true in a language game *is* to stand outside of that language game and make a comment"—in the sense of standing outside all the resources of the language in which this or that "game" is played! To say that this or that is true, say, speaking as the Masons speak—*is not* to say that "true" *means* "true in Masonic talk" (even if what is said *is* true according to Masonic jargon). No. There's a blind spot there, a blind spot that is not essential to Kuhn's and Feyerabend's best formulations of their own position.

The key is this. Putnam claims to be a pluralist, by which he means to say—denying any single, uniquely valid "God's Eye point of view"—that "realism is *not* incompatible with conceptual relativity." He insists, in effect, that this sort of pluralism does not entail anything like the Protagorean formula of the *Theaetetus*[11] or the objectivist view that we *do* know the real world as it is apart from our inquiries and know that there is only one finally valid account of its properties. He treats such claims as beyond our resources. He intends his pluralism as a third way. He has touched on something quite important here. But it cannot help him in his own account.

There are two disastrous weaknesses in what Putnam says. For one, if he's right about his pluralism, then, contrary to what he says, the same will hold for incommensurabilism: realism will be found to be compatible with incommensurabilism *if*, as may be shown, it requires no more than extending without let Putnam's idea of "conceptual relativity" to alternative epistemologies as well. That is the stunning challenge Kuhn and Feyerabend put their finger on. It has been completely overlooked by Putnam and Davidson (for very different reasons), which means in effect that it has been completely overlooked in the analytic literature.

This is a most strategic matter because: (1) both pragmatism and analytic philosophy are prepared to abandon all forms of foundationalism and cognitive or facultative privilege; (2) *if* relativism and incommensurabilism may be shown to be coherent and self-consistent (as I believe is true), then there can be no blanket objection against admitting relativistic and incommensurabilist considerations in formulating an adequate theory of scientific objectivity; and (3) it follows that admitting pluralism as a viable reading of objectivity (opposing the God's eye thesis) cannot in principle preclude admitting relativistic and incommensurabilist versions (or analogues) of pluralism. But that is just what Putnam neglects to mention. Its omission threatens to subvert the force of his entire argument against "objectivism" and relativism (or incommensurabilism). It is hard to believe that the attack on relativism could have been allowed to proceed in such a careless way.

The other weakness is just as telling: Putnam (but also Davidson) never broaches the epistemological issue on which, alone, his own "third" option depends and may be shown (as he must somewhere suppose) to be relevantly different—that is, different in a justificatory way—from the incommensurabilist alternative that he neglects. The connecting premise is simply missing. Incommensurabilist alternatives *are*, nevertheless, a distinct species of pluralist alternatives: they depend on epistemological possibilities neither Putnam nor Davidson are willing to bring under the cognitive tent.

The evidence is buried in the following thought-experiment by Putnam:

If the sentence, "points are mere limits" is a contrary of the sentence "points are not limits but parts of space, [where each] sentence occurs in a systematic scheme for describing physical reality . . . *though the two schemes are in practice thoroughly equivalent,* then [it may seem as if] we are in trouble. . . .But the whole point of saying that the two schemes are in practice thoroughly equivalent is that, far from leading us to incompatible predictions or incompatible actions, it makes no difference to our predictions or actions. [Furthermore, a given] sentence in one [scheme] can be correlated in an effective way with a "translation" in the other scheme, and the sentence and its translation will be used to describe the same states of affairs.[12]

There is nothing wrong with Putnam's proposal, except this: How does Putnam know that the two sentences describe "the same states of affairs"? Can he really assure us that there are no epistemologically incommensurable schemes—*never* are—so that we can always in principle decide whether we are or are not addressing "the same state of affairs"? (Think of Quine's notion of the "inscrutability of reference," which is more radical than Putnam's conjecture here.) Imagine that Kuhn could claim an ally in Quine, against both Putnam and Davidson! There's a point of the greatest importance there, but also the danger of incoherence. (I return to Quine in the final chapter.)

The lacuna just noted is the precise point of Kuhn's and Feyerabend's challenge, the point of the puzzling Priestley/Lavoisier controversy. Kuhn and Feyerabend hold that there *are* such cases—which then require resolution by measures that cannot be canonical.

Putnam never reaches this question. What he offers (interesting in its own right) is simply that *for any accepted description of a given state of affairs,* we are always free to introduce *another* scheme for individuating or parsing *the same world*—another ontology, if you please—that can be made "translationally" equivalent (Putnam's term) to the sentences of the scheme with which we begin (because Putnam's term is Quine's in the context of the fundamental problem of *Word and Object:* "the indeterminacy of translation"). Quine's formulation is genuinely radical, applied within the field linguist's limitations. But it risks impenetrability when it is made to presuppose, as it clearly does in Quine's *Pursuit of Truth,* the unexplained fluency of "holophrastic sentences."[13] Putnam never invokes the principle of the inseparability of metaphysics and epistemology, which, at the time of writing, was the leading theme of his ill-fated "internal realism."[14]

That principle is also, as it happens, a particularly strategic theme in the important interval of discovery that spans Kant and Hegel and comes to rest in Hegel, in superseding the transcendental assurances on which Kant had relied in the first *Critique*. In short, Putnam ignores a theme that implicitly links his increasingly pragmatist version of realism with its unacknowledged Hegelian sources—which, in much the same way, informs Kuhn's and Feyerabend's view. Hegel's doctrine, you realize, is well on its way to making provision for both relativism and incommensurabilism—at least implicitly. This is a marvelous irony all around!

In fact, the inseparability *is* implicated in the modest pluralism Putnam now invokes. But if it is, then, unless principled objections may be brought to bear (a possibility neither Putnam nor Davidson pursues), the same inseparability will bring in its wake the unwanted complications of relativism and incommensurabilism. Pluralism will then not be able to withstand the subversive invitation of these heterodoxies. Alternatively put: pluralism (Putnam's sort of pluralism) will finally be seen to be the same objectivism Putnam has always opposed; what it concedes will be largely irrelevant to the deep challenge Kuhn and Feyerabend press: a tolerance for our fragmentary and transient interests that are content (in Putnam) never to make us demonstrate the convergent unity and compatibility of the plural strands of theory we may pursue. But that is hardly an argument.

The post-Kantian discovery is far more important than Putnam's rejection of his own internal realism.[15] For, of course, it is the constructivist reading of the inseparability of metaphysics and epistemology, precluding as it does any assured or privileged fixity of "the same states of affairs," that ultimately provides the dialectical bite of Kuhn's and Feyerabend's incommensurabilism. Kuhn may not have been aware of the conceptual connection, and Feyerabend may not have been interested in acknowledging any such reliance; and both may be challenged in their reading of particular episodes in the history of science. But it is there all the same and makes possible *their* thinned-down intuitions. Cast in Hegelian terms, we may simply say that our pertinent beliefs are informed (actually formed) by the *geistlich* resources of our home culture, the same culture in which we ourselves are first made linguistically competent. But then there cannot be any *a priori* assurance that the "plural" possibilities that arise (what Putnam calls "cultural relativity") will always converge, must coherently converge, in terms of Putnam's own tame pluralism.

It is in fact not generally recognized that Hegel's account of the "construction" of objects [*Gegenstände*] within the flux of *Erscheinungen*, in the *Phenomenology*, need not be assured of any *a priori* convergence toward "what is" independently real (what Hegel calls *Objekte*). This is not because Hegel subscribes to Kant's "subjectivism" without his transcendentalism but, on the contrary, because he escapes Kant's limitations in both the

Phenomenology and the *Encyclopedia*. Nevertheless, to "escape" is *not* to supersede the inseparability of epistemology and metaphysics *or* the contingencies of a specifically human form of cognition.

II

Though it was remarkably unguarded, Davidson's charge of incoherence[16] leveled against Kuhn's and Feyerabend's original challenge does begin to define the outer limits of what we should understand by incommensurability. Davidson neglects the usual garden varieties, those in fact that do not depend on the vexed epistemological doctrines so many have stumbled over. These common varieties actually help us to see what may be salvaged from the latter. Incommensurability remains, in general, a muddle, even though, setting Kuhn and Feyerabend aside, it cannot fail to strike us as, or as harboring, a perfectly respectable, even ubiquitous, even quietly acknowledged, phenomenon. The reason the entire issue was featured in the derogatory way it was in the analytic tradition is that it was mistakenly conflated with historicism's deeper challenge to the objectivist pretensions of the analytic canon: in effect, what, in the name of realism and naturalism, is hardly more than a late continuation of the fatal "Cartesianism" that spans Descartes and Kant. Clearing the air on incommensurability should help us put the larger issue in a better light.

This needs to be explained. By "Cartesianism" or "Cartesian realism" I mean any realism, no matter how defended or qualified, that holds that the world has a determinate structure apart from all constraints of human inquiry *and* that our cognizing faculties are nevertheless able to discern those independent structures reliably. "Cartesianism" serves here as a term of art, as not confined to Descartes's own doctrine. It ranges over pre-Kantian philosophy, Kant's own philosophy (quixotically), and even over the views of such contemporary theorists as Putnam and Davidson. Twentieth-century analytic philosophy is, in this respect, thoroughly pre-Kantian, or Kantian in that way in which Kant himself is pre-Kantian: it is an unabashed continuation of seventeenth and eighteenth-century philosophy threatened in precisely the same way its ancestors originally were. The unyielding lesson of Kant and the post-Kantians is that Cartesianism is incoherent in all its forms. Hegel is usually credited with formulating (in his *Phenomenology*) the most compelling sketch of a *reductio* of Cartesianism up to the early nineteenth century. The main feature of Hegel's strategy, which, in American philosophy, is preserved (almost without attribution) among the classic pragmatists (particularly Dewey) retires altogether the very idea of reference to a "noumenal" world or a world the properties of which are separable from whatever *they* are said to appear to be to human inquirers, and reinterprets "appearances" (*Erscheinungen*) as open to the recovery of no more than a "constructed" realism, that is, a realism shorn of the recuperative use of the "Cartesian" habit of opposing or disjoining "appearance" and "reality" completely. (*If,* that is, "realism" is a proper term for rendering the sense of the *Phenomenology's* argument.)

It is apparently difficult to grasp (in the analytic tradition) that the post-Kantian *reductio* and the advocacy of a constructive realism are simply *not* equivalent to any form of idealism—in that sense in which Kant and many of the post-Kantians (Schelling, for instance, also Peirce!) *are* idealists. Hegel's essential theme, that appearances (*Erscheinungen*) count as the "appearings"-of-the-world-to-us, so that the things we say we encounter in the world (*Gegenstände*) are what we construe to be objectively persistent among our *Erscheinungen,* on whatever constructed conception we are able to defend against alternatives, is entirely straightforward, though hardly straightforwardly stated. If you grasp Hegel's ingenious adjustment, you grasp the sense in which constructivism need not be idealism, as well as the sense in which to abandon Kant's transcendentalism (including Hegel's possible longing for a historicized replacement) is to expose the illicit transcendental longing of Putnam's pluralism. The essential clue (which is already in good part in Hegel) is caught by the idea that the constructivist account of independent "objects" must be matched by a constructivist account of cognizing and active "subjects." But *that* is an idea completely inimical to the Cartesian drift of late twentieth-century analytic philosophy. Putnam's pluralism counts as a particularly telling piece of evidence of the vulnerable Cartesianism of a great deal of American philosophy—*a fortiori,* of most American philosophy of science.

The opponents of "realism" usually intend as their target some version of the "Cartesian" doctrine. One must take care, therefore, in recovering the term, in agreement with the so-called "anti-realists" (of various stripes), to appreciate both that some among them (Michael Dummett, for instance) are also "realists" in a recuperated sense.[17] They are *not* "idealists" in either the sense akin to Kant's (whether transcendentalist or not) or in the sense favored by certain German and British Idealists (Schelling or T. H. Green, for instance). They may remain Cartesians of a sort, as does Dummett, no less than Davidson. Otherwise, the recuperated sense, in accord at least with the central resolution of both the Cartesian and Kantian paradoxes offered in Hegel's *Phenomenology* (the original site of the full resolution of both paradoxes—admittedly too problematic a text to rest an argument on directly) must be constructive (or constructivist) which, for some commentators (Michael Devitt, for one[18]), is, erroneously, sufficient to convert the anti-realist into an idealist.

"Constructivism" signifies: (1) that there can be no principled disjunction between epistemology and metaphysics, or between the evidentiary roles of cognizing subjects and cognized objects in assessing the objectivity of truth-claims; and (2) that whatever (constructively) is construed as ontically independent of human inquiry is, as such, *epistemically* (not criterially) dependent, in accord with (1). The great shift in modern philosophy ushered in by Hegel replaces transcendental constructivism (Kant), which is effectively an idealism, with a constructivism that depends on human resources and escapes idealism. But if we abandon (as we must) all forms of cognitive privilege, admit the coherence of incommensurability, *and* historicize cognitive resources, we cannot fail to see that we are but a step away from admitting the viability of Kuhn's and Feyerabend's incommensurabilism. Analytic philosophers—notoriously, Davidson and Putnam—ignore these dialectical linkages. That means a loss of nearly two hundred years' work, even if we suppose that Hegel sets the problem that we have yet to solve. The point is simply this: the incommensurabilism issue (like those of relativism and historicism) sets conceptual constraints on what we should count as an adequate philosophy of science, which affects, therefore, the prospects of scientism.

The connection with the views of Kuhn and Feyerabend is simply that they, as opposed to Putnam and Davidson, subscribe to a realism (if we may call it that) that implicitly eschews Cartesianism, favors some form of constructivism, and does so on the basis of a historicized account of our cognizing abilities. In this regard, they are "Hegelian" in spirit (though not explicitly), very probably more radical then Hegel, certainly more radical than the pragmatists, though in a way that extends the pragmatists' own critique of Cartesianism. Once you have these themes in hand, it is relatively easy to see how Putnam simply ignores the incommensurabilist option (assuming, that is, that incommensurabilism can be coherently formulated).

The rejection (as by Davidson) of incommensurability on grounds of its patent incoherence or paradoxicality or self-contradiction presupposes something akin to the thesis of a closed universe—most typically, a closed physical universe, as among the supervenientists, of whom Davidson and Jaegwon Kim are perhaps the best-known exemplars[19]—conceptually constrained at the very least by prior necessities of thought that simply rule incommensurability out of bounds. The supervenientist presumption (the idea that determinate mental changes necessarily supervene on determinate

physical changes)—or, better, the closed-universe presumption on which
supervenientism itself depends—shows very clearly that if we allow such
conceptual limitations to constrain our account of reality *a priori* (or count
them as metaphysical discoveries themselves), we will be forced to argue in
the Cartesian manner.

Davidson presumes that there *is* an obvious necessity *de cogitatione* that
systematically precludes the bare conceptual eligibility of the incommensurability thesis. Allow that to stand unchallenged for the moment, though it
is also completely undefended: it turns out to be the essential nerve of
Davidson's entire objection. All modal detractors (as we may call them),
those who agree with Davidson, argue that the defeat of incommensurabilism need never concern itself with anything like the historicity of thought
and cognition or the historicity of a realism fitted to the sciences, which, of
course, are featured in Kuhn's "different worlds" conjecture.

What I reported a moment ago about Putnam's pluralism and his attack
on "solipsism with a 'we'" could never have been directed against incommensurabilism (or relativism) if he had not, at some subterranean level of
thought, supposed that there *was* a condition of conceptual closure that
ruled out such historicized developments as those Kuhn and Feyerabend
claimed to find. Make no mistake about it: Kuhn's and Feyerabend's account
of incommensurabilism is an extreme epistemological option that cannot
be matched by anything that may be found in Hegel or the pragmatists—*a
fortiori,* by anything that may be found in analytic philosophy.

I see no other plausible explanation of Putnam's blind spot than his resid-
ual Cartesianism (or transcendentalism). It explains his appeal to his *Grenzbegriff* and it is a corollary of Davidson's explicit objection against Kuhn.

Here, I must say candidly: Davidson's presumption has never been successfully demonstrated and rests on an utter misreading of Kuhn's original
texts; also, against both Putnam and Davidson, the prospects of Kuhn's conjecture about paradigm shifts cannot be freed from the empirical evidence
about epistemological incommensurabil*ism* in the history of science itself
(as in Kuhn's famous example of the Priestley/Lavoisier controversy) and
that, apart from incommensurabilism, the incommensurabil*ity* debate (the
debate about ordinary conceptual incommensurability) should provide
specimens that do not rely, philosophically, on the other. To admit all this,
which seems eminently reasonable, yields an instant advantage. For, if conceptual incommensurabilities are as uncontroversial and widespread as we
all imagine, then it is but a step to make the case that incommensurabilism
(epistemological incommensurabilities) is likely to appear *within the range
of ordinary incommensurabilities*! If so, then Putnam and Davidson must be
whistling in the wind.

The elementary point is this: semantic incommensurability *is* linguistically ubiquitous, utterly beyond dispute; it is also conceptually, theoretically, philosophically quite benign. Hence, *any* attack on the bare phenomenon cannot fail to be a blunder. Furthermore, *if,* as seems to be true as well, incommensurability of the specifically epistemological sort obtains from time to time *within* the span of "garden variety" incommensurabilities (say, in the Priestley/Lavoisier case), then the opponents of incommensurabil*ism* (the defense of second-order epistemological incommensurabil*ities*) had better look to their own devices. They may find themselves completely outflanked.

You must remember that Kuhn took Galileo to be his principal exemplar of a practicing scientist, someone actually familiar (as a result of his own training) with the very different "worlds" of Aristotelian science and the emerging dynamics of late medieval science that led directly to Galileo's contribution regarding the pendulum. Kuhn could never have consistently supposed that the fair admission of incommensurability entailed the unintelligibility of one such paradigm scanned by the partisans of another, or the incomparability of two such paradigms, or even the impossibility of translating the terms of either paradigm by way of an idiom that made room for the other. If you admit this much, you cannot fail to admit that a considerable part of the incommensurabilism dispute cannot be made to support the dire philosophical charges usually brought against Kuhn. Admitting that much is (of course) not equivalent to vindicating Kuhn's specific thesis about paradigm shifts (or his version of incommensurabilism, or his weak defense of his own thesis). That must be remembered. But it is still the first step in the argument.

The strategic point is almost trivial: *if* conceptual incommensurabil*ity* is a commonplace and not a problem in terms of intelligibility or translation or truth-claims, then, if we abandon cognitive privilege and historicize the inseparability of metaphysics and epistemology, it will be very probable (it will certainly be more than abstractly possible) that incommensurabil*ist* epistemologies will arise from time to time *within* the space of garden variety incommensurabilities! Second-order challenges will then arise out of our first-order practices. That amounts to a *reductio* of Putnam's pluralism—*and* Davidson's attack on alternative "conceptual schemes" (which I have yet to introduce properly).

III

Let me put this more manageably. If you hold that nature is a closed system, meaning by that that science progressively grasps the single inclusive order that *is* the independent world (call that "objectivism" or "Cartesianism"), the incommensurabilism thesis will be ruled out at once, but *not* for the reasons

Davidson suggests, namely, that (1) *completely* independent (read: *not* in any way or degree intertranslatable) conceptual schemes cannot even be grasped (which is true enough but irrelevant) or (2) that *partially* independent (different) conceptual schemes risk the anomaly of being independent *parts* that are too independent to be parts of any one scheme (which is surely a dreadful confusion).[20]

The reason is simpler and more telling than Davidson imagines: for, *if* the independent world can be discerned as it is independently, without interpretive props of any kind, then it *is* a system of sorts, and then it *is* coherent *qua* that system, and then there would cease to be any Kuhnian-like role for epistemological incommensurabilities (in effect, incommensurabilism proper) to play—that is, *at* the point at which we do grasp the way the world is! But *if* that prospect—which (as I say) is now often called "objectivism"[21]—were indefensible or unconvincing or inaccessible, then whatever we construed *as* the independent world (on our best evidence or reasons) would always be subject to interpretive intermediaries that we could never altogether eliminate.

Then, though we might indeed hope to grasp the inclusive system of the whole of nature, we could never rule out a plurality of partial, competing accounts of the independent world—which is all that would be initially needed to allow Kuhnian-like incommensurabilities to flower. Although, of course, that alone would hardly establish Kuhn's (or Feyerabend's) thesis. (Bear in mind that more innocuous or elementary incommensurabilities than Kuhn's would always obtain.)

Our picture of the objective world would then be a *construction* and, because of that, large-scale incommensurabilities could never be ruled out. That would *not* be because the world was constructed or "mind-dependent" in any purely ontic sense (in effect, idealism's characteristic claim), but because whatever, on epistemic grounds, we rightly judged to be *ontically independent* would count as such *only on* the sufferance of its being *epistemically dependent* (that is, confirmed). This condition cannot be satisfied except in the constructivist way; that is the price of rejecting Cartesianism. But if that is so, then, construed epistemically, the idea of a closed universe is itself a constructive idealization; hence, it cannot be invoked in any convincing way to defeat incommensurabilism. There's the pivot of the matter. I take this to pose the deepest question about exactly what Hegel managed to formulate as his recovery of the "objective" world. My own intuition is that his account should yield in the relativistic direction, whether his actual texts finally support such a finding or not.

What these considerations show—perhaps surprisingly—is that the outright rejection of incommensurabilism, as unintelligible or paradoxical, or self-defeating or incoherent, is no more than a vestigial corollary of Cartesianism itself; also, that constructivism (which opposes Cartesianism and which cannot fail to tolerate the possibility of incommensurabilism) is *not* necessarily a form of idealism at all but only a denial (in effect, a denial of the closed Cartesian universe) of the belief *that* metaphysical and epistemological (or, semantic or logical or psychological) questions *can* be disjunctively pursued.

The bare admissibility of the incommensurabilism thesis is bound to the acceptance of something akin to the following triad: (1) the inseparability of epistemological and metaphysical questions regarding the objective world; (2) the indefensibility of objectivism; and (3) the epistemic inescapability of contingent interpretive intermediaries. (Putnam actually favors such a triad but restricts the application.) The first item is the most general lesson implicated in the defeat of Cartesianism, laid down by the contributions of Kant and Hegel, without our being forced to adopt their particular doctrines; the second concurs with Kuhn's rejection of epistemic neutrality in the correspondentist sense, the natural mate of the first; and the third is the inference that, on the strength of the first two assumptions, no viable realism can be more than a constructive and historicized realism (a constructivism), and not for that reason alone a form of idealism (which would be a perverse reading of the first assumption).

This does not quite tell us what to count as a viable specimen of incommensurabilism in the Kuhnian sense, but it permits us to retrieve, without controversy, ordinary forms of conceptual incommensurability on which the other builds, namely, whatever admits the absence of a common metric (expressed in integers) by which, say, the sides of a right triangle would, if commensurable, be able to be measured by the same metric—hence, by extension, the absence of any suitably analogous conceptual instrument that behaved not unlike a metric, in the way of straightforward comparison, subsumption, generalization, or the like (as in speaking of the different visual appearances of the sky). The important lesson is, first, that incommensurability (among attributes) is widespread; second, that it has nothing, as such, to do with being unintelligible, incomparable, untranslatable, or even eliminable; and, third, that it is so bland a doctrine that its bare admission is even reconcilable with nature's being a closed system.

Let me put the last remark a little more perspicuously: incommensurabilities associated with the Pythagorean case are so simple that they have almost no bearing on the larger issues theorists like Davidson and Putnam bring against Kuhn and Feyerabend; correspondingly, Kuhn and Feyerabend's objections to treating science's picture of nature as a progressively completed account of a single closed system makes room for deeper incommensurabilities than those envisaged by the simple case. These two observations count as a gain, because they confirm that the *a priori* rejection of large-scale epistemological incommensurabilities is a direct consequence of advocating some version of the very objectivism Kuhn and Feyerabend intended to contest. It's the failure to see that Kuhnian-like incommensurabilism hangs on a deeper puzzle than do Pythagorian and similar incommensurabilities that befuddles the debate.

Let me put another argumentative nail in place to suggest how to move from the elementary cases to the Kuhnian case. If, say, the lengths of the sides of a right triangle are incommensurable with that triangle's hypotenuse, then so, too, are the sets of different colors and different lengths of textile swatches vis-à-vis one another (that is, colors and lengths). The lengths of the right triangle's sides plainly remain comparable—the hypotenuse being longer than the other sides—though they remain incommensurable in the technical sense; and the color of any swatch will (trivially) be incommensurable with its length, and vice versa, in the obvious sense that lengths do not fall under the category "color" or colors under the category "length." To be sure, the *categories* "color" and "length" can be compared as distinct categories that range over the same particulars (swatches of fabric) and may belong, coherently, to a larger descriptive scheme of categories: all such incommensurabilities will be marked within a linguistic practice apt for doing so.

So it is reasonably clear that to think (with Davidson) of conceptual schemes that are utterly or "partially" unrelated to one another—"conceptually incommensurable" only in *that* Pickwickian sense—is to confound utterly *any* ordinary sense in which incommensurables are admitted. Finally, if all this is so, then incommensurable concepts (as distinct from the incommensurabilist doctrine) must be ubiquitous, benign, paraphraseable, not necessarily encumbered by the historical drift of paradigms or the historicity of thought itself.

This is not yet the place to pit Kuhn and Davidson against one another. But you will find it helpful to remember that, when he attacks Kuhn's and Feyerabend's views on incommensurability, Davidson unaccountably conflates Kuhn's well-known rejection of neutrality with the "failure of intertranslatability" and with the bare admission of conceptual incommensurability.[22] This is a multiple blunder: because incommensurables *are* translatable *qua* incommensurables; because their being translatable does not presuppose or entail any neutral stance or language; because the so-called untranslatability of incommensurables signifies no more than that translation cannot overtake incommensurability itself; and because, on Kuhn's own thesis, incommensurability does not imply *any* failure of language at all.

Here is what Davidson says—famously:

> The failure of intertranslatability is a necessary condition for difference of conceptual schemes; the common relation to experience of the evidence is what is supposed to help us make sense of the claim that it is languages or schemes that are under consideration when translation fails. It is essential to this idea that there be something neutral and common that lies outside all schemes. That common something cannot, of course, be the *subject matter* of contrasting languages, or translation would be possible.[23]

Obviously, Davidson is committed to some version of neutrality, *unlike Kuhn*, for he (Davidson) holds that if there were incommensurable conceptual schemes (which he opposes), then translation would *necessarily* fail. Hence, if translation succeeds or is possible, as Davidson obviously believes, then there are no incommensurable conceptual schemes. But surely the Pythagorean case shows that Davidson is mistaken: ordinary incommensurables are indeed translatable. We need to know what, on Davidson's view, a "conceptual scheme" is. Davidson nowhere defends his charge. The best one can say in his behalf is that he may have wished to fall back to objectivism. (In a way, that *is* true.) Kuhn's cases simply do not require "independent" conceptual schemes in Davidson's sense: Davidson's conjecture is a complete red herring. Davidson neglects to consider the garden variety specimens already sampled. But *they* hold the master key to the entire puzzle.

I must enter a very large stage whisper here: I have not yet officially acknowledged that Davidson's principal target in his attack on Kuhn and Feyerabend is really his own mentor, Quine, as the author of the "indeterminacy of translation" thesis in *Word and Object* and the eventually articulated account of the epistemic "neutrality" of the perceptions represented by the "holophrastic sentences" of Quine's *Pursuit of Truth*.[24]

Now, Quine's thesis is more of a mystery than a false doctrine. There *is* a touch of the neutral in the "holophrastic," I don't deny. But no one, as far as I know, has ever made entirely explicit just what Quine actually affirms. It is more likely that Quine assumed a robust measure of objectivity in scientific description than that he was prepared to pursue specifically evidentiary questions in the epistemologist's dogged way. He builds on the assumption; he never attempts to make it a verdict deliberately arrived at. But it was, indeed, this tendency in Quine that Kuhn wished (in his generous way) to demonstrate was impossible to defend. Davidson flags (without attribution) the fact that Quinean "neutrality" introduces a "danger" to what he himself advances as a replacing canon. The argument about "the very idea of a conceptual scheme" fails to do justice to either Quine or Kuhn.[25] And yet, alas, its influence exceeds its plausibility.

Actually, once you realize that Quine *is* the target of the charge formulated in Davidson's "third dogma" of empiricism, you see at once the coded meaning of Davidson's and Putnam's own dispute, the obvious (but still indefensible) deformation of Kuhn's and Feyerabend's accounts of science, and the utter irrelevance of Davidson's opportunistic use of the scheme/content disjunction in attacking the important epistemological puzzle Kuhn and Feyerabend have unearthed in the name of incommensurabilism. But, here, it is the substantive issue that I mean to salvage. I leave for another occasion the matter of correcting a philosophical injustice. Also, I think it fair to say in Quine's behalf that Davidson offers not the slightest reason to suppose that Quine would be willing to construe his own admission of incommensurability (in the "indeterminacy of translation" issue) along the lines Davidson has laid out.[26]

It may help to mention that Quine's thesis requires: *(a)* an epistemic grounding of the indeterminacy of translation (as in choosing between two would-be translations of, say, "Gavagai!") in some holistic or holophrastic discrimination; *(b)* there being no determinate criterion at the holophrastic level as to how to choose between one translation and another (where each is judged to be satisfactory to the grounding discrimination); and *(c)* the possibility nevertheless of comparing alternative translations of particular propositions taken pair-wise (at least in terms of truth-values). This begins to show that Davidson has not really grasped the complexity of Quine's position, which cannot be said to rule out the compatibility of incommensurability and translatability. Though I do admit Quine never quite helps us to see precisely what his thesis comes to.

You must bear in mind that, for Kuhn, Galileo (Kuhn's exemplar in the matter of mastering epistemological incommensurables) is, in effect, a bilingual completely at home among well-articulated, relatively large-scale explanatory systems that *are* epistemologically incommensurable. Kuhn admits no massive "failures" of language; no neutral world; and, above all, no closed encompassing language or conceptual scheme of any kind. These features are imputed, whole cloth, in Davidson's account, to Kuhn. Objectivism (or Cartesianism) requires that we *read* Kuhn in this dismissive way. But if the foregoing analysis is reasonably correct, then incommensurabilities are always *local* (no matter how extensive or ramified), always *relationally defined* (relative to some favored metric or conceptual analogue); hence, always capable of being *mastered* both monolingually (so to say) and bilingually.

Furthermore, *if* Kuhnian-like incommensurabilities accord with our most elementary specimens, then we should admit that *they* (the garden variety cases) neither presuppose nor require any neutral, inclusive, single, conceptually closed scheme or language; or that *their* detection presupposes or entails the violation of any neutral scheme or language. All viable languages admit bilinguals and lesser or dependent counterparts: as in mastering dialects, idiolects, classificatory schemes, explanatory theories. Hence, *if* Priestley and Lavoisier lived in "different worlds," as Kuhn notoriously affirms,[27] then *they could* still understand one another. *They* would never need to share a neutral language: in fact, there is in principle no difference between the interlinguistic and the intralinguistic.

IV

Now, what I claim is this: *all* the forms of incommensurability are variations of the two kinds of cases I mentioned just above, namely, the Pythagorean case and that of different color swatches of different sizes. The most quarrelsome case, which I am keeping in the wings for the moment, is of course Kuhn's and Feyerabend's, occupied with the historical drift and evolution of thought. I take the latter case to depend on the separate fate of objectivism, but I insist that its bare coherence requires that it be brought into accord, conceptually, with the simpler cases (or with others comparable to them).

Here, a fresh advantage suggests itself. The simplest cases are clearly occupied with predicative distinctions. Could there be a form of incommensurability, then, that holds even among normally compared predicates—colors or spatial relations—taken separately? Of course there can! There are some convincing comparative studies that help to extend the argument—involving the prelinguistic perceptual training of infants growing up among different languages—that yield obviously incommensurable distinctions that are legibly codified nevertheless.[28] The matter is complicated, to be sure, by the learned/innate disputes made famous by Noam Chomsky, as well as by disputes about the role of prelinguistic social learning. But I waive such questions here, except in the sense of leaving them deliberately unresolved—though not in any tendentious way. It is certainly possible that Chomsky's master notion of an innate underlying universal grammar (or UG) is mistaken: in the sense, first, that syntax may be inseparable from semantics, and, second, that, for any such grammar (UG), a given natural language may violate its putative constraints. In fact, as we have seen in chapter 1, Chomsky has signaled a decision to abandon the model of UG for which he is so well known.[29]

In any case, it has been shown that the spatial use of the prepositions *in, on,* and *under* (in English) relies on very distinctive "containment"/"noncontainment" and "support" features (mingling semantic and syntactic considerations) critical for the systematic description of objects ("the cup is on the table," "the picture is on the wall," "the leaf is on the tree," "the band-aid is on the shoulder," "the napkin-ring is on the napkin"); that the use of cognate German prepositions (*auf, an, um*) is more sensitive than English as "to whether a relationship of contact between two objects involves a relatively horizontal surface [*auf*], a vertical or otherwise nonhorizontal surface or contact point [*an*], or encirclement [*um*]." The corresponding distinction, in Dutch, between *op* and *aan,* it is said, "has less to do with orientation than with *method of attachment.*" Spanish apparently bypasses the "on-to-in" continuum by using *en* for both ("an apple EN a bowl," "a cup EN a table"). Several Mixtec (middle-American Indian) languages, which lack prepositions and other locative markers, apparently express something like the relevant spatial relations by way of "an extended and systematic body-part metaphor" (that separates, in addition, animal and human body-part analogies), in some cases (and in some cases not) requiring contact and support, or adjacency, or other configurations.[30]

All these regularities seem to be equally easily learned and yet, of course, the classifications in each language need not be strictly "commensurable" (though they remain comparable) with those of the classificatory schemes of other languages (in different degrees and in different respects) and in a way that might even be replaced by a more inclusive commensurable scheme. Certainly, the reported features of the Mixtec languages suggest how widespread the incommensurability may be, even with regard to the most elementary categories of description. For example, it is said to be particularly difficult to learn the languages of the peoples of the South Pacific islands, apparently in large part because their categories embody the exotic practices and beliefs of notably local societies: under such circumstances, it is very likely that predicative incommensurabilities are bound to arise, which would be difficult to fathom; in fact, it is likely that such languages may not exhibit the high degree of grammaticality (tending toward universality) that characterizes the usual linguistic specimens of Western theories of language. These considerations suggest entirely reasonable empirical objections to Chomskyan linguistic universals of any known kind. But they do not, of course, work directly against the apriorism of Chomsky's rationalist conception of what a science is. (Frankly, the latter seems to me to afford a very much weaker philosophical strategy than the former, but it is the one that Chomsky is driven to by his own scruple.)

To return: incommensurabilities of these last sorts remain both real and benign and are both paraphraseable and replaceable in principle. The important point to remember is that, if (as I would insist) we eschew all appeal to Platonic Forms or natural essences, the commensurability of categories between natural languages will be hostage to the tolerances of what to count as the perceived similarities or acceptable extensions of given general predicates (whether construed intralinguistically or interlinguistically). But that means that incommensurabilities of this third sort lurk everywhere, cannot be eradicated, and produce no particularly paradoxical effects on our fluency (though we must be careful).

It takes but a step to realize that we can afford to allow this sort of phenomenon to be subject, further, to historical drift, as a result of actual collective usage—which even Wittgenstein admits (in a very thin way), though he is no friend of historicism or historicity.[31] If you concede that the paradigm of perception—the human case—is "enlanguaged," cannot be divided between a nonlinguistic sensory element that is first "given" and then linguistically reported (which would, of course, invoke Cartesianism again),[32] then the bare admission of incommensurabilities at the reporting level (subject, further, to historical drift) would effectively confirm the coherence of epistemological incommensurabilities of Kuhn's and Feyerabend's sorts. That would clinch the issue. (I should add here at once that Quine's carefully crafted idiom of "ocular irradiation" and "stimulus meaning" certainly encourages the idea of a disjunction between the sensory and the linguistically interpretive. But Quine himself *never* actually disjoins the two.[33])

I have, at the very least, provided four grades of incommensurability that are clearly more fundamental than the grand sort of conceptual incommensurability Kuhn and Feyerabend feature and Davidson has so effectively (but misguidedly) attacked. They seem to me to form a family of the following sort. First of all, they are clearly intelligible, describable, ubiquitous, open to fluent natural-language use. Second, their being such presupposes a more inclusive linguistic practice in which incommensurables may actually be sorted, though there is no reason to suppose the encompassing language forms a single or inclusive classificatory system or can be counted on to be neutral in the objectivist's sense. Third, the kinds of incommensurability in question are all predicative in nature, hence subject to the intractable difficulties known to affect the local problem of discernible predicative generality.[34] And, fourth, the three sorts of elementary incommensurability (as we may call them) are all subject, on empirical grounds, to historical change and divergence, without any loss of natural-language fluency and without overcoming the constant threat (if it be a threat) of continuing conceptual incommensurability.

I see no way to gainsay these distinctions. They confirm the general finding that the analysis of incommensurability should be separated, without prejudice of any kind, from the analysis of Kuhn's and Feyerabend's cases, except for the important conjecture that the latter cases (Kuhn's and Feyerabend's) may be shown to be extreme instances of, or to depend on, the grades of incommensurability now gathered, and except for the argument that merely historicizing thought normally will not make any of our specimens paradoxical or incoherent. (Bear in mind, furthermore, that all this counts against Putnam's pluralism.)

If all this be conceded, then a decisive part of Kuhn's and Feyerabend's argument will have been shown to be coherent, for the historicized drift of categories will be seen to be a contingency affecting commensurable and incommensurable predicates alike. If the historicity of thought is not inherently paradoxical, then, so far at least, the Kuhnian case will be as benign as the other sorts of incommensurability already collected. I am not claiming (here) that Kuhn's and Feyerabend's deeper incommensurabilist arguments actually hold (though I am prepared to defend them), only that they cannot be faulted simply because they involve incommensurable predicates and entail the historicity of thinking.

It's worth remarking that the familiar critics of Kuhnian incommensurability do not normally attack on grounds of historicity's incoherence; they argue, as Davidson does, on grounds of the supposed formal incoherence of conceptual incommensurability, which, as I have already suggested, presupposes the modal necessity of something like the Cartesian or objectivist position (however cut down it may be).

In any case, it is a striking fact that Davidson almost never pursues epistemological questions in depth, or questions of scientific perception; so that his animus against Kuhn and Feyerabend is almost certainly based on abstract philosophical objections against admitting any pertinent puzzles that would oblige him to turn to epistemology itself! This helps to explain how his worries about Quine's "indeterminacy of translation" thesis may have led him to an easy but entirely indefensible conflating of Kuhn's and Quine's puzzles. They are altogether different in the sense that although Quine's view[35] does indeed make room for incommensurability (as in the parsing of "Gavagai!"), Quine's "translations" depend on some supposed common perception (represented by "holist" or "holophrastic" sentences); whereas

Kuhn's conception is more daring in that the incommensurability he considers (Priestley and Lavoisier's, for instance) directly affect what would otherwise be a commonplace. Admitting this (in Kuhn's case) has *nothing* to do with violating Davidson's injunction against invoking the scheme/content dogma.

If, further, all the forms of cognitive privilege (that might have buttressed our claims of neutrality and conceptual closure) fail—and there is almost no one today practicing in the analytic manner who would be willing to champion foundationalism, apodicticity, conceptual "totalizing," or cognitive privilege—then it is a foregone conclusion that historicity cannot be ruled out as impossible or improbable. There seems to be *no* demonstration of the supposed incoherence of historicity that does not rest (by way of a *petitio*) on the claim that the basic categories of thought must be invariant and known and universally present in all natural languages. Anything less would instantly lose the modal force of the intended objection.[36] Reflect, for instance, on the implications of Davidson's unsatisfactory conjecture that "most of our beliefs are true."[37] Davidson must mean at the very least that the beliefs of different peoples must, even if construed from our own perspective, be predominantly true. But how does he know that? And how would it be possible if epistemic incommensurabilities and historicized divergences obtained? He nowhere addresses the question.

If predicative generality is labile in the logical respect remarked, that is, if it is linguistically encumbered, never more than consensually grounded, always subject to historical drift, then invariance cannot be more than a construction of convenience. You see, therefore, how difficult it is to recover the Cartesian argument (the conceptual closure argument). Alternatively, you see the sense in which the objectivist's attack on incommensurabilism harbors some secret form of Platonism. I am prepared to argue (but will not do so here) that it is the same underlying Cartesianism that infects both Chomskyan linguistics and Davidsonian scientism, although those two doctrines are as opposed to one another as any one might imagine.

v

This brings me, finally, to Kuhn's and Feyerabend's well-known claim. We may now risk addressing their particular texts directly, without fear of losing the essential thread. I've laid a proper foundation for separating the bare predicative issue from the inevitable complications of Kuhn's and Feyerabend's respective theories of science, that is, their incommensurabilism. By the same token, we may examine Davidson's analysis more closely. For, certainly, Davidson's reading of Kuhn and Feyerabend has dominated the analytic camp's reception of their best-known texts. In fact, Davidson cites them and provides what many regard as the strongest reasons for supposing *that there are no "basic"* (Davidson's word) *conceptual incommensurabilities:* apparently, there can't be any!

I'm afraid I shall try your patience here: the argument cannot avoid a fussy textual turn. I enter the quarrel in order to ensure a final reckoning regarding the connection between Kuhn's and Feyerabend's views and the elementary forms of incommensurability already laid out.

Here, then, is what Davidson cites from Feyerabend:

> Our argument against meaning invariance [this is Feyerabend speaking] is simple and clear. It proceeds from the fact that usually some of the principles involved in the determination of the meanings of older theories or points of view are inconsistent with the new . . . theories. It points out that it is natural to resolve this contradiction by eliminating the troublesome . . . older principles, and to replace them by principles, or theorems, of a new . . . theory. And it concludes by showing that such a procedure will also lead to the elimination of the old meanings.[38]

If I understand Feyerabend's remarks and Davidson's analysis properly, Davidson acknowledges the case Feyerabend describes but asks us to consider,

> only whether, if such changes were to take place, we should be justified in calling them alterations in the basic conceptual apparatus. . . . What is clear [Davidson says] is that retention of some or all of the old vocabulary in itself provides no basis for judging the new scheme to be the same as, or different from, the old. So what [he adds] sounded at first like a thrilling discovery—that the truth is relative to a conceptual scheme—has not so far been shown to be anything more than the pedestrian and familiar fact that the truth of a sentence is relative to (among other things) the language to which it belongs. Instead of living in different worlds, Kuhn's (probably then, also, Feyerabend's) scientists may, like those who need Webster's dictionary, be only words apart.[39]

Bear in mind that Davidson advises us (just before offering his comments) that *he* "think[s] our actual scheme and language are best understood as extensional and materialist," and that "if we were to follow this advice, . . . [neither] science [n]or understanding would be advanced [by Feyerabend's case], though possibly morals would."[40] Of course! The implication is that there *is* a "basic conceptual apparatus" in natural language and human thought and that, admitting *that* (Davidson's objectivism), the incommensurabilities Kuhn and Feyerabend feature cannot possibly serve to demarcate different conceptual schemes *in the "basic" sense* and cannot lead to the discovery (which Davidson assumes *they* intend) that, say, "truth is relative to a conceptual scheme." You see how insouciantly Davidson admits that his objections are "cooked" in the interests of scientism. But he offers nothing in the way of an argument.

I remind you, also, that Davidson's disjunctive treatment of facts and values goes completely contrary to pragmatism's objection to any such policy. I chalk that up to Davidson's Cartesian tendencies, which hardly fit with Rorty's improbable efforts to construe Davidson as a pragmatist. It is not unimportant in this regard that Rorty favors Kuhn where Davidson does not.

I put it to you that Davidson's countermove is an *obiter dictum*, an undemonstrated and utterly indemonstrable "first" principle, if meant to be categorically affirmed. Furthermore, it actually concedes the possibility of incommensurabilities in the benign sense already supplied. But, apart from all that, it shows very clearly that Davidson harbors a privileged view of the conditions of cognition (of reality), which his usual efforts (as in "A Coherence Theory") refuse to permit us to invoke in epistemological debate—on pain (apparently) of generating an insuperable skepticism!

I admit this is a harsh judgment against Davidson. But it is a fair one. Let me offer two considerations straight off. For one, Feyerabend *never* invokes a "basic conceptual apparatus" that could be explicitly formulated or would be coextensive with the whole of a language or the entire closed system of nature. What Davidson cites from Feyerabend concerns changes only in ideal explanatory theories or congruent changes in the meaning of both descriptive and explanatory terms—made necessary under the pressure of finding that some original theory *cannot* explain (possibly cannot even make sense of) a phenomenon that rightly calls for explanation. For instance, Feyerabend notes, more or less in agreement with Kuhn, that the inertial motion Galileo and Descartes consider "does not make sense, nor can it be formulated" within "the Aristotelian theory of change."[41] Failure to be formulable in the terms of one theory despite being formulable in those of another, failure to capture what is descriptively intelligible in observed events by means of a theory thought capable of explaining such events, failure to eliminate inconsistencies between two theories said to be separately adequate (in a formal sense) as explanations of the same events, count as specimen instances of what Feyerabend treats as incommensurabilities. Feyerabend never works from would-be first principles or necessities *de re* or *de cogitatione*. He responds to contingent puzzles as they arise, improvising solutions ad hoc as he comes upon the need for them. It would be entirely out of character for Feyerabend to have adopted anything like Davidson's "third dogma" as a guiding principle.

Furthermore, in the paper cited, Feyerabend *nowhere* draws conclusions remotely like Davidson's, viz., that "truth is relative to a conceptual scheme." That thesis *is* incoherent on its face (as Davidson very well knows), *if,* by "relative to a conceptual scheme," he intends something close to what Myles Burnyeat proposes as a reading of Socrates's account of Protagorean relativism in the *Theaetetus,* namely, that "true" means "true-for-x" (where "x" signifies one or another speaker, or even one or another conceptual scheme)—what I have already termed "relationalism" in reviewing Putnam's account.[42] Otherwise, at best, Davidson's point is trivial. There's all the difference in the world between defining truth in the relationalist way and acknowledging that the confirmation of truth-claims cannot fail to be relativized to one or another society's evidentiary practices. Relationalism is a second-order theory; the other is the bare admission of a first-order fact, nothing more (as such or as yet) than what Putnam dubs "cultural relativity."

Certainly, Davidson opposes Feyerabend on the grounds that Feyerabend's account entails the threat of an incoherent relativism. *Although,* of course, a coherent incommensurabilism would also entail "true"'s playing an explanatory role in epistemic contexts—which Davidson unconditionally resists.[43] If so, then even Davidson's account of canonical science cannot justify denying truth an explanatory or legitimative role—without our insisting, however, that truth must, as a result, have a criterial role as well.

But, now, it turns out that Davidson's insistence that conceptual incommensurability is intrinsically incoherent *is* also Cartesian (in the sense supplied); for the objection to incommensurable conceptual schemes depends on the supposed fact that "different conceptual schemes" cannot be "alterations in the basic conceptual apparatus" of our entire truth-seeking inquiries: they would need to be *compared* with the categories of our former scheme, and then, *putatively within the resources of our "entire" language,* we would still not be able to say whether they were "the same as, or different from, the old." The "old" *what?* you ask. Is it the "part" of the "whole" language we are using or the concepts there invoked that harbor "the basic conceptual apparatus" we are alleged always to employ? The matter remains a complete mystery: Davidson never tells us what the supposed apparatus includes or how that may be discerned.

In any case, the objection is entirely pointless, because, as I have already shown, conceptual incommensurabilities belong—benignly—to natural languages as such and are themselves open to translation and comparison. Furthermore, Davidson could not possibly advance his objection against Feyerabend unless what he calls "the basic conceptual apparatus" *were* demonstrably necessary and inviolable. He's much too adroit to admit any such commitment on his own part, but I'm afraid it lurks in the neighborhood of everything he does admit.[44]

In effect, Davidson mismanages Feyerabend's entire argument: he discounts Feyerabend's claim on grounds that could never have had a place in the latter's philosophy, and he himself disregards the *local* reading of incommensurability (which he implicitly concedes). The whole point of Feyerabend's brief is to show that a purely deductive model of explanation and the corollary notion that changes in explanatory theory do not (or never) entail changes in the meaning of descriptive and theoretical terms goes entirely against the history of science.

The intended lesson is that the failure of these two doctrines is sealed by the actual epistemological incommensurabilities that have occurred at critical moments in the history of the physical sciences, which, by their appearance, preclude a closed system of nature and "a basic conceptual apparatus."[45] Feyerabend is entirely right in what he offers in evidence against such theorists as Rudolf Carnap, Carl Hempel, Ernest Nagel, and Nils Bohr. Davidson's charge is a complete nonstarter. As a consequence, Davidson never actually addresses the logic of incommensurability, though that may be hard to believe. I see no way to avoid the verdict.

VI

You realize that Feyerabend's challenge calls into question any realism that proceeds without interpretive intermediaries, that presumes to avoid constructivism, that embraces Cartesianism, that resists *ab initio* the very idea of a viable relativism. In a word, Feyerabend's claim goes entirely against the official views of figures like Quine, Davidson, and Putnam—utterly against the entire analytic canon. Yet, I venture to say that there is no knockdown refutation of Feyerabend's incommensurabilism. On the contrary, one senses an underground admission that there are no conceptual resources secure enough to dispatch the upstart claim.

But if you accept this way of answering Davidson, you must concede as well that Feyerabend's brief (which is close to Kuhn's) does not alter the table of the four grades of incommensurability (already given) in any fundamental way. What we see from Feyerabend's account is that if incommensurabilities arise in the elementary settings mentioned, then they are bound to arise in disputes about much larger explanatory theories. Incommensurabilities are in a sense always "local," always relativized to particular linguistic resources, intelligible as such, empirically motivated though not captured in any narrowly empirical (or empiricist) way, above all never keyed to intranslatability, or such as to presuppose completely separable conceptual schemes, but only to such schemes as result from normal changes in scientific practice and the historicity of thought. The idea of large-scale incommensurabilities that remain "local" does not entail any paradox or important novelty regarding their analysis, though it does affect the bearing of history on the theory of explanation—and of knowledge and understanding and truth and meaning. The puzzle of the historicity of thought is at least as important as the puzzle of local incommensurabilities.

Consider, now, what Davidson cites from Kuhn:

Philosophers [this is Kuhn speaking] have now abandoned hope of [finding a pure sense-datum language], but many of them continue to assume that theories can be compared by recourse to a basic vocabulary consisting entirely of words which are attached to nature in ways that are unproblematic and, to the extent necessary, independent of theory. . . . Feyerabend and I have argued at length that no such vocabulary is available. [This goes somewhat against Pierre Duhem but accords in a limited way with Quine.] In the transition from one theory to the next words change their meanings or conditions of applicability in subtle ways. Though most of the same signs are used before and after a revolution—e.g. force, mass, element, compound, cell—the way in which some of them attach to nature has somehow changed. Successive theories are thus, we say, incommensurable.[46]

Davidson's instant comment runs as follows: "'Incommensurable' is, of course, Kuhn's and Feyerabend's word for 'not intertranslatable.' The neutral content waiting to be organized is supplied by nature."[47]

This is at least as strange as Davidson's remarks about Feyerabend. For one thing, Kuhn is clear that *he* does not oppose translation *anywhere*. Where, in the context of incommensurability, he warns about translation—in fact he makes the point immediately before the passage Davidson cites (which is from the essay "Reflections on My Critics")—Kuhn confines the sense of his remark to what he calls "the point-by-point comparison of two successive theories [which] demands [he says] a language into which at least the empirical consequences of both can be translated without loss or change." Many have sought such a language, he continues, which they suppose is "neutral" (for instance, the language of "pure sensation-reports"), or suppose possesses "a 'universal character' which would display all languages for expressing them as one." Then comes the line that Davidson cites: "Feyerabend and I have argued at length that no such vocabulary is available."[48] Nothing could be plainer. Kuhn clearly holds that both he and Feyerabend oppose *any* "neutral content waiting to be organized" or *any* neutral language for descriptive and comparative use. There is, he says, no "basic vocabulary"; *a fortiori*, there is no "basic conceptual apparatus." Davidson misleads us here.

Note that this demurrer does *not* mean that incommensurable statements are not translatable, or intertranslatable. Where they are translated ("point-by-point"), they require "compromise" (Kuhn says), precisely because of the problematic intertranslatability of sentences from different languages. Notice, please, that a few paragraphs later Kuhn actually adds that:

> To me at least, what the existence of translation suggests is that recourse is available to scientists who hold incommensurable theories. That recourse need not, however, be to full restoration in a neutral language of even the theories' consequences.[49]

Davidson ignores the point—deliberately falsifies it, one must suppose. Kuhn goes on to enlist Quine's famous "indeterminacy of translation" thesis; chides his own critics for being too vague about translation "point-by-point"; acknowledges the comparability of incommensurable theories throughout; and emphasizes the very sensible view that whatever will finally count as an adequate translation will depend on interests that are bound to require and allow compromise.[50]

Davidson unaccountably foists on us the misleading equivalence of "incommensurability" and failure of "intertranslatability"; and, where Kuhn expressly remarks that he and Feyerabend reject neutrality, Davidson assigns Kuhn the gratuitous view that "nature" somehow supplies the "neutral content" that our incommensurable schemes will thereupon "organize." What Davidson means is that *Kuhn's* incommensurabilism must presuppose a neutral language in which different conceptual schemes can be mapped as different; hence, it must presuppose a condition that obviates incommensurabilism itself. Very clever, but where is the argument? (Think of this as an analogue of Putnam's *Grenzbegriff*.)

There is no warrant for these glosses, and there is no "neutral content" to be had. Davidson constructs, and duly defeats, a so-called "third dogma" of empiricism (beyond Quine)—the "dualism of scheme and content," which he wrongly assigns to Kuhn and Feyerabend[51] and wrongly assigns to Quine.[52] In fact, there may be no one who ever really favored the "dogma" Davidson defeats. The only plausible candidate seems to be Benjamin Whorf; but Whorf cannot be compared with Kuhn and Feyerabend on the history of science and may not have intended his remarks in the way Davidson construes them.[53]

There is more that could be said about Davidson's unusual explication, but it would take us too far afield from the incommensurability issue. Suffice it to say that Davidson's notion of "conceptual relativism" relies on the paradoxical "relationalism" already mentioned, wrongly characterizes Kuhn's account of incommensurability, and then dismisses the pure fiction he has himself invented—and foisted on Kuhn!

I am bound to say in all fairness that Kuhn defends the incommensurabilism issue rather poorly, though he collects the important specimens of explanatory incommensurability. What needs to be recovered is the answer to the important question of what we should understand by an objective science under the condition of the historicity of thought. But I see no reason to take up the defense of Kuhn's specific picture of science here—especially where Kuhn is prepared to retreat to the sociology of science and Feyerabend to endorse his well-known brand of anarchism.[54]

Two further caveats are in order. For one, there is no warrant whatsoever for introducing—as a proper instance of incommensurability or its principal form—Davidson's case of "completely" or "partially" independent conceptual schemes (in the sense he intends). Where admitted, it is totally inoperative, marks no more than the limit of bare intelligibility. For another, granting that, there is no ground for any additional disjunction between so-called "incommensurability of *meaning*" and "incommensurability of *standards.*" On this question, Ronald Giere has the following to say:

> In the process of creating a normal science research tradition, a scientific community develops "norms," "rules," or "standards." These help determine, among other things, what counts as a significant problem and what counts as a solution. But Kuhn's doctrine of the priority of paradigms (that is, exemplars) holds that the standards are determined by the exemplars, not the exemplars by the standards. It follows that a new solution to a problem, one appealing to a new exemplar and thus violating the standards of the older research tradition, could not be recognized as a solution by that tradition.[55]

But that's a misunderstanding and yields too far in Davidson's direction. At best, it trades on an equivocation: "not recognized" sometimes means no more than "not officially countenanced" though intelligible enough to those who work within the tradition—Lavoisier and Priestley, say, within the tradition of eighteenth-century European chemistry. Giere simply ignores the principal question. In a word, Giere never rightly considers the question of historicity. Presumably, Priestley and Lavoisier understood one another's theories and Galileo understood both Aristotle's account of "swinging stones" and the medieval sources of his own account of pendulums.

In the relevant sense, pertinently motivated changes of standard may well entail changes of meaning. It's not the sheer priority of recognizing the need for a new standard that is invariably decisive—which may then usher in a solution that "could not be a solution within a [given] tradition"; it's rather that what *is* a promising or adequate solution *cannot, for deeper epistemological and methodological reasons,* be captured *commensurably* by the terms favored in the canon of the older tradition. It *can* be "recognized" by the apt agents of that tradition. It has nothing to do with whether the scientists of the older tradition are able or unable to *understand* the solution of the new "paradigm." It's merely that the new solution would not have been "countenanced" by the older one, given *its* epistemological stance.

"A solution to the problem of atomic spectra," Giere offers, "that invokes quantized values for the exchange of energy, for example, could not be a solution within a classical tradition that presumed continuity. In recognizing a new solution as indeed a solution, therefore, scientists are creating a new tradition, and thus new standards. But their prior decision to accept the new solution is then not governed by any standards at all. It is a truly revolutionary act in the classical, political sense."[56] Perhaps. But it *is* governed by the conditions of intelligibility that the champions of both "traditions" effectively draw on and that Kuhn rightly commits himself to in the remarks I have cited. In the sense at stake, incommensurable changes of meaning may (often do) implicate incommensurable standards; and incommensurable standards may (often do) entail incommensurable meaning-changes. That's all that's needed.

Giere cannot mean—or does he?—that, in the puzzle cases Kuhn collects, the issue never turns on weighing *epistemological incommensurabilities* (that is, the incommensurabilist's specific claim). If he denies that there are any such incommensurabilities, he has yet to provide the argument; and if he admits them, then his own argument misses the mark.[57] The least sympathy for Hegel's contribution settles the issue at a stroke. Giere's oversight is no more than a variation of Putnam's oversight (already remarked). Extraordinary. Yet both are pragmatists: which is to say, pragmatists are just as prone as analysts are to being blindsighted—Davidson, for instance. In any event, since pragmatists are committed to being anti-Cartesians, they cannot afford to disallow relativism and incommensurabilism, if those views prove to be viable. There's the difference.

VII

It needs to be said that the key to Kuhn's and Feyerabend's distinction rests with their explicit repudiation of neutrality (*not* objectivity) and their implied rejection of any discernible conceptual closure regarding the physical world that disallows the inventive possibilities of science and epistemology that supply the ground for challenging any would-be closure. Neutrality makes no sense except in terms of an epistemology able to demonstrate the undistorted correspondence between the independent world and our would-be science. But that cannot be shown, on pain of all the familiar paradoxes of the "Cartesianism" that runs from Descartes through Kant.

The very idea of the conceptual plenitude of our natural-language resources (Davidson's thesis) signifies that no creative science could possibly generate concepts incommensurable with our "basic" vocabulary—for if it did, so the argument goes, the resultant science would be unintelligible. But then the argument presumes, indemonstrably, that the conceptual resources we *now* possess (in effect, possess at every stage of our continuous history) *is* constitutive in some robust way in the conceptual or causal closure of the world. That closure (which we need never actually master) apparently ensures the ultimate neutrality of our evolving science; furthermore, the continuing intelligibility of science itself, even under radical change, is said (as by Davidson) to confirm the absence of any "basic" incommensurability. But remember: we can never actually formulate what the "basic" vocabulary includes. To be able to do that, we should already possess a clear sense of the closure of the world under the conditions of causal explanation.

That would be a very tidy theory, you must admit, if it could be used at all. But it suffers from two serious flaws at least. For one, it has no relevance whatsoever for appraising either first-order theories like Priestley's and Lavoisier's or second-order theories like Kuhn's and Feyerabend's regarding the incommensurability of competing first-order theories. The reason is plain. *If* the theories in question *are* intelligible and comparable and paraphraseable, then, *on Davidson's account, they are commensurable with our "basic" concepts* even if they are locally incommensurable with one another! (And, of course, even if—or, conveniently enough, because—they are unknown or unknowable.)

That they are commensurable *in Davidson's sense* would be little more than a trivial consequence of their being intelligible. But if so, then Kuhn's and Feyerabend's incommensurabilities *are* clearly commensurable with our basic vocabulary—in the same empty sense in which commensurable but competing first-order theories are said to be. Second, Davidson provides no further account of incommensurability that demonstrates its incoherence. To put the point another way: *on* Davidson's theory, *if* there were incommensurable theories *of the Kuhnian sort, they would be translatable* relative to our "basic" concepts, *as a condition* of their being incommensurable locally! Since we cannot know what the "basic concepts" are, relative to the inclusive closure of the world, those concepts can never be invoked; as a result, Davidson's complaint (against Kuhn and Feyerabend) must be completely irrelevant. I take that to be a *reductio.*

I am *not* claiming that Davidson holds that there is *one* conceptual scheme that we actually possess that collects the basic vocabulary postulated. No, not at all. Rather, what I suggest is that he believes that whatever is intelligible in the conceptual history of science, including differences in competing theories, *entails* a "common" network of concepts answering to the objective work of an ongoing science. In that sense, there is a "common" vocabulary that we *must* share, but it cannot be assigned a determinate set of concepts or any explicit content, since that would signify that another conceptual scheme *might* be formulated in opposition to it, and that, Davidson thinks, is impossible because it is incoherent.

Thus he says, at the very outset of "On the Very Idea":

> Even those thinkers who are certain there is only one conceptual scheme are in the sway of the scheme concept: even monotheists have religion. And when someone sets out to describe "our conceptual scheme," his homey task assumes, if we take him literally, that there might be rival systems.[58]

This is the essential move, Davidson believes, to dismantling "conceptual relativism." He does not mean that there is only one system: he means that there cannot be "rival" systems; and if there cannot be rival systems, then the concepts we use must accord with what is "basic" to the "neutrality" or objectivity of *our* science (such as it is) *and* signifies the only kind of neutrality that makes sense. For Davidson, it appears to signify a kind of necessity that stands confirmed without any further determinacy—without even the possibility of fathoming its conceptual content.

But consider Davidson's deeper argument:

> The dominant metaphor of conceptual relativism, that of differing points of view, seems to betray an underlying paradox. Different

points of view make sense, but only if there is a common co-ordinate system on which to plot them; yet the existence of a common system belies the claim of dramatic incommensurability.[59]

Now, that's a fatal *non sequitur*. For one thing, neither Kuhn nor Feyerabend is committed to supporting anything like Davidson's "dramatic incommensurability"; and, for another, our ability to compare two different points of view does not entail that "there is a common co-ordinate system" that we share in making that comparison, *if* that is supposed to override the incommensurability of Kuhn's and Feyerabend's examples.

It's true that our language permits us to *compare incommensurable points of view;* Kuhn and Feyerabend concede that much: witness Galileo. But comparability does not eliminate Kuhnian incommensurability and does not drive it to the limit of unintelligibility. Furthermore, there is no sense in claiming a "common co-ordinate system" if we cannot state what that system is; and if, *per impossibile,* we *can* specify the details of that system, then *there is one conceptual scheme* after all—and that, Davidson insists, makes no sense.

Perhaps these are petty quarrels, but they are tactical maneuvers in the service of a larger strategy that means to keep alive the double theme Kuhn and Feyerabend espouse: that is, the rejection of neutrality in the guise of an objectivity free of the constituting function of our conceptual schemes, and the rejection of the idea that nature forms a closed system of such a sort that the concepts of an objective science must match that system, and, matching it, ensure neutrality thereby. (You may even be tempted to suppose that Davidson is espousing a sort of transcendentalism *manqué.* I think he is. Just as Putnam is.)

Nevertheless, neutrality remains a Cartesian vestige that cannot escape its original paradox. Davidson's entire effort is a strategy to save as much of Cartesian realism as possible while giving up everything epistemological that would have returned us to the old Cartesian and Kantian paradoxes. So he is content to insert the parenthesis: "Perhaps I should add that I think our actual scheme and language are best understood as extensional and naturalist."[60] This is to warn us about the subversive possibilities of Kuhn's and Feyerabend's heterodoxy. But, clearly, it also signifies that, for Davidson, there must be a "basic conceptual apparatus." No wonder Davidson closes the argument in the following way:

> In giving up dependence on the concept of an uninterpreted reality, something outside all schemes and science, we do not relinquish the notion of objective truth—quite the contrary. Given the dogma of a

dualism of scheme and reality, we get conceptual relativity, and truth relative to a scheme. Without the dogmas, this kind of relativity goes by the board. Of course truth of sentences remains relative to language, but that is as objective as can be. In giving up the dualism of scheme and world, we do not give up the world, but re-establish unmediated touch with the familiar objects whose antics make our sentences and opinions true or false.[61]

This is the Cartesian motive all right, but not its argument.

The essential issue is elusive to the last. The resolution of the incommensurabilism question, you realize, cannot be achieved by any merely "factual" discoveries, as if by a patient review of the history of science itself, because the ultimate question asks whether *that* history should be read in a way that admits incommensurabilism from time to time or drums it out of play altogether. The question is insuperably philosophical.

Davidson had made a valiant attempt to support the second reading, but it backfired badly. If you ask what can be said in incommensurabilism's favor, the answer comes in three moves: the first (the bulk of what has been offered here) shows that the principal counterstrategies, those offered by Putnam and Davidson, fail hands down; the second shows the ubiquity of conceptual incommensurabilities *and* the reasonableness of subsuming epistemological incommensurabilities (the theme of incommensurabilism itself) among the common garden varieties (even if rarer than most); and the third shows that if Cartesianism must be rejected (as it must) and the broad lines of Hegel's recovery of the grounds for a viable realism accepted (in effect, the recovery of what realism must finally mean if it is to be recovered at all), then realism can only be a constructivism that is not foundationalist or transcendental, is historicized, and is hospitable to relativism and incommensurabilism. That is quite a lot. But it cannot be disallowed if, as appears to be the case, the entire argument against the translatability of incommensurables—including epistemological incommensurables—has simply collapsed.

The upshot is that Kuhn and Feyerabend have hit on a genuinely fresh vein of inquiry that analytic philosophy has resisted (almost without compromise) through the whole of the last century. That may be the last outpost of Cartesianism. But if historicism can be revived, and that has yet to be seen, then English-language epistemology is likely to proceed along lines distinctly opposed to its own past history.

The curious fact remains: relativism, incommensurabilism, historicism, constructivism (in the epistemological sense) have been largely avoided in twentieth-century English-language philosophy: as much among the classic pragmatists and "second-wave" pragmatists (Putnam, for example[62]) as among the analytically-minded (Davidson, preeminently). This marks a very deep gap in contemporary philosophy that Kuhn and Feyerabend brought to professional attention in a most compelling way. They themselves have been drummed out of play, however, and essays like Davidson's "On the Very Idea" as well as Putnam's would-be "pluralism"[63] betray the widespread, deliberate avoidance, among philosophers at large, of airing all the coherent options that are before us. The new century must understand that it is under an inherited obligation to make amends. For if the rebuttal is valid, the issue will find new champions in new corners of the world.[64]

3

Restoring the Bond between Realism and Truth

I

Slowly but surely, analytic philosophy is coming to the end of its tether on the theory of truth. It is, however, loath to air the implications of its restrictive policies. By and large, it has chosen to confine its account in the narrowest possible semantic terms, detaching the use and sense of "true" as far as possible from the analysis of knowledge, scientific explanation, even the social history of scientific inquiry, all in a vain attempt to isolate scientism from the subversive penetration of the play of human interests and practical success—in a word, the penetration of one or another constructivism along broadly Hegelian lines. The result is a blizzard of extreme measures which, at the moment, favor truth's indefinability—most notably, in Donald Davidson's account, which claims to provide what is needed beyond the magisterial economies urged in Alfred Tarski's so-called "deflationary" theory.[1] The epithet is seriously misleading, as is Davidson's confidence that he has incorporated, without distortion, Tarski's important contribution in a more complete account of truth of his own devising. The analytic stalemate takes other forms as well, as in Paul Horwich's "minimalist" account (going beyond disquotation), which also derives from Tarski;[2] as well as the blithe dismissal of attempts to treat truth as having some explanatory or normative role with regard to knowledge and causal explanation, as, notoriously, in Richard Rorty's "postmodernist" account—a mistaken reading, as it turns out, of Davidson's own view of truth, as Rorty now acknowledges.[3]

The distortion that these theories encourage lies with the impression conveyed by them that second-order cognitive questions are either altogether useless (Rorty) or of very limited use, if we are to escape the threat of skepticism (Davidson). The conviction they convey is that "true" is no more (or hardly more) than a "semantic" counter of the narrowest possible sort, quite incapable of bearing the full weight of questions about the validity of

science or ordinary knowledge. Nevertheless, precisely *which* more fundamental concepts might be usefully pursued with an eye to understanding
science itself—how and to what advantage—is never actually spelled out.
My own impression in reading Davidson and Rorty (when they speak in the
"naturalizing" manner) is that they hope to escape intensional complications that they would otherwise not be able to discharge by means of featuring the disquotational, even approximately deflationary, treatment of
"true." Rorty, who sees the threat at once, is inclined to be more reckless than
Davidson in clearing the decks; for his part, Davidson is more cautious and
circumspect, though plainly sanguine about eventually reaching an adequate extensionalist account.

It's true that we cannot return to *any* version of the tradition that disjoins
the cognizing powers of enlanguaged humans and the cognized features of
the "external" or "independent" world (which, already in medieval times,
was named *adaequatio*). Let's call that failed tradition "Cartesianism," regardless of what actually stands in for cognizers (beliefs, propositions, sentences, mental or intentional states) and what stands in for the cognized
world (facts, states of affairs, actual things). To admit an *epistemological* gap
between mind and world of any of the sorts mentioned that bear on a responsible use of "true" is to produce conditions for an insuperable skepticism affecting any would-be science or body of true beliefs that we claim to
rely on. This important finding (the threat of skepticim) was first compellingly developed *and overcome,* in modern times, in the post-Kantian period that features the work of Fichte and Hegel, reaching its apotheosis in
Hegel's *Phenomenology,* at least as far as the initial cognitive site of the "objects" discerned in experience and sensory perception is concerned (*Gegenstände*).[4] This is the decisive, generative novelty of Hegel's account of
Erscheinungen, which replaces in a relatively perspicuous (but incomplete)
way Kant's own problem-ridden notion of our first sensory "representations" (*Vorstellungen*), which cannot by themselves rightly overcome Kant's
own pre-Kantian disposition. The plain fact is that much of late twentieth-
century analytic philosophy has never escaped the Cartesian paradoxes: fear
of epistemology is the decisive symptom.

What Hegel makes painfully clear, in the *Encyclopedia,* is just how strenuous it is to overcome Cartesianism in a compendious way that answers all
the essential questions that must be met and does so without committing us
to more than a society of ordinary human beings! Hegel does not quite succeed, but he comes as close as any theorist of his time. More than that, we
actually begin to see how his characteristic conceptual excesses regarding the
would-be *Subjekt* of cognition and activity might be replaced without dis-

advantage by reinterpreting the very life of *Geist* (even the world as incarnated Spirit) as an instructive metaphor. I would like to think that that was Hegel's own intention. It is certainly the principal achievement of Dewey's somewhat pedestrian pragmatism in *Experience and Nature,* though the textual connections are no longer legible.

What both Fichte and Hegel grasp is the unavoidability of reconciling the cognitive agency of individual human subjects among themselves. Hegel, in particular, acknowledges the link between the confinement of consciousness to individual subjects and the collective, constructive, evolving nature of the conditions under which a society of cognizing subjects *can* make sense of their shared achievement (*Geist*). Hegel does not satisfy us here. We ourselves require a close explanation of the sense in which the "societal" is collectively shared—hence no more than predicative—the sense in which individual human subjects are first formed, as linguistically apt ("secondnatured") selves, by way of internalizing a common language and a common culture apt for affirming and communicating their truth-bearing beliefs among themselves. Hegel never advances an explicit account, and in just these terms, both analytic philosophy and pragmatism are remarkably thin.[5]

Efforts are now afoot to reinterpret Hegel in ways that might enrich the analytic treatment of truth (and realism and knowledge) compatibly with the kind of deflationary zeal sampled just above. But such efforts require a proper sense of whether the intended economies will or will not lead us astray (however innocently), or whether the Hegelian resolution of the Cartesian *aporia* is or is not reconcilable with such spare economies. The answer is not altogether clear, though I think it must be unpromising.

In any case, arguments from the "Hegelian" side are very different from those that tend toward deflationism or minimalism, that seek to isolate "truth" entirely in formal or semantic terms.[6] The "Hegelians" (I use the epithet as a term of art) wish to integrate the analysis of truth—I would say, "holistically"—with the analysis of knowledge and reality, on the promise of overcoming the Cartesian paradox. But they require, remember, a reconciliation (1) between cognizing subjects and cognized world that admits no epistemic gap, (2) between the "consciousness" (Hegel's term) of any single cognizing subject and that of another, and (3) between the cognizing agency of any such subject and the collective cultural (or enlanguaged) life of a society of suitable subjects (the mysterious *Geist* Hegel forever invokes, completely absent in analytic accounts).

All of these themes—(1)–(3)—can, I believe, be rendered in an acceptable form confined to ordinary human persons. That is what I mean to signal in favoring Hegel over Kant and pragmatism over post-Kantian Idealism. Kant fails in the direction of positing a peculiarly abstract cognizing and active Subject functioning, distributively, through all the members of the human species. Hegel fails by assembling "everything" that is the world, the history of human culture, every human being's capacity to communicate his perception, experience, feeling and emotion, conviction, purpose, action, judgment and the like, among the rest of humanity, as, finally, a system of graded predications of one universal Subject somehow engaged in self-reflection! Yet Hegel is incomparably closer to an adequate account than Kant, and closer still than the whole of analytic philosophy.

The most important strategies among recent "Hegelians" (not Hegel directly) may be called *realist*. Implicitly, the "Hegelians" proceed as follows: they deny (1) that a viable realism must be, or must depend on, any specifically Kantian or pre-Kantian form of idealism; they promote (2) a constructive realism that nevertheless overcomes the gap between cognizer and cognized (and so remains open to a charge of idealism); and they do all that (3) in a way that unites truth, knowledge, and reality epistemically. These minimal conditions are classically satisfied in Hegel's *Phenomenology* and *Encyclopedia* and certain post-Hegelian accounts (notably, also, in American pragmatism, especially Dewey's). There are, of course, certain essentially formal or abstract solutions content to affirm that the "gap" *has* indeed been overcome, without supporting their claims in any *epistemically* robust way. They are for that reason definitely not "Hegelian" solutions.

One of the most impressive of the failed ("pre-Hegelian") efforts is advanced in Ludwig Wittgenstein's *Tractatus*.[7] There, Wittgenstein pursues in a superb way the radical idea that "The world is the totality of facts [*Tatsache*], not of things [*Dinge*]" (1.1). What is remarkable in the *Tractatus* is that Wittgenstein sketches a spare realism along correspondentist lines without the least intrusion of any enabling epistemology. We are invited to reflect on proposition 1.1 in the context of such remarks as these: "A proposition [*Satz*] *shows* [*zeigt*] its sense. A proposition *shows* how things stand *if* it is true [*wahr*]. And it *says* [*sagt*] *that* they do so stand" (4.022); "Reality [*Wirklichkeit*] is compared with propositions" (4.05); and "Propositions cannot represent [*darstellen*] logical form: it is [rather] mirrored [*spiegelt*] in them. . . . Propositions *show* the logical form of reality. They display it" (4.121). But the *Tractatus* is, very plainly, a metaphysics and an epistemology *manqué:* it cannot be regarded as an autonomous semantics of any kind.

We cannot do better than begin with Wittgenstein. His dicta are cast as necessities of thought, binding (implicitly) on whatever may be contingently true about the world and our knowledge of the world—but they are not otherwise characterized. Certainly they are not defended as forming an explicit metaphysics or epistemology. The meaning of "facts" (*Tatsache*) is not explained by Wittgenstein, except to note that commonplace facts entail "atomic facts" (*Sachverhalten*), that is, all the logical possibilities that belong to the nature (*Natur*) of an object (*Gegenstand*), which is itself never more than simple (*einfach*), since objects form the (changeless) substance (*Substanz*) of the world (*Welt*) (2.0123, 2.02, 2.021). It is on the basis of considerations of these sorts that Wittgenstein is led to say, pointedly (in the *Notebooks*):

> "p" is true, says nothing else but p. [But] "'p' is true" is—by the above—only a pseudo-proposition of signs which apparently say something that can only be shown.[8]

This shows that, in spite of the fact that Wittgenstein is driven to affirm 1.1—because he finds that he cannot otherwise affirm what he takes to be the true propositions of the *Tractatus* (displacing "objects" by "facts")—he does not explain or defend his "ontology." Max Black remarks (presciently, it turns out) that Wittgenstein experienced considerable difficulty in "find[ing] a way in which the propositional fact '*aRb*' shall mean [the state of affairs] *cSd*, when there may be no such fact in the latter. There seems [Black adds, lightly paraphrasing Wittgenstein] to be a gulf between thought and reality—and yet the thought 'reaches right up to' reality, because it has a truth-value, is made true or false, as the case may be, *by* reality."[9]

In effect, Wittgenstein *closes* the Cartesian gap, by "metaphysical" fiat—for the sake of a conception of reality that *he* favors (and we might not). The implication is (it is also the point of the remarks cited from the *Notebooks*) that *any* alternative conception of how we arrive, responsibly, at a point at which we can affirm what is true about the world requires not only that the gap be closed—my item (2), offered in behalf of the "Hegelians"—but also must, if closed, be closed in an epistemically operative way (3). Black's remarking that when Wittgenstein says that "a thought" (or proposition) "has a truth-value" he (Wittgenstein) signifies that it is "made true . . . *by* reality" ("'reaches right up to' reality") effectively anticipates the convergence between Wittgenstein's formal account and recent variants, more Kantian than "Hegelian," like John McDowell's (directed against the "deflationists," Davidson and Rorty particularly) and between the convergence Wittgenstein's and William James's views (however inexpert James finally proved to be).

In the "Notes on Logic" (September 1913) appended (as Appendix I) to the *Notebooks,* Wittgenstein reflects on both Frege's and Russell's logics and tellingly remarks:

> Neither the sense [*Sinn*] nor the meaning [*Bedeutung*] of a proposition is a thing. These words are incomplete symbols. It is clear that we understand propositions without knowing whether they are true or false. But we can only know the meaning of a proposition [*Bedeutung:* what it "names" or refers to] when we know if it is true or false. What [by contrast] we understand [*Sinn*] is the sense of the proposition.[10]

Taken all in all, this shows very neatly how Wittgenstein was able to anticipate the fatal equivocation of the disquotational account of truth. In effect, what Wittgenstein is emphasizing is that, although

"p" is true, says nothing else but p,

"p" says or asserts something that is substantive, "which can only be shown"; on the other hand, he continues, the formula "'p' is true" pretends to say what can only be shown. I take this to mean that the semantic, epistemological, and metaphysical dimensions of "true" cannot be analyzed apart from one another. For what is said (affirmed) by "p" earns the right to be assigned the truth-value "true" if what is said *is* as it is said to be (can be shown). That difficult unity of conception is precisely what is lacking in or threatened by recent American analytic accounts of truth—what is more promisingly remembered in Dewey's pragmatism, even if more haltingly in James's.

This much agrees in a formal way with Aristotle: "To say of what is that it is, and of what is not that it is not, is true"[11]—except that, in the *Tractatus,* Wittgenstein does not touch at all on resolving the epistemological question. (He could not do so, except by Cartesian means, while holding to his formal correspondentism.) He does acknowledge in the *Notebooks,* however, the need to invoke the question. That is the point of distinguishing knowing the *Bedeutung* of what is said (reference to a determinate reality) as opposed to understanding the *Sinn* of what is said, which (on Wittgenstein's view) requires grasping all the conditions on which what is said might be *either* true *or* false. (Hence, if he had abandoned correspondentism, he would have been obliged to consider the analysis of truth in specifically epistemological terms.)

I can put this in a more pointed way. When we assert p, or say that p is true, we are saying something that can in principle be shown (by, say, a cognitive instantiation of Wittgenstein's "*zeigt*") about the real world, that would justify applying the predicate "true" to what was said; but doing that would require something that could not *be* said (on Wittgenstein's account): it would have to be "shown," if indeed the picture theory of truth proved valid or could be demonstrated. But if we rejected correspondentism (which is surely unavoidable by this time), we would need, and would need to formulate, some suitable realist replacement in accord with which we could give a fuller sense of what "true" signifies epistemologically and metaphysically—doubtless, a constructivist account of what we take to be independently real. Wittgenstein's use of "zeigt" manifests his own unwillingness to overcome the gap in the Cartesian way, though he himself was unable to add anything more of an epistemologically recuperative sort in the Tractarian manner.

On this reading, the deflationists are utterly mistaken, because they fail to see that, *whatever* counts as confirming the fact that things are as they are said to be, mere assertion (or the formal use of "is true") could never justify the normative assignment of "true" *to what was claimed to be thus and so and is now found to be so*! The formal equivalence of "p" and "p is true" says nothing about the validation of the realist standing of our claims. The deflationists confuse the semantic import of the words "is true" (viewed without regard to the outcome of any inquiry) and its role in collecting or marking the successful outcome of a particular inquiry. That is what I mean by saying that the analysis of "true" is "holistic": it cannot, except derivatively, segregate its so-called semantic and epistemological and metaphysical roles. *Prima facie*, therefore, accounts of truth that follow Davidson's lead are bound to be defective; they never come to terms with the epistemological side of "true."

The matter is never merely additive: thus, the deflationists arbitrarily favor an exclusively bivalent logic, though it is certainly possible that, in one context of inquiry or another, the usual semantics of "true" may be insufficient to accommodate some intended, even unavoidable, epistemological constraint or latitude (as in making concessions to relativism and incommensurabilism or to a many-valued logic). That is an adjustment Tarski would have been willing to consider, but clearly not Davidson. In any event, such possibilities cannot be precluded *a priori*.

The deflationists insist that "true" *is* a semantic distinction—and so it is. But it works, as such, only in a context in which realist concerns are able to be met; hence, it works only in contexts in which the semantic, the epistemological, and the metaphysical are operatively inseparable though they remain conceptually distinct. Hence, even where Wittgenstein is right to emphasize the difference between what can be "said" and what can only be "shown," he, too, misleads us, by failing to acknowledge all that is entailed in admitting that what can be "shown" has a structure that we can actually know answers to the truth of what we say. For instance, human perception is "enlanguaged," informed by the very language we use to advance our truth-claims, even though our merely perceiving (something) is not actually asserting (anything). The linkage cannot be explained in a merely formal way—"semantically." That is the *pons* of Wittgenstein's *Tractatus*. We cannot relevantly *say* what we claim to say if, in so saying, we cannot rightly claim to know what (*we say*, with Wittgenstein) can only be *shown*! At the very least, semantics cannot be autonomous. How could anyone who confines the analysis of "true" in a way that disjoins the semantic from the epistemological possibly know that, in contexts of assertion, we are necessarily committed to a bivalent logic? (That is surely one of Frege's mysteries.)

Imagine, then, that some form of cognitive privilege were accessible— that, in principle, correspondentist claims could always be confirmed, and, indeed, all claims would be correspondentist or would depend on correspondentist grounds: if so, then of course a disquotational reading of "p is true" would be "semantically" unproblematic in a Tractarian world (would support deflationism), but it would not be because "true" was a merely semantic notion. Furthermore, if the picture theory could never be vindicated, or if we could never ensure any uniquely correct body of knowledge (to the effect that what was claimed to be thus and so *was* indeed so), then clinging to the disquotational or, more problematically, the deflationary thesis would suddenly risk losing the import of the epistemological use of "true" altogether—as by discounting the bearing of opposed versions of realism *on* the "semantics" of truth! All *that* must already be implicated in the correspondentist theory.

This is precisely what John McDowell has in mind (has at least in mind) when he explains, in the Introduction recently added to his John Locke lectures (1991):

> A belief or judgement to the effect that things are thus and so—a belief or judgement whose content (as we say) is that things are thus and so—must be a posture or stance that is *correctly* or *incorrectly* adopted according to whether or not things are indeed thus and so. . . . This relation between mind and world is normative, then, in this sense: thinking that aims at judgement, or at the fixation of belief, is answerable to the world—or how things are—for whether or not it is correctly executed.[12]

I say, "has at least in mind," because, although McDowell salvages the epistemological import of "true," the would-be realist sense in which "true" is used, he does so only in a "formal" way. He adds nothing in the way of a substantive epistemology beyond our being "answerable to the world." We never learn his specific epistemological strategy, though we know that he means to make room for one: he may yet be vulnerable to the charge of favoring Cartesianism in spite of his intended opposition. For what, we may ask, does McDowell mean by the remark, "*correctly* or *incorrectly* adopted according to whether . . ."? He nowhere tells us how that question is to be answered, unless we are to suppose that his "Kantian" overcoming of the Cartesian (and canonical analytic) *aporia* is enough to show the way. Of course, it is not. That is precisely what I mean by the lesson of Hegel's example (which McDowell cites but never really uses or matches). In a word: McDowell (who may have formulated the best of the analytic approximations to the Kantian-Hegelian solution at the present time) "solves" the problem (the Cartesian *aporia*) semantically but not epistemologically. Yet, what is surely needed *is* a sufficient epistemology.

We may ourselves allow the disquotational maneuver, *if* we acknowledge that it does not disallow the epistemological import of "true"; and we may concede that McDowell has indeed made provision for the difference between the semantic and epistemological aspects of "true," *if* we hold in abeyance the qualifying condition needed, which McDowell may not be willing to support or able to vindicate. For example, if (as I believe) the conditions for applying "true" in a realist way are "constructions" and not "discoveries," then McDowell will have missed the epistemological lesson in warning, however blandly, that we must inquire as to whether thinking in the way of making a truth-claim *is or is not* "correctly executed." Being "correctly" executed does not entail or presuppose a prior (or *a priori* or "discoverable") condition of normative correctness: it is itself a constructive detail internal to a constructivist form of realism. There is ample evidence in *Mind and World* that McDowell would not agree. I am quite prepared to say, I should add, that Dewey's solution (in *Experience and Nature*) is very nearly the best sketch (no more than a sketch) of a solution that American philosophy has thus far yielded—it is essentially a "Hegelian" solution, though Hegel can hardly be discerned in Dewey's account.[13] In any case, to acknowledge Dewey's feat is to strengthen our sense of the opposed strategies of the "Hegelian" and the "Cartesian."

In short, what Dewey provides, but McDowell does not, is a good grasp of the kind of second-order (validating) reflections by which we characteristically decide to treat our truth-claims as true—subject to a continuing and open-ended review. *That* McDowell advances the realist cause without anything like an epistemological policy (as distinct from a table of the constitutive factors that must be present) suggests a straightforward *discovery* and, consequently, a sort of improved Cartesianism. In any case, McDowell's account is deficient just where it ought to be robust.

Rorty rightly poses the question whether McDowell's attaching the idea of "answerability to the world" to the meaning of "true" is not itself "philosophically sterile."[14] Of course, Rorty is a super-deflationist himself. He holds that "'true' has no explanatory uses" at all and that "there are no relations of 'being made true' which hold between beliefs and the world" (of a validative or otherwise normative sort).[15] Rorty and McDowell could not disagree more between themselves, though there is more to the issue than either cares to admit. It is worth remarking that Max Black, who tends to say very little that he does not weigh with care, uses the expression "being made true," which James introduced, without any sense that he (Black) must be committing himself, in interpreting Wittgenstein, to an untenable theory of truth.[16]

The deflationist notion underlying the disquotational account of "true" is problematic, however, since, on the one hand, we do tolerate disquotation (where it plainly distorts nothing) precisely because we realize that we have the world in mind, not merely sentences; and since, on the other hand, the would-be "semantic" conception of "true" is (as in the analytic tradition) often taken to be separable from its epistemological (and metaphysical) role, which yields a false reading of disquotation itself. Quine is marvelously clear on the matter: "the utility of the truth predicate is precisely the cancellation of linguistic reference. The truth predicate is a reminder that, despite a technical ascent to talk of sentences, our eye is on the world."[17] Quine, of course, tends to read his own thesis in a "Cartesian" spirit, though he inclines ineluctably toward some form of "idealism," as in the "indeterminacy of translation" thesis (or perhaps better: the indeterminacy conjecture);[18] and McDowell tends to read his overcoming the Cartesian gap in a dampened Kantian way (that is, along "idealist" lines) though, as in favoring his own form of naturalism ("natural Platonism"), he inclines ineluctably in the Cartesian direction once again.

II

Aristotle's account of truth is remarkably sensible, if we read what he says (in *Metaphysics* Gamma) without committing ourselves to his theory of knowledge or his theory of reality, all the while admitting that a robust use of "true" does entail a commitment to some reasonably determinate practice regarding making and confirming truth-claims. In this sense, the meaning of "true" may be said to be realist in import or to signify the realist intent of a claimant. In other words, to say "p is true" (or to say "p") is to say that the world is as it is said to be—but not to say (or imply) how that is rightly or necessarily determined: it would make no sense if, speaking thus, one did not suppose there was an acceptable way to decide the claim. So it is surely part of the meaning of "true" to make provision for disputes about what realism may require epistemologically and metaphysically, where suitable answers (whatever they may be) *would* justify the "normative" use of "true"—meaning by that that it could be determined *that* the world is as it is said to be!

In that sense, "true" *is* an epistemic concept. That is, "true" remains an epistemic concept regardless of which particular realist theory we prefer—so long as we prefer *some* robust form of realism in accord with which we believe we are able to know the way the world is. In that case, once we acknowledge that the realist question is seriously and coherently disputed (not dismissed), as Rorty would have it,[19] "true" cannot fail to have an explanatory role! That is precisely what, in his initially bungling way, James perceived—and secured for pragmatism: which infuriated Peirce but actually enlarged the resources of pragmatism when compared with those of analytic philosophy.

That, minimally, is also what McDowell's notion of "answerability to the world" signifies: it identifies an ingredient part of the meaning of "true," but it fails to deliver the actual epistemology it seems to promise. In short, it is part of its semantic analysis that the meaning of "true" include reference to the epistemic determinability of an agreement (or "correspondence" or "adequation") between what is claimed about the world and the way the world is (so long as these notions do not function criterially). This is all that realism requires in the bare semantic analysis of "true": a normatively vindicated *relationship* between cognizer and cognized, possible or actual. But of course we want to know what that relationship is!

Read this way, "correspondence" is benign enough, a formal notion that does not invoke epistemic privilege, does not entail determinate criteria, does not require subscribing to an ineliminable Cartesianism. McDowell is worrisome, nevertheless, because *he* insists so pointedly on the conditions of correspondence being "correctly or incorrectly adopted." That seems too sanguine, too casual about the profoundly disputed nature of what *is* real. Certainly, McDowell hardly meets our doubts.

Would he, for instance, be willing to accept a constructivism that would never pretend to vindicate a correspondentist discovery of the way the world is? Could he tell us why or why not? In what pertinent respects might he agree or disagree with Dewey's answer?

Yet, Rorty also misleads us when, worrying about where McDowell may lead us, he counters: "Brandom [that is, Robert Brandom], is content [in *Making It Explicit*] to think of normativity, of the possibility of correctness and incorrectness, in terms of human beings' answerability to one [an]other."[20] If McDowell ventures beyond what a mere semantic analysis could ever support (as by his Kantian explication), then Rorty has surely shied away too nervously from what we may be entitled to claim. If what he says in Brandom's name is a reasonable alternative, then it may also be inferred from McDowell's proposal; or, if that's not so, then we are really at sea and Rorty has failed us. Rorty never explains, in epistemic terms, what "answerability to one another" entails or how that is even possible. He cannot, therefore, substitute his formula (or Brandom's) for McDowell's (or Kant's or Hegel's). Answerability to one another surely implicates answerability to the world, if the first is not to be merely arbitrary—for instance, content with any agreed-upon consensus or "ethnocentric solidarity."

We know from the history of early modern philosophy that Cartesianism is untenable and inadequate as a master version of realism. But we cannot pretend to draw that finding from the bare semantics of "true." Nevertheless, *if*, in saying "p is true," what we say (speaking with McDowell) implicates that what we utter is "answerable to the world," then "true" has a normative sense answering to the requirements of realism—where those requirements (whatever they are) can be decided (if they can be decided at all) only by way of invoking pertinent practices in accord with our epistemological tradition. (That is what McDowell never rightly provides in spelling out his abstract formula—which is why he seems to be a Cartesian or a Platonist or a transcendental Kantian.)

There's a great difference between saying that the meaning of "true" implicates "our answerability to the world" and saying (or insinuating) that the full realist intent of "true" is not really a contested notion after all: whatever would be "correctly or incorrectly adopted" can always be spelled out on demand! But it *is* a contested notion—which signifies that Rorty's clever rejoinder to McDowell cannot be taken seriously; that is, answerability to one another cannot be taken seriously, since "true" has a realist intent and Rorty's alternative precludes our answerability to the world. Moreover, McDowell's analysis of belief in terms of "adopting" the "correct" posture regarding what to believe(relative to "whether or not things are indeed thus and so") fails to acknowledge the profoundly contested standing of realism itself.

Let me put the matter as plainly as I can: (1) "true" cannot be confined merely to the role of a formal semantic function, since, on any reasonable view, it does have realist import; and (2) since it has realist import, though realism is itself profoundly (perhaps perennially) contested, *no* descriptive expression can be directly paraphrased *in terms of its truth-conditions,* the conditions under which it truly applies, *by merely articulating its meaning in normal use.* What follows from (1) is that "true" may be treated disquotationally, but it cannot be construed in a deflationary way; what follows from (2) is, precisely, that it would be a profound mistake to confine the theory of meaning within the terms of a theory of truth, since we usually know the meaning of what we say even when we are at a loss as to what its "truth-conditions" are—apart from merely trivial answers.

Rorty may be taken to be the fair target of (1); Davidson is surely the most important target of (2). The fact is: *no* known theory of truth *can* specify (except trivially) the meaning of ordinary sentences. For the time being, I remind you that Davidson's account of truth is the best-known, perhaps the most influential such theory in the whole of late analytic philosophy. Davidson is committed to an uneasy denial of (1) and an unequivocal denial of (2). I believe he is mistaken on both counts.

If all this must be admitted, then, on the argument of the post-Kantians, a satisfactory realism cannot fail to be a *constructivism* (*not* an idealism in the classic sense): that is, (*a*) realism will prove to be a second-order conjecture about the epistemological and metaphysical constraints under which our first-order truths are judged to be such and our first-order inquiries are made to conform; (*b*) whatever contributes to the realist standing of our truth-claims cannot be separately assigned to the "subjective" or the "objective" side of that relationship (whether in the manner, say, of Descartes, Locke, or Kant); and (*c*) "answerability" signifies our continuing critique of what, under conditions (*a*)-(*b*), we are prepared to project, posit, constitute, or sustain as a program or policy normatively suited (by our lights) to continued realist success.

If you grant this much, you see at once how little McDowell can affirm if what he is offering *is* no more than a semantics of "true," or how much remains disputatious *if* he is advancing an epistemology; or how easily Rorty's counterproposal can be absorbed by McDowell's proposal; or how reasonable it is to suppose that "true" possesses a normatively determinable realist sense that is not in the least "philosophically sterile." If you see all this, you see the fatuousness of Rorty's "postmodernism" and the inadequacy of every deflationary semantics. For, to abandon cognitive privilege of every kind *is* to require continual second-order normative guidance (more, certainly, than under conditions of privilege); and to concede the point is to embrace constructivism. Constructivism is flatly incompatible with deflationism.

The theory of truth, therefore, is a substantive part of our inquiries into what a viable realism would require. When Rorty sides with Brandom—Brandom having already sided with an earlier Rorty—what could he possibly mean by "answerability to one another" if he does not mean "relative to our realist needs"? How does he avoid conceptual anarchy or irrelevance when, say, we consider how to adjust our science wherever we are confronted with the need for a "paradigm shift" or the bewildering possibilities of the history of science? There you may find another benefit of the incommensurabilist thesis.

Consider a small example. In countering McDowell's conception of a "space of reasons" (essential to McDowell's realism), Rorty argues: "Because most of our beliefs must be true, we can make no sense of the idea that a great gulf might separate the way the world is and the way we describe it."[21] In context, we are led to believe that Rorty shares the implied force of this line of thinking with Donald Davidson and Wilfrid Sellars, two very different realists whom he nevertheless admires. But Sellars is one of the most extreme eliminativists American philosophy has ever spawned—in fact, Sellars declares as openly as you please:

> According to the view I am proposing, correspondence rules would appear in the material mode as statements to the effect that the objects of the observational framework *do not really exist—there really are no such things.*[22]

Here, Sellars could not possibly subscribe to Rorty's line of argument: *most* of our beliefs—perhaps even all of our *beliefs* (in the sense assigned "the manifest image") are *false!* Rorty (I'm afraid) distorts Sellars's view in the service of his own argument. But he also says, in developing his stand against McDowell, that "Sellars himself was all too inclined to describe nature in Democritean terms as 'atoms and void' and to invent pseudo-problems about how to reconcile the 'scientific' with the 'manifest' image of human beings."[23] Extraordinary! Rorty undercuts the very point of urging that "most of our beliefs" are true! (Most of pre-modern science is obviously false.)

Of course, Rorty's line of thinking comes originally from Davidson's version of realism, which is notoriously tangled:

> My coherence theory [Davidson declares] concerns beliefs, or sentences held true by someone who understands them. I do not want

to say, at this point, that every possible coherent set of beliefs is true (or contains mostly true beliefs). . . . All that a coherence theory can maintain is that most of the beliefs in a coherent set of beliefs are true. . . . [Yet s]ince no person has a completely consistent body of convictions [we must ask:] coherence with *which* beliefs creates a presumption of truth?[24]

There is no ready answer. Davidson hardly subscribes to the overly strong presumption Rorty applies against McDowell. On the contrary, Davidson explicitly says, "I do not hope to define truth in terms of coherence and belief." His first step in explicating truth (which he says "is beautifully transparent compared to belief and coherence") is to adhere to what he regards as "the disquotational feature enshrined in Tarski's Convention T, [which] is enough to fix its domain of application."[25] (I shall come back to that.)

Nevertheless, Davidson says more carefully (more recently), though not quite carefully enough, that

Tarski's Convention T . . . stipulates that a satisfactory definition of a truth predicate 'is true' for a language *L* must be such as to entail as theorems all sentences of the form

S is true-in-L if and only if *p*

where '*s*' is replaced by the description of a sentence and '*p*' is replaced by that sentence or a translation of the sentence into the metalanguage. [It follows that] there can be no definition of 'For all languages *L*, and all sentences *s* in *L*, *s* is true in *L* if and only if . . . *s* . . . *L* . . .' In other words, [Davidson explains,] Tarski justified the application of a truth predicate to the sentences of a particular language only by restricting its application to the sentences of that language.[26]

What Davidson neglects to mention is that Tarski's Convention T applies only to languages or fractions of idealized languages that conform with certain severe constraints of extensionality. Tarski was well aware that natural languages hardly supported his convention.[27] Furthermore, though it is true that Tarski restricted the application of "true" to what can be affirmed in one or another particular language *L*, Davidson is surely seriously wrong to hold (either in his own name or in Tarski's) that Convention T "defines" (or provides a "satisfaction" condition for) "true-in-*L*." It does (and can do) no such thing! For that would signify that Davidson was committed to a relationalist theory of truth rather similar to the theory attributed to Protagoras in

Theaetetus. (Davidson was perhaps careless here: he undoubtedly meant a satisfaction condition for "true" *for* the sentences of *L*. But there is a deeper objection to Davidson's account.)

Tarski advances a *semantic* constraint on "true" that invokes an ulterior *metaphysical* consideration: *if* Davidson means to avail himself of that constraint as a first step in an adequate semantic analysis of "true," *he* must commit himself to the implicated metaphysical condition—but he cannot then segregate the semantic and the metaphysical or the semantic and the epistemological. Tarski was not convinced that the extensionalist constraint could be supported in natural-language contexts, and Davidson has yet to demonstrate that it can. Hence, when he coopts the "disquotational feature" of Tarski's theory, he both trivializes and confounds Tarski's so-called Convention T!

The disquotational feature of "true" is *not* a distinct part of Tarski's theory of truth at all: it's no more than an ordinary feature of "true" in ordinary discourse. The point is that Tarski's theory cannot be a deflationary theory, since the structural "description" of sentences that enter into Tarski's Convention T requires a certain extensionalist analysis of those same sentences. Davidson admits the point obscurely in what I've cited from his retelling of Tarski's story. He does not address the issue directly, which would have had the unhappy consequence (following Tarski's conviction) of obliging him to concede that Convention T would have little relevance for the analysis of natural languages. There would be nothing to build on! Davidson offers no non-vacuous sense in which his own reading of Convention T really does apply to natural languages.

There is no way that Davidson could possibly *use* Tarski's Convention T as a *first step* in defining (or, better, explicating all we need to know about) "true" unless he could generalize *its* lesson broadly enough to apply to all natural languages. Of course, Davidson's argument cannot assure us that the sentences of all natural languages *can* be paraphrased in an extensionalist manner.

In short, there is a metaphysics behind both Sellars's and Davidson's accounts of truth (and cognate notions) that infects the semantics either one of them might care to advance. Davidson eventually came to see that his coherence (or correspondence) theory was a "blunder" (his own term): he abandons the idea that he was ever advancing a "theory."[28] Yet he still insists: "The important thesis for which I argue is that belief is intrinsically veridical. That is the ground on which I maintain that while truth is not an epistemic concept, neither is it wholly severed from belief (as it is in different ways in both correspondence and coherence theories)."[29] But if truth is not "an epistemic concept," where does Davidson's realist assurance come from? It cannot *be formulated at all* on the grounds Davidson supplies, for reasons bearing on the inherent limitation of Tarski's "Convention T" *and* the unreliability of any coherence criterion for deciding truth.

Bear in mind: it's not the generic form of realism that is at stake, it's the actual body of determinate truths that we must be concerned about. If, furthermore, the *semantic* analysis of "true" makes it reasonable to impute a realist *sense* to the predicate itself, it hardly justifies us in supposing (with Davidson) that "belief is intrinsically veridical." It's obvious that it is precisely *because* Davidson subscribes to the latter doctrine and acknowledges an unexplained link between truth and belief that *he* can afford to deny that truth *is* an epistemic concept. He has gained the realist goal without the toil; and he has made no substantive use of Tarski at all, despite appearances. The truth is: belief is not "intrinsically veridical"; intrinsically (that is, tautologically), belief takes truth-values when construed in realist terms. Beliefs are candidates for veridical standing: Davidson has skipped the decisive step, the epistemic or evidentiary step. (Belief, for instance, that there is a God need not take truth-values at all.)

III

It's reasonably clear that, although he rejects his earlier "theory" of truth— that is, rejects the idea that he has any theory at all—Davidson does really cling to a considerable part of his coherence and correspondence "theory." For he says very plainly, opposing Paul Horwich's minimalist proposal:

> I think the sort of assertion that is linked to understanding [that is, understanding the meaning of what is said] already incorporates the concept of truth: we are *justified* in asserting a sentence in the required sense only if we believe the sentence we use to make the assertion is true; and what ultimately ties language to the world is that the conditions that typically cause us to hold sentences true *constitute* the truth-conditions, and hence the meanings, of our sentences.[30]

This would indeed seem to justify construing "true" as "an epistemic concept," though Davidson explicitly rejects the idea. To be sure, Davidson officially insists that "true" cannot be defined. He's right, of course, since he means to follow Tarski who relativizes the use of "true" to one or another language *L;* Davidson adds a plausible argument to the effect that it makes no sense to generalize uniformly over all *L*-relativized uses of "true." Fine. But that means that the impossibility of defining "true" is an artifact of

Davidson's having followed Tarski's thinking about the scope of Convention T (*not* the details of Convention T itself) as a first step to *any* would-be definition, just as it is an artifact of his following Tarski (in the way he does) that it falls out that "truth is conceptually prior to meaning and proposition."[31]

Tarski might have meant that Convention T applies to all languages in the sense that extensionalism is grounded in the nature of reality, though it must be variably applied to different languages because of *their* semantic contingencies. He does not generalize, because he confines his analysis to the semantic regularities of very carefully circumscribed languages. Ironically, it is Davidson who supposes that truth-bearing sentences may be counted on to yield to extensionalist analysis, though he nowhere supplies the evidence.

I am not clear about what is supposed to be at stake in arguing that truth is prior to meaning or meaning to truth. I cannot see how, *au fond,* there can be *any* articulation of what we mean by "true," "means," "believes," "knows," "real" or "exists" that does not implicate the conceptual interrelationship that binds the entire set in an encompassing account that is at once a semantic analysis of one or another of these terms *and* an epistemology and metaphysics of the conditions under which each is rightly assigned its role in the whole of human discourse. This is indeed (or so I believe) the gist of McDowell's notion of "answerability to the world." I see no difference in this regard between the wildly different philosophical systems offered by Aristotle, Kant, Hegel, Sellars, Davidson, McDowell—and even Rorty, despite Rorty's postmodernist demurrer. Intuitively, it seems preposterous to think that the correct account of "true" should depend on whether truth was prior to meaning (as in Davidson's opposing both deflationary and minimalist theories) or whether meaning can rightly claim priority over truth (as in Horwich's minimalism).[32]

Determining meaning seems to require invoking truth, and understanding truth seems to require understanding meaning; and whether *stating* the meaning of some term or predicate must be given in terms of truth-conditions or not seems to depend on what we mean by "must." The idea that Tarski had formulated certain "satisfaction" conditions for the use of "true" said to be neutral metaphysically and epistemologically may say something about Tarski's conception of an effective semantics, but it says nothing about "metaphysical neutrality." That would be a dodge. Once you concede that "true" has realist import, is "an epistemic concept," the quarrel between Davidson and Horwich seems overblown. There is no neutral division between the semantic and either the epistemological or metaphysical analysis of truth that could support Davidson's reading of Tarski. To treat Tarski's thesis as disquotational in any important sense at all is, in effect, to treat his extensionalist constraint as *not* skewed in any quarrelsome way when read in realist terms; that is, it is taken then to be genuinely neutral. Davidson recommends extensionalism rather shyly in fact. But if it is only a recommendation, then we cannot really claim to understand the sense in which he actually means to use Tarski's thesis as "the first step" in the formulation of *his own account* of truth.

There is, then, a benign holism that links all these concepts together: none can really function except in the discursive setting in which the others have their assigned roles. The "priority" question seems little more than a verbal trick: if you admit the existence of "propositions" (which Davidson worries and which Horwich favors), you "can" (if you wish) formulate what we should understand by "understanding" propositions, without explicitly invoking truth; but if you admit a conceptual connection between the use of "true" and one's beliefs (which Davidson says are "intrinsically veridical"), you will also be able to claim, plausibly enough, that the concept of meaning relies on the concept of truth. Still, as we have seen, there is no point to speaking of the semantics of truth apart from realist concerns; hence, there cannot be any adequate deflationary accounts that *really* detach the semantics of truth from one or another enabling epistemology and metaphysics. (Even Horwich's minimalism does not go that far, apart from the purely verbal game.)

Similar considerations seem, in fact, to have played a large part in the admiration with which Tarski's "definition of truth (for certain languages)" was first greeted; for Tarski took great pains to elude the positivist suspicion that "truth is a metaphysical concept and hence ought to be banished from all rigorous and scientific thought."[33] It's true that Tarski does not explicitly invoke metaphysical concepts. But, on the strength of the gathering argument, his semantic analysis of "true" *is* a metaphysics and epistemology "by other means"; and, of course, Tarski's "definition" does presuppose the extensionalist paraphraseability of natural languages, which makes no sense if detached from realist assumptions.

So the prime example of a "formal semantics" of truth is not really confined to a semantic analysis of the familiar predicate "true," except in the Pickwickian sense that its explicit definition does not employ epistemological or metaphysical terms, but only presupposes them in a powerfully constraining way. Convention T might be thought to be completely deflationary, given severe constraints on the use of "true." But no one believes that saying so would be informative, and Tarski did not think of his work that way.

Davidson's use of Tarski has its own difficulties. For one thing, Davidson believes that one must *begin* with Tarski, who had allegedly held the line on a semantic analysis, recognizing all the while that Tarski did not "complete" the analysis of truth itself; truth, Davidson insists, requires admitting a conceptual link to beliefs (said to be "intrinsically veridical") as well as a link to meanings (along the lines suggested). Truth, Davidson holds (not unreasonably) is among "the most elementary concepts we have"; hence, even apart from Tarski's "proof," truth is "an indefinable concept." Still, Davidson goes on, "This does not mean we can say nothing revealing about it: we can, by relating it to other concepts like belief, desire, cause, and action. Nor does the indefinability of truth imply that the concept is mysterious, ambiguous, or untrustworthy."[34]

But now we see that Davidson holds to the indefinability of truth, largely as a result of his accepting the positivist-inspired notion that the semantics of "true" *should* avoid all explicit entanglement with metaphysics and epistemology. That is why the "second" step of linking Tarski's convention with the role of belief (and action and the like) is taken by Davidson to go beyond semantics—hence, to go beyond deflationism and minimalism. (But that, too, is only a verbal gain.) If, therefore, *we* acknowledge that "true" *is* a metaphysical and epistemological concept, no matter what verbal niceties we favor, it no longer seems an insuperable problem to define "true"—it no longer seems important to insist that it *is* indefinable! For example, when he concedes that "the conditions that typically cause us to hold sentences true" are simply the same conditions that cause us to believe that they are true—since belief "*justifies*" us in asserting a sentence responsibly—Davidson cannot deny that *he* is explicating the normative import of a realist reading of "true" (a reading he means to confine to causal episodes). For, his thesis *is* universalized; the condition he isolates is already realist in import; and, the causal condition is taken to behave extensionally.[35]

The "only" worry is that the causal argument cannot distinguish between "veridical" belief and erroneous belief! Something further is needed beyond mere causal connection. Yet Davidson opposes any justificatory or validative or legitimative addition to his account. He fears he would be restoring—by such an addition—an epistemological and/or metaphysical "theory" of truth relative to the "independent" world: *that* would be to court, once more, the skepticism he finds in nearly every robust theory of truth.[36] Surely, that is a hothouse argument.

There remains a disastrous lacuna in Davidson's account. Recall that Davidson holds that it is belief that *justifies* us in asserting a sentence (in a cognitively responsible way) *and* that belief itself is caused by internal and external events that "ultimately [tie] language to the world." All that is fine—tenuous perhaps, but not wrong-headed. It's what Davidson adds to that account, which then shows at once what is missing—*what cannot be admitted, on his own thesis.* For he goes on to say—I have already cited it—that "the conditions that typically cause us to hold sentences true *constitute* the truth-conditions, and hence the meanings, of our sentences." That cannot possibly be right. It cannot possibly be true, for instance, that what, unknown to us, causes us "to hold [certain] sentences true constitute[s] . . . the meanings of our sentences," *if* it follows that, speaking as fluent speakers do, we could then be said to be using language in a standard way without understanding what we are saying!

On one reading of the causal theory of belief, the one Rorty has in mind when he insists that Davidson is a "pragmatist" in spite of his demurrer (in spite of his expressly opposing James's theory of truth[37]), the generic realism of belief is already ensured—it's the point of the notorious remark that "most of our beliefs must be true": we are apparently entitled to be confident that we *are* in touch with the world, for we normally proceed by way of "intrinsically veridical" beliefs. Yet we cannot know, for *that* reason alone, *whether this or that particular belief is true!* And, if we cannot know that, we cannot know that "most of our beliefs are true"; of course, we *cannot* know *that*, on causal grounds shorn of validative power, because even false beliefs are caused.

How then does Davidson explain *how* the causal theory of belief legitimates *any* particular belief's standing *as true?* He admits that "a causal explanation of a belief does not show how or why the belief is justified."[38] But if you give up the coherence theory of truth (as Davidson now does), you have nothing to fall back on (in the realist sense). That is, you cannot—following Davidson's lead—account for the justification of a particular belief, *without exceeding the causal theory of belief itself.* You must provide for a "normative" appraisal of the way beliefs are caused—never mind by what means, since *any* pertinent addition will have to be constructivist—and then you will have exceeded the limitations Davidson imposes on himself and us (and Rorty)—that is, "naturalizing." Only then will you be entitled to make sense of how you sort beliefs as true or false. (They are, after all, uniform insofar as they are merely *caused.*) But to yield in a constructivist direction would altogether undermine Davidson's scientistic intent.

Now, I don't deny that Davidson rejects the realist line of reasoning, that is, our invoking specifically realist criteria: we have been assuming, he says, that a person can tell if all or any of his beliefs are true:

by connecting his beliefs to the world, confronting certain of his beliefs with the deliverances of the senses one by one, or perhaps confronting the totality of his beliefs with the tribunal of experience. No such confrontation makes sense [however], for of course we can't get outside our skins to find out what is causing the internal happenings of which we are aware. . . . Since we can't swear intermediaries to truthfulness, we should allow no intermediaries between our beliefs and their objects in the world. Of course, there are causal intermediaries. What we must guard against are epistemic intermediaries.[39]

This is indeed the nerve of Davidson's naturalism—patently (in fact, explicitly) directed against Quine's (and Dummett's) empiricisms. It might have worked well enough (applied to particular beliefs) *if* the coherence theory of truth had passed muster (which Davidson championed at the moment of advancing the solution just cited). But he has now rejected it, while still subscribing (as we have seen) to the conviction that beliefs remain "intrinsically veridical."

He cannot, however, capture the veridicality of belief on causal grounds alone: he admits as much, it is impossible. *He must then "go epistemic" on truth,* whether he cares to or not. But if he does, then against his own "naturalizing" doctrine—and against Rorty's even fiercer naturalizing[40]—he must deny the adequacy of the causal theory of belief; he must reclaim the realist meaning of "true" and, thus, the "normative" element in the meaning of "true." But that *is* to fall back to something akin to McDowell's "answerability to the world."

What keeps the account from falling back to Cartesianism (*pace* McDowell) is simply that the whole affair must take a constructivist turn (which Davidson implicitly opposes). But if it must, there will be "epistemic intermediaries" galore. Only a constructivism could admit such complications consistently with accepting any robust version of realism. Such a theory could no longer be counted on, however, to behave in a reductionist or extensionalist—or naturalizing—way.

What, for his part, McDowell is trying to save is this: if meaning is inseparable from truth (as Davidson affirms), then the meaning of "true" must meet the constraints of *Bedeutung* and not merely of *Sinn,* in a sense akin to Wittgenstein's distinction, which goes contrary to Davidson's account. But McDowell himself says little more than this, though he seems (in examining Kant's theory) to intend much more. The obvious evidence is that McDowell nowhere explains just *which* sort of interpretive intermediaries he himself favors in the name of realism—or why. That also explains why, finally, one cannot say what the sense is in which McDowell avoids Cartesianism.

Put differently: Davidson faces an insoluble dilemma, which he cleverly finesses by insisting that *belief* is "intrinsically veridical." For, if we are restricted to the causal theory of belief, we must go epistemic, we must admit a normative distinction between justified and unjustified causal connections, which would exceed the resources of naturalizing itself. And if we insist that "most of our beliefs are true," meaning that most of what we sincerely affirm is true (*not* relying on the intrinsic veridicality of belief but admitting the disjunction between states of belief and *states of the world*), then we must go Cartesian and rely (very problematically) on our truth-seeking faculties. To rely on belief is, in any case, to disable the causal theory, because (as Davidson admits) "we can't get outside our skins"; and to rely on the way the (independent) world is must be to fall back on some form of *a priori* or facultative privilege, because (as Davidson also insists) to try to legitimate our realism is merely to court skepticism.

Furthermore, even to entertain these alternatives is to construe "true" *as* "an epistemic concept." In some strange way, Davidson had originally veered off in Michael Dummett's direction, for Dummett had held that the "realist" (as opposed to the "anti-realist") took "true" to be "a radically non-epistemic notion."[41] The idea seems incoherent on its face, as Hilary Putnam convincingly argued.[42] The ulterior reason is the one Hegel supplies against the Cartesians, namely, that in cognitive contexts there cannot be a gap between the "subjective" and the "objective"; effectively, there cannot (as we would now say) be a disjunction between epistemology and metaphysics.

Hegel's own "phenomenological" formulation is superficially difficult to fathom—may, for instance, appear to yield too much to idealism (by featuring the space of "consciousness"); but it lays a proper ground for the slimmer formulations of our own day. Thus Hegel says, in the Introduction to the *Phenomenology of Spirit*:

consciousness is, on the one hand, consciousness of the object, and on the other, consciousness of itself; consciousness of what for it is the True, and consciousness of its knowledge of the truth. Since both are *for* the same consciousness, this consciousness is itself their comparison; it is for the same consciousness to know whether its knowledge of the object corresponds to the object or not. The object, it is true, seems only to be for consciousness in the way that consciousness knows it; it seems that consciousness cannot, as it were, get behind the object as it exists for consciousness so as to examine what

the object is *in itself,* and hence, too, cannot test its own knowledge
by that standard. But the distinction between the in-itself and
knowledge is already present in the very fact that consciousness
knows an object at all. Something is *for it* the *in-itself;* and knowledge, is, *for it,* another moment.[43]

This is quite splendid in its own right. For what it shows, if we can get beyond Hegel's alien prose, is that all the *aporiai* of the Cartesian-Kantian interval are resolvable within (and only within) the terms of a benign holism
that (in contemporary terms) would never permit the semantics of truth to
be disjoined from its epistemological and metaphysical conditions. (That is
precisely what Hegel means by "phenomenology.") The lesson is at least two
hundred years old.

What Hegel is saying is that all distinctions, as of "appearance" and "reality," are internal to the world-as-we-experience-it (*Erscheinungen*) relative
to which *there is no disjunction* between appearance and reality. The independence of the "independent" world is already epistemically internal to the
conditions on which we report the way in which we experience-the-world.
What we take to be the "in-itself" is, therefore, a construction of what appears "for consciousness": that is the sense in which Hegel draws his realism
from his phenomenology. That I take to be the sparest but still compelling
clue to any viable realism since Kant and Hegel. It is not an idealism, because
what we construct is not the actual world but a conception of what, among
our *Erscheinungen,* we *take* to belong to what *is* independent of experience.

In this sense, there is no "given" that is epistemologically or metaphysically privileged; what we *take* to be independently real we construct, which
(to repeat) is not to say that reality is constructed by the human mind.
Davidson, you remember, refuses to countenance constructivism or legitimating reasons for espousing the realist standing of our beliefs—on the
doubtful grounds that "epistemic intermediaries" would drive us back to
privilege and thence to skepticism. But Davidson nowhere explains how the
causal theory of belief, which somehow secures the "veridical" connection
between belief and world, itself escapes the same threat. To admit the threat,
however, *requires* a reconciliation between causal and normative factors.

If you think carefully about what Davidson actually says here, you will
not fail to be struck by the oddness of his demurrer. Surely, the bare request
for supporting evidence or reasons invokes no privilege and invites no skepticism—unless the initiating belief or truth-claim already does so. Or does
Davidson suppose that the bare request to explain *why* any would-be evidence or supporting reasons *are* epistemically pertinent, or valid for the pur-

pose, or confirmatory, already signifies an appeal to privilege or, by a reverse scruple, drives us to skepticism?

IV

I can now assemble a reasonable picture of the central meaning of "true." "True" is a predicate applied to sentences as and when used in asserting how the world "is," viewed according to our lights. It has realist import for that reason, which, determinately specified by what the uttered sentence means, is thought to be confirmable in accord with a normative practice for doing so. Correspondence between what is said or asserted or believed and the way the world is, judged according to our lights about what such a fit requires, entitles the affirmed sentence to be deemed true if it is found to be true. Hence, although the sentence "p is true" is, normally, disquotationally equivalent to "p," *that* "semantic" fact does not explicate the meaning of "true" at all, it presupposes it. Furthermore, there cannot be a purely "semantic" analysis of "true," in the sense in which such an analysis would avoid employing any metaphysical or epistemological distinctions. For the meaning of "true" essentially includes the sense of a realist commitment *and* the propriety of appealing to pertinent normative constraints as to what (by our lights) we should count as true.

The meaning of "true" presupposes a holist space linking a nest of concepts like "meaning," "knowledge," "reality," "belief," "evidence," "experience," "reasons," "justification," and the like, by invoking which the assignment of truth-values ("true" and "false," say) rightly applies. The pretty thing about these considerations is that, although "true" has realist import, it does not signify any particular metaphysics or epistemology—or any methodology or logic for that matter. In this sense, Tarski's proposal regarding a "truth predicate" coextensive with "true"—under certain extreme constraints—may be conditionally eligible as a determinate interpretation of "true" *in* the context of making claims about the real world; but it cannot be said to specify any necessary or neutral or universal semantic feature of discourse about the real world conformable with what has been said about the meaning of "true." As already remarked, Tarski's predicate, formulated in Convention T, is conceptually dependent on a certain realist assumption controversially committed to the adequacy of a thoroughly extensionalist analysis. Tarski was well aware of that. But it cannot then function as a "first step" in, say, Davidson's two-part theory.

If, furthermore, a conceptual holism constrains the analysis of "true" in the manner sketched, then, eschewing cognitive privilege, our analysis comports well with post-Kantian policies (especially Hegel's) to the effect that epistemology and metaphysics (as well as logic and semantics) cannot be disjoined in pursuing what a viable realism would be like. Thus, the analysis being offered here lends weight to the idea (which is not itself part of the general meaning of "true") that a viable realism must be a form of constructivism, need not be a form of idealism, may take plural and even incompatible forms, may not accord with Tarski's Convention T, and may even change substantially under the pressures of changing experience and changing history. Deflationists characteristically ignore these matters, which is to say, they harbor a secret metaphysics and epistemology that they do not care to expose!

The upshot is this. We cannot explicate the meanings of terms in terms of the truth-conditions of the sentences in which they occur, without invoking second-order theories of the realist standing of such sentences. But realism, as already argued, is a profoundly contested notion. (Think, for example, of Quine's doctrine of the "indeterminacy of translation.") Hence, it must be the case that the theory of meaning cannot be given largely or wholly in terms of a realist account of truth; or, more modestly and more pertinently, the meaning of the terms of a particular sentence cannot be given, unless *per impossibile,* in terms of that sentence's actual truth-conditions. For meanings would then be hostage to an unacceptable degree to the contested nature of realism itself. The very fluency of language would be adversely affected. Unhappily, Davidson is on both sides of the fence at once. For he insists on abandoning all non-causal "intermediaries" (legitimative interpretations, say); and yet he also insists that "most of our beliefs are true," despite its being perfectly clear that causal connections cannot function criterially to distinguish between correct and erroneous beliefs.

This, I must emphasize, provides the basis for an important distinction pursued in the final chapter, namely, the distinction between an "internal" and an "external" holism: Davidson's thesis that "most of our beliefs are true" is the key to what, in effect, is his external holism (which needs to be compared with Quine's holism); whereas the constructivist account of truth I favor here is an instance of what I call an internal holism. The post-Hegelian tradition that runs from Hegel, through Nietzsche, through Heidegger, through Dewey, through the Frankfurt Critical school, through Wittgenstein, through Foucault, tends to spawn internal holisms. The difference rests with relying on some form of epistemic privilege obscured in holist terms (external holism); internal holisms are epistemologically benign. Thus, my criticism of Davidson's account of truth is, precisely, that it hides, by various ingenious means, its final reliance on an external holism— the point being that, in our time, Cartesianism is quite capable of availing itself of one or another form of external holism. But I postpone the final reckoning until the final chapter.

To return. To pursue Davidson's concerns in terms of the analysis of belief instead of a direct analysis of truth makes it impossible to regard Tarski's account as a "first step" in the analysis of truth (as Davidson claims); also, it jeopardizes his entire realist program, as far as eluding Cartesianism is concerned.

In this respect, Davidson cites an intriguing example offered by Michael Dummett, which he opposes but does not satisfactorily put to rest:

> The human use of language [he says, advancing Dummett's thesis] must be a function of how people understand a language, so if truth is to play a role in explaining what it is to understand a language, there must be something that counts as a person having "conclusive evidence" that a statement is true. One can appreciate the force of this idea [Davidson responds] while finding it difficult to accept. I have given my chief reason for rejecting it; that it is empty, or makes truth a property that can be lost. But there are other strong intuitions that would also have to be sacrificed if Dummett were right. One is the connection of truth with meaning; on Dummett's view, we can understand a sentence like "A city will never be built on this spot" without having any idea what it would be for this sentence to be true (since the sentence, or an utterance of it, has no truth value for Dummett). Another is the connection of truth with belief: on Dummett's view I can understand and believe a city will never be built on this spot, for my belief will have no truth value.[44]

My own suggestion is that the meaning of "true" *does* have realist import but not in any way that would enable us to paraphrase the meaning of any individual expression in terms of the truth-conditions of the sentence in which it occurs or the conditions that bear on its particular role in that sentence. If truth is contestable in the profound way I think it is, then it would be completely unworkable to link meaning and truth in the close way Davidson prefers. Wherever we ask for an explication of the meaning of sentences in ordinary discourse, we mean to do justice to the fluency of actual communication. Meaning is, normally, an informal and consensual matter (without being essentially criterial); and truth is a profoundly contested matter wherever we argue beyond the mere admission that, generally speaking, "true" does have realist import.

As far as I can see, truth never plays a criterial role: we always step down from truth to the ascription of truth-values; and, there, we find ourselves obliged to accommodate the contested standing of our alternative forms of realism. But if that is so, then scientism will have lost another inning. The work of epistemology cannot be ensured by any merely semantic means. And that is an important theorem favored by internal holism. But now it signifies, ineluctably, that, as soon as you abandon cognitive privilege, scientism becomes subject to the vagaries of epistemology in ways it seems impossible to surmount. In that sense, the very fact that truth is not an independent notion but one that is essentially tied to epistemological considerations—themselves holistically inseparable from metaphysical, semantic, logical, methodological, even psychological questions—confirms at once that the kind of scientisms we have already reviewed (in chapter 1, for instance) cannot fail to be delayed or defeated by the complications besetting truth-claims of any kind. Davidson seems to have tried to tailor the very idea of truth in such a way as to avoid just such entanglements. But the entanglements stubbornly persist.

I have pursued the analysis of "true" in strictest conformity with the rigors of analytic philosophy in order to demonstrate its aporetic standing. The paradoxes that I've uncovered cannot be put to rest without recovering a sense of the entire human world in which science and truth-claims first arise. That is the simplest implication of the tangled subtleties of the different bands of philosophers who have sought to confine the analysis of "true" in semantic ways. The idea was, of course, to neutralize our understanding of its use so that it could conform with whatever strong version of extensionalism might be independently vindicated. It is worth remarking, there- fore, that pragmatism and certain strong currents of analysis within continental philosophy converge at least to the extent of rejecting the adequacy of the familiar analytic accounts. Here, I confine my remarks to contributions toward strengthening the case against scientism.

4

The Unraveling of Scientism

When Ludwig Wittgenstein's *Philosophical Investigations* appeared posthumously and without warning, many who had admired the *Tractatus* as the early century's greatest philosophical feat, fulfilling expectations latent in the work of figures such as Gottlob Frege, Bertrand Russell, and Rudolf Carnap and who were entirely willing to concede the deficiencies of the Tractarian vision and the visions of others, openly cried "traitor!" at the first shock of being confronted with Wittgenstein's profound dissatisfaction with his own masterpiece. Quite literally, I heard these outraged voices on at least one professional occasion in New York City in the 1950s.[1] Perhaps no one, at the moment of that first shock, could have grasped the full import of the remarkable difference between the Tractarian undertaking and what was being offered in the *Investigations* and would continue to be offered in subsequent selections from an unexpectedly large cache of writings that Wittgenstein left behind.

Looking back on that fateful turn,[2] one can begin to see the unraveling of the scientistic vision of Anglo-American analytic philosophy from within its own citadel, the line of investigation that spans Russell and Carnap and the Tractarian Wittgenstein and, more equivocally, W. V. Quine and Donald Davidson, which remains in play (but has been increasingly contested) down to the beginning of the new century. Viewed from that vantage, Wittgenstein's *Tractatus* and *Investigations* may be read instructively as anticipating the need for either of two very different kinds of *holism* that have dominated English-language philosophy ever since, and that explain much about the present state of the discipline and its future prospects.

I hasten to add that the *Tractatus* does not require or implicate any form of holism, though it makes room for a distinct kind of holism that later theorists—Quine, preeminently—found it necessary to invoke. By contrast, the *Investigations* does rely on a form of holism, but it is a benign form diametrically opposed to the kind of holism Quine relies on in one part of his theory (the "indeterminancy of translation" thesis), though not the kind featured in another (the analysis of the "two dogmas" of empiricism). In any case, Wittgenstein's *Investigations* may be the single most important early and obviously informed rejection of the kind of theorizing that the *Tractatus* represents; its appearance coincides with the nadir of American pragmatism's reception and was seen to promise a profound change in philosophical taste.[3]

This is not to disagree with (or confirm) Richard Rorty's dating of what he calls "the shift from the earlier to the later form of analytic philosophy, . . . which began around 1950 and was complete by around 1970."[4] In Rorty's genuinely helpful introduction to the anthology, *The Linguistic Turn*,[5] this counts as a relatively local "turn" within the larger "linguistic turn" that effectively begins at the beginning of the twentieth century with Bertrand Russell. Rorty's point—a perfectly fair one—is that "analytic" philosophy "started out as a form of empiricism" (in fact, favored a kind of foundationalism, as in A. J. Ayer's *Language, Truth, and Logic* [1936]) and took a specifically linguistic turn when it rejected all forms of foundationalism and cognitive privilege. Rorty explicitly enumerates, as the "most seminal" publications of the time, Quine's "Two Dogmas of Empiricism" (1951), Wittgenstein's *Investigations* (1954), and Wilfrid Sellars's "Empiricism and the Philosophy of Mind" (1956).[6]

I find this all to the good (though misleading); but the dialectical contests within the analytic tradition and between analytic philosophy and (say) pragmatism are, I think, better served by reflecting on the two kinds of holism I mean to flag. The *Tractatus*, as I say, does not invoke any holism at all. It is meant to be a self-contained fragment of a larger account of knowledge and reality that it does not itself supply; *that* larger "system," assumed to be congruent with what we are specifically given in the *Tractatus*, is an undefined "part" of an even more inclusive vision of the entire range of human life, about which we are told nothing beyond its being "a limited whole," that is, a "mystical" whole.[7] We are not told what that specifically means or shown that saying so rightly belongs to the Tractarian idiom.

I don't pretend that these are the only, or the only important, forms of holism to acknowledge in twentieth-century English-language philosophy, but they are the principal forms that bear on the contested adequacy and possible redirection of the entire analytic movement in our time. The contrast between them, therefore, suggests a very different line of reflection from the one Rorty favors; for Rorty treats the later Wittgenstein, along with Quine and Sellars, as contributing (thus far at least) to the same "linguistic turn" he flags—the one against foundationalism. Sellars, not unlike the

Wittgenstein of the *Tractatus,* does not invoke any external holism; that is, both he and the Tractarian Wittgenstein are fundamentally opposed to holism. Curiously, Rorty and Robert Brandom, who subscribes to Rorty's reading of Sellars, manage to discount (in effect, dismiss) Sellars's scientism (which champions an alternative "atomism" in place of the atomism of the *Tractatus*). They then isolate Sellars's account of linguistic competence as a kind of "pragmatism" (as Rorty and Brandom agree), which, thus separated from Sellars's original scientism, is made to implicate a form of internal holism that the scientism would never have needed or thought appropriate.[8] Suddenly, the story turns opaque.

External holism began to infect early analytic philosophy when the failure of logicism became a metonym for the general inability of philosophical programs like those of Russell, Frege, Wittgenstein, and Carnap to yield a reasonably determinate degree of closure with respect to the philosophical description of the achievements of the principal sciences. Chastened but loyal to what they believed might be salvaged from the ruin of nearly fifty years of heroic work, they committed themselves to defending (at nearly any cost) the prospects of an exceptionless materialism and extensionalism—and admitted in their hearts, if not explicitly, that they could not succeed without the advantage of certain carefully constructed assumptions (thought to be reasonable, but practically impossible to confirm) that would permit them to show, piecemeal, in a critically responsible way, how particular analyses might advance the cause.[9]

Quine and the Wittgenstein of the *Investigations* are our best exemplars. For Quine's *Word and Object* is the first strong recovery of the systematic possibilities of materialism and extensionalism along these lines, shorn of all forms of privilege and fixity (epistemic, ontic, semantic, logical, methodological), cast in the idiom of "semantic ascent"[10] and made disarmingly flexible (even charming) about a fair contest among competing efforts of every stripe; whereas, Wittgenstein simply abandoned the entire venture of the *Tractatus* and invented, brilliantly, an entirely novel conception of how to understand (by another variant of the "linguistic turn") the verbal and more than verbal feats of intelligence essential to the entire range of human life. Here, Quine embraces the paradigm of an external holism and Wittgenstein, that of an internal holism. At any rate, that is my brief.

Actually, Quine is more interesting than I've made him out to be, because you could argue that, in the "Two Dogmas" paper and elsewhere, Quine is drawn to an internal holism;[11] whereas, in *Word and Object,* his best-known doctrine plainly accords with an external holism.[12] The truth is, as we shall see, that the former is made to serve the latter. Viewed conformably, Davidson may be thought to be a more consistent holist, however much he is drawn in the same contrary directions that Quine is; but what becomes transparent in Davidson's characteristic work is that the internal holism begins to undermine the plausibility of the external holism. That alone obliges us to reassess Quine's position. These are no more than promissory notes, of course, that will have to be redeemed.

But, as you follow the argument, please bear in mind that Quine's extreme economies effectively occupy us in a way that abandons all the detailed analyses of the positivists (and others) grounded in the actual puzzles and practices of the natural sciences. I don't doubt that Quine was familiar with the issues the positivists raised about, say, the role of mathematics in theoretical physics; and he was certainly very well informed about the larger quarrels regarding logic and mathematics. But what Quine produced (viewed this way) was a sort of half-way house that encouraged analytic philosophy to seek to solve its problems in a professional bubble of its own. Even the treatment of the analytic/synthetic distinction (Quine's finest essay, in my opinion) betrays a kind of isolationism, since, as against Carnap's speculations, Quine does not explore the way the distinction is treated in philosophical reflections on the actual work of the physical sciences. You cannot fail to see the danger when you turn from Quine to Davidson. For, in Davidson's analyses, which are more ambiguously committed to scientism than Quine's, it is nearly impossible to fathom just how the answers Davidson gives—for instance, on matters spanning linguistic meaning and the analysis of actions—fit any familiar empirical inquiries that might compare with the gauge of the early work of the positivists and their allies.

II

To put the issue in the bluntest way: external holism is an irremediably question-begging and inadmissible liberty that launches a venture that could not possibly succeed otherwise; internal holism, by contrast, is a relatively benign strategy that is not vulnerable in the "externalist" way and is actually able to mount a telling objection against any thoroughgoing reductive materialism and extensionalism. That is certainly a claim worth pursuing.

Consider Quine, therefore. Quine's most distinctive thesis, "the indeterminacy of translation," is also his most baffling. Just how baffling it is proves to be nothing short of breathtaking, considering the doctrine's strategic importance in Quine's work and the plain fact that it borders on illegibility, if not incoherence. It will need some care and patience in the telling. But, given Quine's executive role in late analytic philosophy, the investment can certainly be justified. Here, then, is the preamble to Quine's thesis—more thesis than a mere conjecture—which, even by itself, has, with good reason, greatly worried his admirers:[13]

> We were [Quine begins] undertaking to examine the evidential support of science. That support, by whatever name, comes now to be seen as a relation of stimulation to scientific theory. Theory consists of sentences, or is couched in them; and logic connects sentences to sentences. What we need, then, as initial links in those connecting chains, are some sentences that are directly and firmly associated with our stimulations. Each should be associated affirmatively with some range of one's stimulations and negatively with some range. The sentence should command the subject's assent or dissent outright, on the occasion of a stimulation in the appropriate range, without further investigation and independently of what he may have been engaged in at the time. A further requirement is intersubjectivity; unlike a report of a feeling, the sentence must command the same verdict from all linguistically competent witnesses of the occasion.
>
> I call them *observation sentences.* Examples are 'It's raining', 'It's getting cold', 'That's a rabbit'.[14]

The first thing that strikes the eye on reading this remarkably obscure passage is that, given Quine's wording—"on the occasion of a stimulation [of our sense organs]"—*there is no observational or perceptual element that Quine specifically identifies,* that is, nothing in the ordinary sense of "perceive" that others could identify as perceived by the supposed percipient himself, and *there is no obvious way, in general or in the context of sensory stimulation, to specify any sentences matching stimulations that could "command the same verdict from all linguistically competent witnesses of the occasion"*—or specify how we could ever know what to count as the same stimulation or the same verdict or the same verdict answering to the same stimulation. The worry is that the seeming rigor of the constraints imposed is the result of restrictions that make sense only on the resources of ordinary perceptions that the new behaviorist and physicalist discipline promptly pretends never to have invoked!

The "occasion" is plainly perceptual, but Quine carefully avoids any explicitly perceptual datum. (Yet it is identified in materialist terms.) Certainly Quine's intention is to address a perceptual occasion, since he speaks of "associating" sentence and stimulation in a way that "should command the subject's assent or dissent outright," indeed "should command the same verdict from all linguistically competent witnesses of the occasion." But he steadfastly refuses to make explicit any evidentiary connection between "occasion" or "stimulation" *and* "sensory perception" in the usual sense, which, as is well known, both Kuhn and Davidson failed to persuade him to elucidate or abandon.[15] It is a further irony that this lacuna in Quine's account should correspond to the essential *aporia* of Cartesianism itself. In Locke, for instance, the gap spans sensory "ideas" and the "qualities" of the independent world; in Quine, the subjective element is replaced by the physical occasion of ocular stimulation, which seems on its face to be an even more profound retreat from reflecting on the problem of perceptual evidence. In fact, on the prevailing view, every would-be pretheoretical sensory source proves to be no more than a late artifact admitted within the theory of perception itself—a source therefore that could never play an evidentiary role. If that worry held, then, of course, there could be no initial "fact of the matter" *on which* the "indeterminacy of translation" issue *could* rightly be grounded *or applied* in any determinate way. As a result, Quine's doctrine may be stalemated at the start.

Quine would oppose any such reading, both because of what *I* am calling his "external holism," which is meant to ensure "a [certain] fact of the matter" on which alone indeterminacy makes sense, applies to *some* delimited part of the world rather than another, and because he means to confine the relevance of the lack of a "fact of the matter" to a choice among translational manuals" already pertinently addressed to the indeterminacy posed by some would-be holist perceptual "datum." What Quine means is that there *is* an initial fact of the matter (associated with the *truth* of holophrastic sentences) that supports the relevance of alternative translations of "observation sentences" within the scope of the admitted indeterminacy, but that this alone is insufficient to dissolve the indeterminacy itself. As he explains in his usual ingenious way: "even the extreme holist cannot hold that *no* single sentence has its empirical content to itself. We can meet legalism with legalism. If the empirical content belongs to the scientific theory as a whole, then it still belongs to a single sentence, the long conjunctive one that states the whole theory."[16] Obviously, this would be a paper victory if we could not relativize "empirical content" (however "holist") to particular stimulus occasions. Quine offers no clear instruction here. (Otherwise, there would only be one observation sentence and that sentence would be utterly vacuous.)

Roughly: "stimulus meaning" is Quine's replacement for protocol sentences in the positivists' sense, and is meant to provide a guess at an empiricist ground for science and ordinary experience alike, which, when viewed holistically (or "holophrastically"), may be fairly thought to have cognitive force *prior* to, and *without* benefit of, *any* interpretive or theoretical intervention. The sticking point is that "holophrastic sentences" *do* appear to have cognitive standing: they apparently answer to "a fact of the matter," though they are not parsed in the way ordinary facts (or sentences affirming ordinary facts) are. Read one way, *they are not* the locus of Quine's explicit holism, since they take truth-values directly (*how*, is admittedly a puzzle); yet, read another way, they constitute the essential holism on which Quine's entire epistemology depends, since there is no fact of the matter as to how they should be parsed (or translated) objectively! I see no possible way in which these two doctrines can be reconciled.

There are a great many puzzles regarding Quine's theory that dovetail here, that would have to be resolved if the indeterminacy thesis could be satisfactorily defended—or even used in explaining the work of the sciences. Too many, I think, to support a favorable reading; but, if so, then the indeterminacy thesis cannot take the form Quine requires—it must collapse—and with its collapse Quine risks his entire philosophical vision. Bear in mind that, rightly interpreted, Quine's indeterminacy thesis is one of the principal targets of Davidson's influential paper, "On the Very Idea of a Conceptual Scheme."[17] For Davidson fears that Quine has segregated "stimulus-meaning" (or "holophrastic sentences") and "analytical hypotheses" (or "translation manuals") in the spirit of a third dogma of empiricism, that of the disjunction of empirical content and conceptual scheme, which accounts for the would-be pertinence and robustness of the indeterminacy issue itself.[18]

Take a moment more to sort out our initial puzzles. I have featured two. First of all, Quine appears to be using "stimulation" in a decidedly problematic way. Along one line of reflection, he clearly assigns occasions of stimulation (of our sense organs) an evidentiary role that captures "empirical content" of some kind: witness his specimen sentences (cited above); along another, he clearly subordinates or erases altogether anything like empirical (or "empiricist") sensory evidence that might have encouraged us to align his view with Carnap's (or, more generally, with anything like the admission of first-person avowals of how things appear to us in accord with the various sensory modalities)—something, say, akin to Hegelian *Erscheinungen* or positivist *Protokollsätze* or, more problematically, Davidson's first-person avowals.[19] In this way, Quine prepares the ground for resolving epistemological questions by referring to the evidentiary bearing of physical and behavioral events alone ("radical translation"). That is, as far as our truth-claims and judgments are concerned. But he nowhere supplies the clue by which to explain *how* such events ever acquire their evidential or epistemic standing in the first place.

Why should we suppose that the threat of the indeterminacy of translation does *not* affect our perception of physical and behavioral "data" in the same way that it affects all other occasions on which it is invoked? Quine, you remember, is quite willing to speak of the assent of "all linguistically competent *witnesses* of the occasion" (of "stimulation"). There are, therefore, two unanswered puzzles here: one regarding what to understand as "perceptually" common to all assenting witnesses and the rationale for doing so; the other regarding the reasons for supposing the perceptions implicated in our "witnessing" are not infected by the indeterminacy problem in the same way ordinary perceptual occasions are. There's a dilemma there. Ultimately, Quine offers no answer to either question.

Second, Quine seems to be affirming that there *is* a "fact of the matter" *at* the holist or holophrastic level of sensory stimulation, in virtue of which "stimulations" do acquire their epistemic standing *and* yield enough in the way of objectivity to resolve the indeterminacy threat as far as an open family of determinate parsings (*of those sentences*) is concerned, but not enough to confirm the objective standing *of any one or another such parsing*—even, for example, as to *what* stimulations *there are* by which to fix the locus in which true holophrastic sentences are, indeed, true, so that we may conjecture (further) as to *what there is* in the world (as by applying Quine's quantificational devices and "analytical hypotheses"). There seems to be an enormous *petitio* here. I do not believe either of these puzzles can be resolved within the compass of Quine's resources.

For his part, Davidson goes too far with his "third dogma" (in correcting Quine), in the sense that Quine plainly holds that "indeterminacy of translation is not intranslatability; it is multiple translatability."[20] And there you have the puzzle: Quine's emphasis is essential, because the indeterminacy thesis *is* the site of his (external) holism and because, if what I have already cited from Quine holds, then his holism cannot be defeated by way of Davidson's objection. (Which is not to say it cannot be defeated: I have just sketched the main charge of the counterargument.)

Quine's holism is simply more resilient than Davidson supposes, even if it cannot finally succeed. "Holism at its most extreme," Quine maintains, "holds that science faces the tribunal of experience not sentence by sentence but as a corporate body: the whole of science."[21] Yet, as we have seen, Quine is not himself an "extreme" holist in Davidson's sense (in "On the Very Idea"), since he also insists that *that* does not preclude any single sentence from having "its empirical content to itself"[22] and because he relies on the truth of holophrastic sentences. Frankly, I cannot see how Quine's thesis (the indeterminacy of translation) can be reconciled with the testing of empirical claims (the tribunal of the whole of science) except vacuously.

In fact, Davidson's charge (nominally directed against Thomas Kuhn and Paul Feyerabend) would entail the equivalence of indeterminacy and intranslatability. In effect, Quine shows us a straightforward way of introducing indeterminacy "by degrees," whereas Davidson requires an all-or-nothing verdict. If you allow gradations here, then incommensurable conceptual schemes (those Quine actually introduces in parsing indeterminacy) *can* make perfect sense on Quine's view—which Davidson has no intention of allowing. In fact, Davidson provides no resources for defeating Quine's maneuver, and Quine never really explains how the indeterminacy thesis serves his behaviorism. Furthermore, Quine *couldn't* really play his hand out along the lines of treating "the tribunal of experience [as] a corporate body: the whole of science": Duhem's more moderate holism would not allow it; and, in any case, it would not support *any* informed choice of "stimulations." We would simply be obliged to fall back to the fluent prejudices of our own language, which of course would obviate Quine's entire apparatus. It would also reintroduce the intensional complications Quine wished to avoid.

The right analysis begins, I would say, with the odd fact (noted above) that, although the empirical content of our most fundamental or primitive observation sentences—those indexed to "stimulations"—are said to keep their "empirical content to [themselves]," such content cannot possibly fail to be a *theoretical* posit about what we should take as primitive (in this regard) when judged from the vantage of later conjectures that have already introduced parsings of *words and terms*—some effective resolution of the indeterminacy of translation—relative to *our* language. But that cannot be Quine's final word, since, on his own account, it would be question-begging *and* would risk the advantage (which he requires and insists on) of maintaining that these elementary sentences *are* indeed directly confirmed *and* reliable *prior* to the application of *any* theoretical parsing (according to our "analytical hypotheses").[23] So they are meant to be a replacement, odd as they are, for reports of sensory experience, often issued as a first-person avowal ("Lo, a rabbit!").

Quine is in grave difficulty here. I venture to say that this most famous of late analytic doctrines is simply incoherent. Undoubtedly Davidson saw the problem—saw also the cleverness of linking Quine and Kuhn—but was guided by his close association with Quine to break the news in a way that only "in" readers would be able to fathom easily (and accordingly, could be counted on to remain discreet about). But Quine's difficulty bleeds into the strongest currents of analytic philosophy—Davidson's as well—and Quine's inability to extricate his principal doctrine from the confusion that threatens to descend betrays the vulnerability of the entire movement, even where its champions resist the indeterminacy thesis itself. You will insist on the evidence, of course.

The relevant objections are surprisingly straightforward, but the textual argument is tangled. I begin, therefore, with a short statement of Quine's that should lead us to all the principal *aporiai* behind the surface difficulties. That has to be seen. Quine needs a candidate run of sentences to mark the occasions for practicing "*radical* translation, i.e., translation of the language of a hitherto untouched people," with an eye to isolating the "stimulus meaning" of a native's uttered sentence.[24] This is expected to yield a body of observation sentences marked in terms of their stimulus meaning, which, on Quine's theory, should fix the "meaning" of what is uttered—*pretheoretically* and as a first pass—for us and for native speakers according to our lights. These sentences have rather unusual properties, however, that lead directly to the indeterminacy thesis. (They are only rarely mentioned.)

Here, then, is the promised remark, the classic site of Quine's so-called behaviorist theory of meaning, except, of course, that Quine opposes hypostatizing meanings and acknowledges that "stimulus meaning" does *not* begin to capture all that we have in mind in any normal understanding of the "meaning" of what apt speakers utter:

> The recovery of a man's current language from his currently observed responses is the task of the linguist who, unaided by an interpreter [a bilingual], is out to penetrate and translate a language hitherto unknown. All the objective data he has to go on are the forces that he sees impinging on the native's surfaces and the observable behavior, vocal and otherwise, of the native. Such data evince native "meanings" only of the most objectively empirical or stimulus-linked variety. And yet the linguist apparently ends up with native "meanings" in some quite unrestricted sense; purported translations, anyway, of all possible native sentences. . . . What is relevant . . . to our purposes is *radical* translation. . . . The task is one that is not in practice undertaken in its extreme form, since a chain of interpreters of a sort can be recruited of marginal persons across the darkest archipelago. . . . The utterances first and most surely translated . . . are ones keyed to present events that are conspicuous

to the linguist and his informant. A rabbit scurries by, the native says 'Gavagai', and the linguist notes down the sentence 'Rabbit' (or 'Lo, a rabbit') as tentative translation, subject to testing in further cases.[25]

By these means, we define "affirmative [and negative] stimulus meaning" and stimulus meaning itself "as the ordered pair of the two. . . . The imagined equating of 'Gavagai' and 'Rabbit' [Quine concludes] can now be stated thus: they have the same stimulus meaning."[26]

Hence, understanding one another is modeled on the field linguist's sparest record of an alien people, and that record is itself constructed by means of the impoverished idiom of "stimulus meaning." Still, what role is being played by Quine's remarking that the field linguist's data are confined to "the forces that *he sees impinging on the native's surfaces and the observable behavior*"? Is that a contradiction or is it merely an arbitrary, pointless restriction? Quine treats the proposal as both neutral and empirically viable. But what he means, of course, is that if *that* option would not work, then the prospect of a thoroughly extensionalist account of science would be dashed. The model must be more than a mere stand-in: Quine spends too much care on the details—in *Pursuit of Truth* as well as in *Word and Object*. But what if it fails? (I believe it must fail.)

The holism of the indeterminacy thesis is what holds the entire labor together, which is what Davidson fears, though he has no suitable alternative to offer. The decisive point is this: "stimulus meaning" is no more than a tendentious selection from larger epistemic resources that sets aside—or pretends to set aside—the unwanted intensional complications it *first* draws on, as through the field linguist's own perceptual habits. It is not entitled therefore to any privileged evidentiary standing. If you read with care what has just been cited, you cannot fail to see that holophrastic sentences, or the "holist" perceptions they putatively report, play no evidentiary role at all distinct from the ordinary resources the field linguist brings to his own work— in effect, ourselves! The entire argument is a house of cards.

That Quine intends his account to isolate what *in terms of his theory* is *pre*theoretical can be gathered directly from his claim that "[f]rom the point of view of infantile learning, as from the point of view of the first steps of radical translation, we do best to look upon 'Mama', 'Red', 'Water' and the rest simply as occasion sentences. [So that a]ll the linguist can claim for his first radical translations is agreement in stimulus meanings, and all the baby learns is to say his word when appropriately irritated and not otherwise."[27]

There you have *half* the argument. But you surely see that the pretheoretical standing of the stimulus meaning of observation sentences is itself an artifact of Quine's theoretical reliance on the constraints he simply imposes on the field linguist's work and on our reading of the baby's first utterances. (Quine is not entirely clear on the matter.) The knockdown reason is that Quine precludes anything that would involve bilingual competence; so that what the native *says relative to what he sees* must itself be constructed in accord with our own (contingent) conceptual schemes (our metaphysics). In this sense, the meaning of what the native says, either in terms of stimulus meaning or in terms of something closer to what apt speakers of a shared language would normally "mean," cannot collect what is *pre*theoretical *for us:* that is, cannot collect what stimulus meaning should come to, before ever raising the question of radical translation. That is the problem of the other half of Quine's theory. For we are not in the same position, understanding ourselves and understanding babies and alien natives.

Quine offers only the barest beginnings of a theory of stimulus meaning for *apt speakers like ourselves,* and what he says is very strange indeed; however, *it is the nerve of his external holism.* We understand ourselves and one another because we are the apt speakers of a home language; we "understand" babies because we construe their initial babbling heuristically, on the model of our own language; and we understand another people because all natural languages have their apt bilinguals. Or, if we insist on denying such resources to ourselves, we treat the "aliens" much as we do our infants, though always with the advantageous concession that *they* are speaking some language and *we are never driven to understand ourselves by way of "stimulus meaning."* We may, as Quine does, pretend that this is not true, but it represents a game within the full play of a community of apt speakers of a given language. Even the ambiguities of "Lo, a rabbit" presuppose our ordinary resources; they cannot be resolved *in any way* by the "prior" resources of stimulus meaning, for stimulus meanings are themselves diminished distinctions offered as adequate within the amplitude of the other!

If you now look back to the passage cited from *Pursuit of Truth* at the beginning of this section, you will see that Quine offers there a sketch of a theory of "the evidential support of science" itself, which requires "sentences that are directly and firmly associated with our stimulations." That might have led you to imagine that the theory of the evidential grounds of science and the theory of radical translation are one and same. They are certainly joined and rely on the same distinctions—stimulus meanings, specifically. But it is the interpretation of the first and not the restriction of the second that produces the condition—the indeterminacy of translation, said to be irresolvable *except "by degrees."* Put another way, the indeterminacy that obtains in the context of radical translation (all the famous turns on parsing

"Gavagai!") is a consequence of the *internal holism* of using any natural language that (on Quine's view) is already infected by the *external holism* originally responsible *for* the indeterminacy of meaning that cannot be completely overcome: that is, cannot yield "a fact of the matter" in choosing in a determinate way between translation manuals. The indeterminacy of translation thesis presupposes a holophrastic "fact of the matter": the holism of the first is meant to be benignly "internal," whereas the holism of the second cannot fail to be "external." Furthermore, the first holism is subordinate to the second, where the second is privileged—so as to ensure an uncontested extensionalism.

Quine's way of putting matters is admittedly idiosyncratic. But the difficulty he has put his finger on is not in the least cranky. For what he's broached by his "external holism" is simply his solution to the old Cartesian *aporia* in another guise, required (as he sees matters) by certain intervening discoveries that cannot be ignored. He has forced the entire analytic tradition—shaped by Frege, Russell, the Tractarian Wittgenstein, and Carnap—to come to terms with the double fact: (1) that there are no separable protocol sentences (of any kind) that could count as the empirical foundation for our sciences,[28] and (2) that *any* account of empirical objectivity must be reconciled with the "internal" holism yielded by generalizing (in Quine's way) the lesson of Pierre Duhem's argument regarding the "tribunal of experience" and by confirming that there can be no "principled" disjunction between analytic and synthetic truths.[29]

What Quine offers in providing the indeterminacy doctrine (his external holism) is a high-wire balance between the needs of an epistemology that accords with constraints (1) and (2) just mentioned *and* the further wish to continue along the lines of a thoroughgoing extensionalism and materialism. There is an admirably honest confrontation in Quine's labor. What nearly all later "analysts" exhibit (who take heart at Quine's "recovery")— Davidson, most particularly—is a willingness to continue to support the scientistic project as before, now under the nominal direction of Quine's *internal* holism (the "Two Dogmas" argument) without bothering to come to terms with the deeper (riskier) penetration of *that* holism by Quine's *external* holism (the "indeterminacy" doctrine). They neglect thereby the point of the entire exercise.

If Quine were right about the empirical backing of science, the obvious vulnerability of his external holism could not fail to place in jeopardy any extensionalist program that thought to escape a constructivist or interpretive intervention—that is, the complication of admitting the undeniably intensional features of perceptual reports, under the control of which *any* extensionalism would fail to establish its independence and adequacy. That is indeed the entire point of Davidson's coded "corrections" in "A Coherence Theory of Truth and Knowledge" and "On the Very Idea of a Conceptual Scheme": to obviate the need for anything like Quine's indeterminacy doctrine.[30]

III

I am not raising a purely textual question here, though it will pay to proceed in a textual way. The point of Quine's initiatives has eluded us too long. Quine is the decisive figure among analytic philosophers at mid-century who seek to secure a thoroughly extensionalist treatment of science and common sense in spite of abandoning the advantages of empiricism's "two dogmas." Quine grasped at a stroke the fact that, if not by privilege, extensionalism would never be recovered except by way of some form of external holism.

You must bear in mind that the Tractarian Wittgenstein and the eliminativist Sellars had hoped to salvage the extensionalist needs of a thoroughgoing scientism without invoking cognitive or empiricist privilege. Unlike Quine, neither invokes an external holism. Wittgenstein abandons the project altogether, turns abruptly to "language games" and *Lebensform*—to what I am calling "internal" holism—which, if permitted, would keep the old extensionalism from ever surfacing again. For his part, Sellars simply announces his atomism, his physicalism and eliminativism, without supporting arguments of any kind, as in "The Language of Theories" and "Philosophy and the Scientific Image of Man."[31] His achievement is a bit like an Escher drawing that finally erases the hand that draws the erasure of the original drawing. The only thing finally clear (and compelling) about Sellars's purpose is that, like Quine, he opposes any and all forms of cognitive privilege.[32] However, he offers no connecting clues to compare with the first two parts of *Word and Object* or the transparency of the *Tractatus*.

What Quine sought to achieve was extraordinarily clever. I doubt it could ever succeed, but it was certainly worth a try. It attempted to work out the only option not blocked by the failure of the century's earlier scientisms. Quine introduces an external holism by which to secure the assured epistemic pertinence of science and common sense without invoking empiricist privilege or risking insuperable intensional complication. That *is* the purpose of *Word and Object*: a brilliant gamble and a marvelous economy.

It's the inherent vulnerability of his external holism, or the dependence of his internal holism *on* his external holism—in effect, the vulnerability of introducing stimulus meanings and holophrastic sentences in the service of the indeterminacy of translation—that jeopardizes Quine's entire vision just when it seems so plausible. If that could be shown, we would be well on our way to demonstrating the fatal weakness of late twentieth-century scientism: whether, say, in Davidson's careful "correction" of Quine's excesses or in the more headlong confidence of Paul Churchland's and Daniel Dennett's computational analyses of mind.

The success of the "Two Dogmas" paper was deemed to have reduced to a complete shambles what remained of Carnap's program: Quine deprived scientism of any reliable semantic grounds for pursuing its extensionalist objective—just the reverse of his intention! Since it had already yielded up foundational privilege of every sort, positivism had been forced to fall back to the resources of analyticity. "Two Dogmas" appeared to make this last appeal unworkable, and Quine emerged with a frankly constructivist policy—of a behaviorist and physicalist cast—that seemed to owe nothing to the failed resources favored in the first half of the twentieth century. That was the golden promise of Quine's pared-down scientism. It could never have succeeded, however, because it never really escaped the empirical privilege it claimed to have abandoned: that is the ultimate lesson so cunningly buried in Quine's external holism.

The decisive key lies, I believe, with the uncertainty of what we should regard as the *empirical* standing of our would-be objective judgments and truth-claims. For Sellars, reports of sensory observation are ultimately addressed to fictions, to what does not exist at all; although, somehow, *that* conclusion is said to rest on a valid interpretation of what our (fictional) folk reports signify about what is finally real. Imagine! For Quine, reports of sensory observation are assigned some suitably reduced "stimulus meaning" in terms of physical and behavioral changes (which is what Quine calls "radical translation"); but it is not in the least clear why such assignments are needed, or are thought more reliable than the perceptual grounds on which they themselves rely, or might be independently confirmed. Quine nowhere explains, for instance, the supposed objectivity of holophrastic sentences. Churchland means to sweep out all "folk" reports of perceptual experience, but his neurocomputational model is never outfitted with more than a piecemeal ability to *simulate* whatever we discern *from* the folk perspective itself. And Dennett simply dismisses any and all reliance on first-person avowals of experience without regard to the adequacy or coherence of third-person reports of physical and behavioral change completely separated from the other.

All in all, theorists of these sorts wished to hold on to some form of empirical adequacy, but they were fearful of yielding in empiricism's direction.

It would not be too much to suggest that analytic philosophy down to the turn of the twenty-first century is bedeviled by that threat, because of the entanglements of both privilege and intensional complication. Quine promised to escape both snares but produced an impenetrable enigma instead. (The need to avoid the same threat reappears in a particularly egregious form in Richard Rorty's postmodernist papers.[33]) The ultimate worry is that the admission of first-person perceptual reports and avowals is, effectively, the admission of "empirical content" that might never be displaced by any device of reductive identity or supervenience or freed from intractable intensional complications. Quine's holism seemed almost to elude the trap.

The entire trajectory of American analytic philosophy from the mid-twentieth century to the beginning of the new century is, as a result, remarkably legible. The old century begins, in Europe, with an enthusiastic but completely unguarded optimism about the systematic extensionalism of the natural and formal sciences. All the pertinent movements are severely pared back by the end of the 1930s, certainly by the 1940s and 1950s, without quite ending the entire undertaking. Suddenly, Quine appears, in the late '40s and early '50s, with the bold and buoyant promise of the "Two Dogmas" paper and "On What There Is,"[34] which links up with the external holism of *Word and Object* (1960). Quine seemed to have eluded all the old stalemates without yielding on essentials. What we now understand of course is that analytic philosophy's procedural rigor should have been separated from its scientism. In a sense, Quine postponed the reckoning for an additional fifty years.

Quine succeeded, of course, beyond anyone's wildest dreams—and moved the capital of philosophical Camelot to the American Cambridge, where, we may say, it has languished ever since. For, precisely because of his yielding in the direction of external holism, Quine actually prepared the ground for the deeper erosion of scientism itself. The argument of the first two books of *Word and Object* suggests a calculated risk. It would not be unreasonable to regard Davidson's oblique but pointed criticisms of Quine as a warning of potential disaster—which, however, lacks the needed clue for repudiating scientism. Davidson retreats from *any* explicit theory of knowledge—on the grounds of avoiding skepticism (or Cartesianism)—hence, from Quine's admittedly florid holism. That is the engine of Davidson's cautious attempts to stem the tide (against Quine)—as in "On the Very Idea of a Conceptual Scheme" and "A Coherence Theory of Truth and Knowledge" and his efforts to bring the notion of truth back to its strictest extensionalist function. Yet however tepid he is at times, Davidson *is* a partisan of the same scientism that Quine champions.

The fact is, you cannot find in either Quine or Davidson any sustained attention to the detailed problems and resources of a theory of science fitted to the actual work of the physical sciences—of the gauge the positivists, the unity of science program, and their followers explored—in terms of which an empirically motivated scientism seemed at least promising. Quine attempted to secure *their* goal by the most attenuated semantic resources imaginable: by way of the constraints of his method of "radical translation" and the privilege made possible by his "holophrastic sentences"—in a word, by the resultant free-wheeling strategy of the "indeterminacy of translation" practiced on "occasion sentences" and "stimulus meanings." If that strategy were to fail, there would indeed be no further fall-back position to count on.

Davidson is a self-appointed monitor of the old guard, responding to divisions within the analytic ranks that "go too far" in risking the recovery of extensionalism itself. That is also the point of his critique of figures like Hilary Putnam, Thomas Kuhn, Paul Feyerabend, William James and the pragmatists, and even, in a more surgical way, Quine himself, Michael Dummett, and (least manageably) Richard Rorty. For his part, Rorty plays the role of a double agent: his sympathies are always with the extensionalists, even the eliminativists. But his natural skepticism leads him to bank on his well-known "postmodernist" conception—a conceptual night in which no philosophical cats are either extensionalist or calico! It is, in fact, in just this setting that pragmatism seriously declined (as Rorty says) on account of the "linguistic turn" and was then "revived" (in the 1970s, in its "postmodernist" form) by Rorty himself in the context of a running quarrel with Hilary Putnam.[35]

The result has surely been a disaster all around: the clear failure of pragmatism's second life to secure more than an opportunistic advantage, the evident arbitrariness of postmodernism, and the continuing inability of analytic philosophy to reclaim extensionalism as a compelling program. The truth is: the advocacy of a comprehensive extensionalism that does not rely directly on the demonstrated adequacy of materialism in the physical, biological, and informational sciences has almost no chance of seeming plausible at all. That is precisely why our reflections on the nature of language, mind, history, and culture are of such importance at the present time.

Quine realized that a systematic extensionalism required a reliable "set of sentences" (in Quine's wording) to vouchsafe our direct contact with a real world that could also be said to be: (1) unquestionably empirical, (2) free of and operatively prior to any and all theoretical or interpretive qualifications (drawn from our contingent and parochial interests), (3) qualified as holistic or "holophrastic," in order to disallow the presumption of any metaphysical or epistemological privilege, (4) still plausible as candidates for prompting universal (verbal) assent or dissent in any people, no matter how diverse their history, and (5) maximally hospitable to extensionalist "translation" ranging over all possible conceptual schemes. A heady prospect, you must admit.

You see the clever parallel with the positivists' *Protokollsätze,* except for the fact that Quine begins at once in a behaviorist way (avoids relying on reports of inner mental states) and disallows any presumed correspondence between the structure of our uttered statements and the structure of "what there is." He introduces his model as reasonably neutral and uncontested and pretheoretical—a holism very different from the Duhemian model he is supposed to have adopted,[36] but one that he advances as a principle of charity nonetheless.[37] Quine's holism is external, or at least that part of the holism that bears comparison with Duhem's is subject to an external holism, whereas Duhem's holism is entirely internal.

Not to put too fine a point on it, Quine's external holism is a form of epistemic privilege *manqué,* which defeats, *before* any empirical testing ever begins, what might otherwise comprise the principal reasons for opposing extensionalism itself: for instance, (*a*) the seeming disjunction between "occasion" sentences and "stimulus meanings" that might, nevertheless, be counted on to preserve the stimulus content of the first;[38] (*b*) the benign disjunction between translational sentences and the original "non-verbal stimulations" that the first would be expected to match perspicuously;[39] and (*c*) the curious notion that stimulus sentences *(read as observation sentences)* can be treated holistically, that is, as not involving the use of *words* at all, since (on Quine's view) "words" betray our theoretical bias and practical interest—commit us to one ontology or another! Quine's entire position may be summed up here in the marvelously pregnant remark: "Occasion sentences and stimulus meaning are general coin; terms and reference are local to our conceptual scheme."[40] The only trouble is that this thesis—meant to collect the advantages of (*a*)-(*c*)—is palpably incoherent. Word and sentence are indissolubly linked, though they are indeed not the same.

It also begs all the questions that would otherwise worry opponents of extensionalism. Once you have items (*a*)-(*c*) before you, you see how reasonable Davidson's worries about Quine's "orthodoxy" are, and how "The Very Idea of a Conceptual Scheme" applies to Quine every bit as much as (if not more appropriately than) to Kuhn and Feyerabend. Ironically, *if* you concede Kuhn's rejection of epistemic "neutrality," Kuhn's worries about

Quine's odd use of "stimulus meaning," as well as his emphasis on the historicity of science,[41] you begin to see the arbitrariness of *both* Quine's original external holism *and* Davidson's attempt to correct the Quinean excesses by insisting on excluding, in realist contexts, *all* interpretive (as opposed to causal) intermediaries between cognizer and cognized.

Normally, one would suppose that the philosophical repudiation of interpretive intermediaries in the work of the natural sciences was tantamount to the advocacy of a form of empiricist privilege, but Davidson is dead against the latter. It's in this sense that he tries to match Quine's daring tit for tat by replacing "radical translation" by "radical interpretation" and Quine's "two dogmas" by his third. But neither maneuver has had a happy history. For the same reason, he tries to *replace* any constative model that features "empiricist" content by a purely *causal* (materialist) account of "empirical" belief and judgment. Causal processes, for instance, often produce mistaken judgments; so causal intermediaries alone cannot replace interpretive intermediaries that presume to correct for causal error. Again, having given up the reliability of correspondentist criteria, Davidson can appeal to little more than one or another form of coherentism (which he realizes cannot possibly be adequate to the task[42]).

If we agree that the admission of interpretive intermediaries cannot but adversely affect the extensionalist program, if Davidson cannot claim a neutrality firmer than Quine's, if causal explanation is itself subject to the same interpretive view that "stimulus meaning" and "occasion sentence" are, then Davidson cannot possibly strengthen extensionalism's hand by any internal holist means opposed to Quine's admittedly dubious external holism. Davidson simply does not address the realist question effectively enough. He worries too much about the skepticism risked by speaking of realism at all. Quine's holism fails, because it is incoherent and implausible, but not because it refuses to broach the epistemological questions realism poses. Davidson's holism fails, because it concedes inherent epistemic limitations that it cannot overtake by the use of resources that it is unwilling to exceed. But that *is* to defeat the extensionalist program Quine and Davidson share under Neurath's, Duhem's, and Quine's (own) constraints. That is also to risk the ineliminability of intensional complications.

Look more closely, then, at how we might object to Quine's assumptions in (*a*)–(*c*). There is no known account of natural language that fails to characterize a sentence as a string of words, even if we admit one-word sentences (as Quine does)—"Gavagai!," say. Furthermore, there is no obvious way to admit assent or dissent to (or from) a particular affirmation that does not require *some* use of words ensuring relevance of response—in effect, denotation. (In fact, to deny this would require that assent and dissent were themselves "holophrastic," which would defeat Quine's project at the start.) Quine seems to admit all this. But if so, then there can be no disjunction between "sentence" and "word" such that there *are* sentences that are true or false and capable of being known to be, but are nevertheless entirely "holophrastic," that is, *not* rightly parsed in terms of one "translation manual" or another. Quine appears to deny this.[43]

There is also no way, avoiding (as Quine intends) any reliance on bilingual competence, to treat the dawning assent of children, or our attempts to understand alien speakers, in terms of linguistic resources different from whatever we invoke in accounting for our own linguistic abilities. Hence, "stimulus synonymy" not only presupposes our "translation manuals," but there are no "further" evidentiary sources to call on unless they first apply to our own claims. If so, then there *are* no "further" sources of understanding! Bilingualism, of course, implicates our translational theories and interpretive intermediaries. But that means that Quine would need to provide a very much stronger account of "stimulus meaning" relative to "occasion sentences" than he actually does in order to gain the extensionalist prize. He might even be driven back to protocol sentences (which he wisely avoids), and he would in any case need to fix the sense of "stimulations" *epistemically,* which he nowhere seriously attempts to do and which no one seriously believes can be done. Furthermore, as far as I can see, we *never* rely on "holophrastic sentences" and wouldn't know how to do so if we tried.

Davidson himself, in the "Coherence" and "Conceptual Scheme" papers, opts for a form of internal holism—which is not to deny that he also favors an external holism. In fact, he believes he can preserve the same rigors of objective truth and extensionality Quine had hoped to secure by his own external holism. Davidson might have yielded in Wittgenstein's direction (in the sense favored in the *Investigations*), but that would have completely obviated the strong "naturalizing" program of the "Coherence" paper and the cognate role he ascribes to truth. There's no sense in which extensionalism could be strengthened in that direction.

But these are blunderbuss difficulties, justified, to be sure, but not quite in touch with the details of what Quine offers in his account of holophrastic sentences.

IV

Come closer, then, to Quine's specific formulations.

On infants' learning a first language, for example, which you may reasonably suppose Quine treats as strengthening his account of the role of stimulus meaning, Quine has the following to say:

> The infant's first acquisitions in cognitive language are rudimentary observation sentences, including 'Mama', 'Milk', and the like as one-word observation sentences. They become associated with stimulations by the conditioning of responses. Their direct association with concurrent stimulation is essential if the child is to acquire them without prior language, and the requirement of intersubjectivity is essential in order that he learn the expressions from other speakers on appropriately shared occasions. . . . But the two requirements, intersubjectivity and correspondence to stimulation, assure us that any observation sentence *could* be learned in the direct way.[44]

This is surely doubtful. For how could we *ever* know directly—without interpretive intervention—*that* an infant was responding to a present "stimulus" as opposed to being prompted by a competent speaker? How could we ever know *what*, under real-time conditions, to count as one stimulus or another? And how could we decide either question without some strenuous theory that would compensate for extensional uncertainties, irregularities, divergences, and errors? If this is what an extensionalist epistemology requires, then it is surely doomed. (Just imagine the results of disallowing Platonism with respect to predicates.)

I come now to what seem to be the most baffling pages of Quine's entire *oeuvre*. Quite literally, I cannot make sense of what Quine says, though there is no doubt that what he says must affect the final assessment of the indeterminacy thesis. You must review the text in the light of two considerations: one, that it was Quine who, through the publication of *Word and Object* primarily—hence, through the supposed advantages of the indeterminacy thesis—provided mid-century analysts with an engaging new blueprint for extending the extensionalist program, liberated once and for all from the unproductive visions that dominate the first half of the century; the other, that Quine's innovation sprang from the perception that, once we agree to promote extensionalism in an empirically responsible way, once we abandon every form of privilege, once we yield up the would-be advantages of the analytic/synthetic disjunction, we cannot go forward without the charity of some form of external holism neutral and hospitable enough to permit extensionalism to avoid certain potentially crippling difficulties at the outset.

The idea is not to permit the extensionalists to bypass bona fide responsibilities, but only to avoid hobbling their efforts in unreasonable ways. So the burden rests with Quine's rationale for securing an initial measure of perceptual and linguistic objectivity that extensionalism may fairly claim for itself (and for any other account of science or ordinary inquiry) on the strength of which to advance its own interests. Fine. But there's the rub. You cannot find a coherent rationale in *Word and Object* or *Pursuit of Truth* for "stimulus meaning," "observation sentence," "holophrastic" and "theoretical sentence" that *can* justify the initial advantage Quine delivers to the extensionalists.

No doubt the charge will strike you as unlikely. But what if it were true? Take the question step by step. First of all, as we have seen, Quine features "observation sentences." But what are observation sentences? Well, Quine says, "the notion of observation is awkward to analyze." This is already a warning shot, since we might have supposed that "observation sentences" were keyed to prior observations. But that's not quite right: "a gulf yawns [Quine reminds us] between [observable objects and events] and our immediate input from the external world, which is rather the triggering of our sensory receptors." (There you have Quine's acknowledgment of the Cartesian paradox.) Quine opts, therefore, for "the triggering or stimulation itself and hence [as he says, for our] speaking, oddly perhaps, of the prediction of stimulation. By the stimulation undergone by a subject on a given occasion I [Quine] just mean the temporally ordered set of all those of his exteroceptors that are triggered on that occasion."

By this remarkably oblique strategy (perhaps, also, the assumption of some very uncertain causal laws), Quine claims to have dropped "observation . . . as a technical term." "Observable," he says, "is whatever would be attested to on the spot by any witness in command of the language and his five senses." And "observation sentences" themselves are defined, therefore, in a way that makes no reference to observation's being "theory-laden" or "theory-free."[45] Quine obviously relies here on some very improbable causal laws imagined to capture the regularities linking linguistic assent and sensory observation, without ever addressing ordinary observation itself. If you think about it, that is an absolutely unbelievable gamble. A sort of behavioral (or, better: behaviorist) fiat now defines what is to count as observation in the first place; and yet, of course, Quine also means to confirm the reasonableness of his conjecture by tracing, along empirical lines, the natural history of a child's actually learning a first language. Quine never extricates himself from this dilemma.

I cannot see how any of this works. *If* it worked at all, it would preclude any speaker's *assent*, since, surely, to assent to an observation sentence (in ordinary circumstances) would require that the speaker had an understanding of what "observation" meant *relative to assenting,* rather than to the "triggering" of "our receptors." If assenting is not intentional, it is not the familiar notion at all; if it is intentional, Quine's proposal regarding radical translation is irrelevant or wildly unreliable *or* is itself no more than a restrictive way of formulating results under the ampler resources of natural discourse.

How could any version of stimulus meaning possibly determine a speaker's pertinently assenting? *If* "assent" (or "attesting") amounted to what *we* (observers) judge to be the "triggering" of observation on another's part, then, surely, the burden shifts to *our* being prepared to assent or attest to the truth of the claim that another person had observed something! That could hardly be marked off by stimulatory "triggerings." There would be no gain there. *Observed exactly what?* you ask. We could never really say—unless it would be enough to say, "probably observed some part of the world."

Remember that "observation sentences" are *not* indexed to observations in any ordinary perceptual or experiential sense; rather, they are indexed to the "triggering" of our sensory receptors. In one sense, they are "theory-free" precisely because *they* do not implicate ordinary observations that observers might *report,* for if they were reported they would be "theory-laden." In another sense, however, they *are* "theory-laden"—ineluctably so—since they are *not* indexed to observations in the ordinary sense; they are indexed, rather, to *our* theory-driven specification of what to count as "stimulations"; only then do (or can) *our* reports count as "observations" of *their* stimulations (or their observations).

In fact, Quine holds that "what qualifies a sentence as observational is not a lack of [theoretical or theory-laden] terms, but just that the sentence taken as an undivided whole [a holophrastic sentence] commands assent consistently or dissent consistently when the same global sensory stimulation is repeated. What relates the observation sentence to theory, on the other hand, is the sharing of embedded terms."[46] But then, of course, to be "theory-free" is to be an artifact of *our theory* of what to count as the "triggering" of our "sensory receptors." Yet what, I ask you, is a "global sensory stimulation" and how would we ever know whether we had discerned "the same global sensory stimulation" on two occasions? I see only too easily how very nearly any answer could be self-deceptively protected from disconfirmation.

The whole affair requires an operative account of similarity of stimulation, of the reliability of pertinent causal regularities, of the conditions under which physical objects and behavioral responses can be properly identified, *and* of the assurance that collecting matters this way is not itself tethered to varying but unmonitored interpretations of all the constancies alleged. For, if that could not be counted on, "observation sentences" could not possibly play the role Quine assigns them. I cannot see, admitting all this, how Quine could claim that observation "drops out" as a "technical notion": it is, rather, merely embedded in a deeper theory for the sake of an impoverished and unreliable formulation that counts on its being hospitable to scientism. The entire doctrine rests on the function of holophrastic sentences, which plainly use ordinary perceptual terms. Quine, of course, denies that holophrastic sentences *have* terms at all. But what could that possibly mean? And what would it then mean to assert a holophrastic sentence?

From all this Quine draws the cold comfort that in a certain sense observation sentences "are all theory-laden, even the most primitive ones, and there is [also] a sense in which none are, even the most professional ones." Take, he suggests, the "primitive ones,"

> the entering wedge in language learning. They are associated as wholes to appropriate ranges of stimulations, by conditioning. Component words are there merely as component syllables, theory-free. But these words recur in theoretical contexts in the fullness of time. It is precisely this sharing of words, by observation sentences and theoretical sentences, that provides logical connections between the two kinds of sentences and makes observation relevant to scientific theory. Retrospectively those once innocent observation sentences are theory-laden indeed.[47]

I cannot find the argument that shows that there are any words that are *shared* between observation sentences construed as indissoluble "wholes" and any ordinary sentences. Where, that is, what counts as the "syllables" within those "wholes" (the ones that are "primitive" observation sentences) *are* (somehow) the same as what may be found in "theoretical sentences": the same *what?*—syllables which, in "theoretical sentences," count as words? *That* children *begin* to learn language by way of verbal "wholes" (holophrastic sentences, apparently), which, by definition, are "theory-free," is surely *a part of Quine's own theory*: it cannot possibly explain what anyone could be doing *in* originally issuing a holophrastic report or in using it to vouchsafe perceptual objectivity. If it serves to avow an observational datum ("Lo, a rabbit," "Mama"), it cannot be part of Quine's explanatory machinery that eschews observation in the ordinary sense; and if it is the latter, it cannot mark the beginning of our mastery of perceptual language. Suppose, furthermore, that Quine is simply mistaken about how children learn their first language.

If I understand Quine correctly, *words* require the parsing of sentences with regard to "what there is" in the world (our conceptual theory or ontology, say): *their* presence in sentences is never theory-free. Hence, where sentences *are* theory-free, there are no words. But if so, how can there be a "sharing" of words by "observation sentences" and "theoretical sentences"? To be perfectly honest, what Quine says here looks very much like a contradiction.

But there's more:

> [Even the] observation sentences . . . of specialized scientific communities are . . . two-faced, even though learned by composition rather than direct conditioning. What qualifies them as observation sentences is still their holophrastic association with fixed ranges of sensory stimulation, however that association be acquired. Holophrastically they function still as theory-free . . . though when taken retrospectively word by word the self-same sentences are theory-laden. . . .[48]

I can see dimly how, if we wished, we might indeed treat a *given* "scientific" sentence "observationally." But I can't see how doing that would make *it* theory-free or "holophrastic." Surely not, if it remained the same sentence! Think of sentences about the path an electron takes in a cloud chamber. But I also can't see how that would help us in the reverse direction, that is, where we are said to *begin* with holophrastic sentences *and then* treat *them* as the same sentences that, by inventing their constituent "words," count as theory-laden. Quine actually claims this as an advantage for his account: "Starting with sentences as we have done rather than with terms, we see no bar to a sharing of vocabulary by the two kinds of sentences; and it is the shared vocabulary that links them."[49] But there's no vocabulary *to share*. Would Quine be willing to adopt a Platonist account of predicative similarity sufficient for invoking a common predicable linking holophrastic and theoretical sentences? Certainly not. But if not, then I see no way of bridging the difference between a holophrastic and a "theory-laden" sentence and no way to speak of "sharing a vocabulary." How could "sensory stimulations" do better? Here you can begin to see the crudity of the proposal.

To recapitulate. We cannot begin with sentences *tout court* rather than with words: for natural-language sentences are inherently composed of words—even one-word sentences. Again, if we could begin with holophrastic sentences, then there would be no *vocabulary* that they and their matched theoretical sentences could meaningfully share. Also, and most important, if these objections hold, then the indeterminacy thesis must fail utterly. Because, of course, *there would then be "no fact of the matter" regarding the sharing of vocabulary!* Quine, you remember, wishes to hold that there is no fact of the matter *in the choice of translation manuals;* he plainly believes there *is* a fact of the matter in matching holophrastic and theoretical sentences— sharing a vocabulary in that sense. The choice of a manual is indeterminate, but (apparently) not the relevance of the empirical testing of the sentences produced by applying one manual or another. But that has been ruled out.

There you have the *reductio* of Quine's entire program—in particular, the *reductio* of the indeterminacy of translation thesis. For, *if there is no sharing of vocabulary, then the indeterminacy problem cannot arise; and if there is a sharing of vocabulary, then there can be no indeterminacy of the sort Quine invokes.*

But that means that Quine's external holism cannot be conceded to provide a margin of neutral charity. The trouble with Quine's argument is that his holism is really a camouflaged form of cognitive privilege—in fact, a form of empiricist privilege: we are to permit him to match, as far as observational objectivity is concerned, the vocabulary of holophrastic and theoretical sentences by purely materialist or behaviorist means; and we are to do so in such a scrupulous way that we still acknowledge, as a problem *internal* to our practice, the matter of rationally choosing one "translation manual" or "analytical hypothesis" over another.[50]

The entire scheme cleverly favors extensionalism *at the start*—and, indeed, as a way of resolving the Cartesian puzzle to boot. Quine's solution is decidedly idiosyncratic. But it touches on all the questions that must be resolved, once we give up epistemic privilege, cognitive foundations, substantive or *a priori* necessities, indubitabilities, and similar advantages. Hence the failure of Quine's proposal signifies the reasonableness of thinking that any newfangled scientism that abandoned privilege would still need to secure its own advantage by one or another form of external holism—that is, to redeem with one hand the privilege the other gives away! That, we now see, is impossible to ensure in anything but a hopelessly question-begging way.

Quine has built into his notion of "ocular irradiation and similar notions"[51] enough of a realist picture of perception that is free of intentional complications and theoretical constructions (a "direct realism," in effect) in order that when he broaches his theory of understanding linguistic meaning, he is unashamedly a "behaviorist" (eschewing "intentions"). As a result, he is prepared to concede, as must then be true, that our policy of "radical translation" (the policy of restricting ourselves to behavioral and "stimulus-linked" cues in the "translation of the language of a hitherto untouched people") leads directly to the "indeterminacy of translation" thesis.[52] "There is nothing in linguistic meaning," Quine affirms—late in his career as well as early—"beyond what is to be gleaned from overt behavior in observable circumstances" (where "observation" is itself defined in the manner already sketched). The same behaviorism (akin to B. F. Skinner's) appears in Quine's important paper, "Ontological Relativity," which actually begins with a very clever effort to conflate Dewey's use of the term "behavior" (meant, by Dewey, to offset dualism) with his own use of the term (meant to disallow any first-person use of "mental" terms in science that might be thought to strengthen the hand of those who support a "private language"—which, of course, *is* a form of dualism). By this extraordinary maneuver, since he gives us to understand that all mental terms are afflicted in the private-language way, Quine suggests (incorrectly) that he *is* a sort of pragmatist and that Dewey had already inclined (in his William James lectures at Harvard) in the same behaviorist direction![53]

What you must bear in mind is this: Quine's extensionalist theory of meaning is *not* a consequence of his "analytical hypotheses" at any stage of conjecture; it is, rather, an *a priori* certainty which itself directly yields the indeterminacy problem—*which* (since "there is no fact of the matter") in turn yields all the puzzles of interpretation, *which,* by the original posit, must already be congenial to extensionalist "translation"! The result is that Quine recoups the privilege that he seems to have willingly abandoned. In doing that, he goes against his admitted admiration for Neurath's boat image—that is, for keeping science and philosophy "afloat," rebuilding "[if] we must . . . plank by plank":

> There is every reason [Quine admits] to inquire into the sensory or stimulatory background of ordinary talk of physical things. The mistake comes only in seeking an implicit sub-basement of conceptualization, or of language. Conceptualization on any considerable scale is inseparable from language, and our ordinary language of physical things is about as basic as language gets.[54]

But if there is no "sub-basement," then (with Neurath) there is no "basement" either! We are always *in medias res*—"afloat," as well as we can manage to be. Quine's unearned advantage becomes entirely transparent when we realize that he is deliberately displacing Carnap's treatment of meaning, by appealing to something apparently more basic—holophrastic sentences rather than words:

> There remains [Quine explains] a significant contrast in the uses the two of us [that is, Quine and Carnap] make of subjunctive conditionals: I limit them to my investigator's considered judgment of what the informant would do if stimulated; Carnap has his investigator putting such conditionals to the judgment of the informant. Certainly my investigator would in practice ask the same questions as Carnap's investigator, as a quick way of estimating stimulus meanings, if language for such questions happened to be available. But stimulus meaning can be explored also at the first stages of radical translation, where Carnap's type of questionnaire is unavailable. . . . [M]y theory has to do primarily with sentences of a sort and not, like Carnap's, with terms.[55]

But this of course is just another statement of Quine's doubtful privilege. Carnap's procedure is the procedure of bilinguals or apt speakers of a common language; Quine's pretends to hold fast to third-person "observations" that lack intensional complication altogether and provide in an unmarked way (let it be said) for the observational consensus of his own "investigators." (All the repressed puzzles must then flood back into our little boat.)[56]

If I am right in my analysis, then Quine *cannot* rightly contrast Carnap's method with his own in the comfortable way he does: because, of course, there cannot be any disjunctive preference of sentences over words. That helps to draw attention once again to Quine's peculiar strategy and the slackness of his argument. (All this comes clear in the restatement of his argument in "Ontological Relativity.") He takes "terms" to convey intentions regarding alternative ontologies that could be fitted to the same stimulatory and behaviorist clues that "radical translation" employs: there, "there is no fact of the matter" regarding the exclusive validity of one ontology over another. That is what Quine means by "inscrutability of reference" (in the "Ontological Relativity" paper). But then, to ensure some pertinent perceptual access to the world itself, free of intentional complication, Quine is obliged to introduce "holophrastic sentences"—relative to which, of course, there *is* a fact of the matter: a fact, however, that is both neutral to the problem of choosing between one translation manual and another *and* is capable of vouchsafing the relevance of *ever* making such a choice in the first place! It is also worth remarking that, in the "Relativity" paper, "inscrutability" is clearly applied to our choice of terms and predicates; Quine always slights the problem of the "indeterminacy" (or, "inscrutability") of reference to singular things. All of this collects the extraordinary tenuousness of the seemingly robust doctrine of radical translation.

v

Late twentieth-century scientism favors "the linguistic turn," though, on the whole, it is surprisingly negligent about whether natural languages can be convincingly paraphrased in any thoroughly extensionalist way. (Tarski was more than merely skeptical.) Quine obviously thought that first-person perceptual reports and avowals constituted a threat to that objective, and so he precluded or tamed them (or thought he had effectively precluded or tamed them) by the ingenious devices of his external holism. Davidson thought he saw a related danger in the theory of truth, and moved against any explanatory role for truth and against any normative analysis of "true" that might have adversely affected its extensionalist use. Quine attempted an extensionalist treatment of both denotation (or reference) and predication. But he offers almost nothing in the way of a theory of predicative similarity apt for accounting for our epistemic fluency. He favors a "Darwinian" idiom, to be sure: he speaks, for instance, of a child's having "a prior tendency to weight qualitative differences unequally," if the child is to be capable of learning any language at all.[57] He admits the "hopeless neurological complexity" of trying to account for perceptual similarity in neurophysiological terms.[58] And, in general, he waves his wand in the direction of explanations drawn from "evolutionary genetics."[59]

Davidson is more guarded though sanguine enough. He holds rather strictly to extensionalist constraints on the truth predicate,[60] that is, he disallows all intensional qualifications—for instance, by denying any intrinsic explanatory role for "true." Yet he does claim conceptual resources going well beyond Tarski's semantics, and he plainly believes the difficulties affecting intentionality can be met by supervenientist measures, in spite of the fact that (on his own view) psychophysical laws are "anomalous."[61]

Still, predicative similarity *is* a serious problem for the extensionalist: I take it to be insuperably intensional, even insuperably holist (in the internal holist sense). Furthermore, when Quine turns to "solve" the puzzle of singular denotation or reference, he commits a blunder the history of philosophy had compellingly tagged centuries ago, again and again, namely, that individual or singular things cannot be identified or reidentified numerically by predicative means alone.[62] Reference or singular denotation is, I believe, ineluctably intensional as well, rather along the lines Duns Scotus favored when he concluded (with humor, I suppose) that *haecceitas* was knowable but not in this life! If these (and allied) problems cannot be solved algorithmically—I believe they cannot be—then, let it be noted here, in passing, the scientistic use of computationality will never succeed. I am myself prepared to argue that strict computationality (computationalism), like extensionalism, is simply false if, as I believe, reference or the identification of singular things, predicative similarity, context, relevance, the specification of meanings and the sufficient conditions of truth cannot be fixed algorithmically or by extensional means alone. I know of no promising argument that favors the opposite verdict.

Again, wherever epistemological distinctions are obviously successful even if irreducibly intensional, as reference and predication appear to be, *some* form of internal holism will be required. That, for instance, is the simplest explanation of Wittgenstein's turn from the *Tractatus* to the *Investigations:* the appeal to "language games" and the *Lebensform* (or *Lebensformen*)[63] is a frank recognition that there remains an ineliminable element of consensual conformity (that is not itself criterial but provides a ground for criteria, wherever wanted) in confirming the validity of our cognitive practices—whether, say, in extending a mathematical series or in assessing the propriety of particular practical judgments.

Wittgenstein himself is stunningly candid about the reversal of his convictions. Here, for instance, is one of the best-known of his conceptual cameos, which begins to show the compelling difference between internal and external holism:

> 241. "So you are saying that human agreement decides what is true and what is false?"—It is what human beings *say* that is true and false;, and they agree in the *language they use. That is not agreement in opinions but in form of life* (*Lebensform*).
> 242. If language is to be a means of communication there must be agreement not only in definition but also (queer as this may sound) in judgments. This seems to abolish logic, but does not do so.—It is one thing to describe methods of measurement, and another to obtain and state results of measurement. But what we call "measuring" is partly determined by a certain constancy in results of measurement.
> 481. [. . .] here grounds are not propositions which logically imply what is believed.[64]

What needs to be grasped is that, in some attenuated way Wittgenstein could hardly have been aware of, his remarks intuitively salvage the essential nerve of Hegel's original displacement of the pre-Kantian and Kantian treatment of realism—hence, are meant to obviate every form of skepticism; and yet, of course, the logical informality of Wittgenstein's internal holism (for that is what it is) generates a fresh suspicion that external holism and intensional complications are themselves the ultimate source of an insuperable skepticism![65] There's the irony of the classic contest: both Cartesianism and its post-Kantian defeat are thought to lead to skepticism!

The charge cannot hold, of course, *if* all the forms of privilege are rejected (recall Quine) *and* if the various versions of the holism of our *Sitten, epistemes, Geist, Lebensform,* language games, societal practices, traditions, and other collective regularities (for that is what they are) provide a convincing sense (though not a criterion) of viable conformity with ongoing operative practices and "rules."

The Quine of *Word and Object* and *Pursuit of Truth* and the Wittgenstein of the *Investigations* are the clearest exemplars we have of the opposing forms of external and internal holism—are, in particular, exemplars of the paradoxicality of the first and the relatively unproblematic (but debatable) standing of the second. The Wittgenstein of the *Tractatus,* the Sellars of "The Language of Theories," the Carnap of the *Aufbau* have no need for holisms of any sort: they count on one or another form of privilege or indubitable necessity and one or another form of logical atomism. But they either fail outright, or fail to support their implicit claims to complete the arguments for their own versions of extensionalism. One need go no further than Carl Hempel's masterly review of the positivists' account of the logic of scientific discourse.[66]

By contrast, internal holism (when not subordinated to external holism) never exceeds (never pretends to exceed) the enabling conditions of our practices of inquiry and judgment. Hence, the very norms of truth are a construction internal to the viability of deeper cognitive practices, open, of course, to historical change and critical reform (which, by the way, are hardly Wittgenstein's concern). That remains, nevertheless, the common understanding that informs Hegel, the later Wittgenstein, Dewey, Heidegger, Foucault, and Kuhn, who could hardly be said to form a single school of thought! But they do indeed share the essential clue to the unraveling of scientism: the unresolved objections against any blanket extensionalism.

For his part, Davidson offers a theory of what he calls "radical interpretation" partly to supplement, partly to displace, Quine's theory of "radical translation," partly to answer questions affecting extensionalism that Quine did not attempt to answer.[67] There are indeed objections to Davidson's proposals. But he himself is frank to admit:

Of course my project does require that all sentences of natural languages can be handled by a T-theory [a theory of truth in accord with Tarski's Convention T, of which more in a moment], and so if the intensional idioms resist such treatment, my plan has foundered. It seems to be the case, though the matter is not entirely simple or clear, that a theory of truth that satisfies anything like Convention T cannot allow an intensional semantics, and this has prompted me to try to show how an extensional semantics can handle what is special about belief sentences, indirect discourse, and other such sentences.[68]

Davidson's work is always initially plausible—but risky—and, on analysis, is almost always unable to deliver an adequate extensionalism. Of course, if reference and predication are irreducibly intensional, his program cannot but founder, as it would if the extensionalist reading of supervenientism regarding intentional properties could not be demonstrated or even shown to be empirically testable.[69] But, beyond even that, Davidson *nowhere shows* that "all sentences of natural languages can be handled by a T-theory": Tarski has the gravest doubts about the prospect, which Davidson regularly ignores or simply overrides.[70]

Seen in retrospect, Quine characteristically risks his semantic analyses in a frontal way; Davidson tenders his own semantic programs (which are almost never detailed) much more tentatively; and both are roundly challenged by such uncompromising critics as Jerry Fodor and Ernest Lepore for yielding unnecessarily in holism's direction. Fodor and Lepore, however, think of holism as a consequence or implication of one or another *semantic* program; never as an independent premise drawn from larger considerations—for example, to meet the needs of a defensible realism. The result is that they confine *their* work "dialectically" to what is or is not strictly semantically entailed in the narrowest possible sense—which misses the entire point of invoking holism (whether external or internal) in some larger epistemological space. Thus, against Davidson's account, they straightforwardly conclude:

> The strategy of the arguments [we examine is] to infer meaning holism from proposed solutions to the problem of choosing among extensionally adequate T-theories under the conditions of radical interpretation. . . . We've argued that the extensionality problem resists all the solutions we've surveyed [drawn from Davidson's program]; hence, barring further candidates, the strategy fails. And we have also argued that [on the] proposals considered, the principles in-

voked to solve the extensionality problem do not in fact imply
holism; specifically, they are compatible with the languages for
which they choose T-theories being punctate [that is, not
"anatomic": in effect, not holist].[71]

But this falsifies the essential point of Davidson's conjecture (Quine's,
also), because Davidson's holism (and Quine's) is inferred from the social
nature of natural-language use *in* the context of realist inquiries, *not* from a
constitutive condition of radical interpretation (or radical translation) or as
an implication of any narrow-gauged semantic analysis. Fodor and Lepore
have simply missed the mark—probably in their own extensionalist zeal.[72]

Fodor we know to be a modularist in something like Chomsky's sense;
hence, we have good reason to think that he views semantic analysis as separable from epistemology in essentials. Furthermore, given that he subscribes to a kind of scientism akin to Chomsky's, it is not surprising both
that he opposes Quine's holism regarding the analytic/synthetic distinction
and that, in doing that, he falls back haltingly to a "punctate" rather than a
holist resolution.

Davidson means to avoid altogether Quine's "indeterminacy" thesis and
reliance on "holophrastic sentences," "stimulus meanings," and "translation
manuals."[73] Fair enough: he sees Quine's proposals as threatening our realist concerns along extensionalist lines—in effect, risking "the unintelligibility of the dualism of a conceptual scheme and a 'world' waiting to be coped
with"[74] (in effect, the "third" dogma of his "Conceptual Scheme" paper).
But, in grasping the threat of Quine's *external* holism (which cannot fail to
affect the internal holism of a choice of translation manual), Davidson is
convinced that we still require—for realist reasons that escape skepticism—
the "charity" of an alternative *external* holism, which (in turn) is meant to
facilitate the holism internal to his own use of Tarski's Convention T. If I am
not mistaken, Fodor and Lepore miss all this, though they do not miss the
debatable details!

The essential thread is not difficult to isolate, though it takes a bit of patience. An "internal" problem arises for Davidson that is decisive: the attempt to apply Tarski's Convention T *in realist contexts under the condition
of "radical interpretation."* (It is not a problem that would even be recognized
from a purely abstract reading of Davidson's program that sees it as no more
than a "semantic" program.) Certainly, a "punctate" treatment of Convention T *is* "possible," *but it's not possible under the conditions of applying "radical interpretation" to our realist inquiries.*

Two constraints arise that Davidson acknowledges and that make this obvious. First of all, on Davidson's account, radical interpretation "should rest on evidence that does not assume knowledge of meanings or detailed knowledge of beliefs"; but *that* (he claims) does not negate the fact that "an interpreter may plausibly be taken to be able to identify [a speaker's believing what he says] before he [the interpreter] can interpret, since he may know that a person intends to express a truth in uttering a sentence without having any idea *what* truth."[75] This same constraint directly affects Davidson's intended use of Convention T, threatens in effect to make it unworkable in the context of objective inquiry. It's for this second reason that Davidson advances his *internal* holism (a holism of beliefs). But, as I say, even that problem arises because of a deeper realist question that (as Davidson recognizes) requires a prior form of *external* holism (that he believes is able to elude all the difficulties he finds in Quine's alternative picture).

Now, "a theory of truth in Tarski's style" (a T-theory) entails that "for every sentence *s* of the object language, a sentence of the form:

s is true (in the object language) if and only if *p*

[where "i]nstances of the form (which we shall call T-sentences) are obtained by replacing '*s*' by a canonical description of *s*, and '*p*' by a translation of *s*."[76] The classic T-sentence is given as

T. "Snow is white" iff snow is white.

Where (as Davidson reads Tarski and as Tarski intends) T is true in English, and Convention T cannot be applied except in a language-relative way. For it is entirely conceivable that T might not be true in (say) Swahili. Okay. But, according to this understanding, it is also perfectly possible to satisfy Convention T by,

T'. "Snow is white" iff grass is green.

That is, Tarski's account (thus construed) is no more than "extensionally adequate." Both Davidson and Fodor (and Lepore) acknowledge the limitation.[77] Davidson's conclusion is that truth-value cannot be all that matters. Convention T must be brought into line with our realist concerns—but now under the constraint of radical interpretation (which, inherently, cannot appeal to Tarski's translation condition: *it would entail knowledge disallowed by Davidson's proposal [his radical interpretation]*):

If we know [says Davidson] that a T-sentence satisfied Tarski's Convention T, we would know that it was true, and we could use it to interpret a sentence because we would know that the right branch of the biconditional translated the sentence to be interpreted. Our present trouble springs from the fact that in radical interpretation we cannot assume that a T-sentence satisfies the translation criterion. What we have been overlooking, however, is that we have supplied an alternative criterion: this criterion is that the totality of T-sentences should . . . optimally fit evidence about sentences held true by native speakers. The present idea is that what Tarski assumed outright for each T-sentence can be indirectly elicited by a holistic constraint. If that constraint is adequate, each T-sentence will in fact yield an acceptable interpretation.[78]

This might work, Davidson believes, because the extensionalist grounds on which radical interpretation itself works would, within the holism of an entire language, trade off the "material equivalences" of the "grass is green" variety, until we arrived at a more and more finely tuned matching of native beliefs and particular T-sentences. The idea seems entirely plausible. The difficulty lies elsewhere: Davidson's (internal) strategy depends on how we ensure our realist confidence *in the truth and extensionalist structure of what is believed-true*! And this is a worry that Davidson nowhere satisfactorily resolves.

A specimen problem arises, for instance, in the supposed extensionalist treatment of beliefs about intentional states: if, say, supervenientism fails, then it's a foregone conclusion that extensionalism will fail as well. But that's an empirical question internal to realism itself. The deeper question concerns how to ensure the objective truth of *what* is believed *and* the *a priori* reasonableness of thinking that, no matter how that is secured and however difficult the "internal" analysis of beliefs may prove to be, we *do* (Davidson affirms) have sufficient reason to count our beliefs as true *and* as amenable to extensionalist treatment. That is what I mean by Davidson's external holism, which directly conflicts with Tarski's view of natural languages!

Davidson is entirely explicit: what "justifies the [entire] procedure [of radical interpretation] is the fact that disagreement and agreement alike [regarding candidate beliefs] are intelligible only against a background of massive agreement." This is the gist of Davidson's notorious doctrine that "most of the beliefs in a coherent total set of beliefs are true."[79] I take it to signify a form of external holism very different from Quine's. Otherwise, the doctrine might have been read in Wittgenstein's way, in accord with the *Investigations;* but that would have jeopardized Davidson's extensionalism.

What Davidson offers is more like a transcendental or *a priori* argument cast in such a way as to make extensionalism plausible. He *has* in a way eluded Quine's difficulties, but he has generated his own. Put in the briefest way: he not only needs to ensure the truth of the belief that most of our beliefs are true, but the belief as well that those beliefs support an extensionalist analysis or are amenable to being paraphrased in an extensionalist way. Whatever else one may say, the reasons for thinking the first to be true have very little (if anything) to do with supporting the second. Tarski would never have countenanced it; neither would Wittgenstein; and Quine finesses the doubt by a frank apriorism that he nowhere earns.

Fodor and Lepore are at their best here, for they notice that Davidson's arguments "are more or less transcendental in style [in that they have] premises that are simultaneously epistemological and metaphysical." "The basic idea [they opine] is that [according to Davidson] it is metaphysically constitutive of facts about content that they must be accessible to someone in the epistemological situation of *a radical interpreter* and that radical interpretation is impossible unless principles of charity are invoked."[80]

This is exactly right. Still, I find a weakness in their analysis: although they see the doubtfulness of Davidson's premise (with ample cause), they do not seem to realize that once semantic analysis is caught up as an essential part of the realism question, the further question whether some form or other of holism will be needed is an issue utterly different from that of the merely "dialectical" or "semantically" restricted challenge they put to Davidson (and Quine and others). What they object to is internal holism—hence, the holism of Quine's attack on the analytic/synthetic dogma *and* Wittgenstein's speaking of "language game" and *Lebensform*. It is only incidentally that they notice the external holism of Davidson's "transcendental" treatment of the veridicality of beliefs. In short, they are themselves scientistic opponents of Quine's and Davidson's own scientisms. But they are opposed to Wittgenstein as well, and that cannot be for reasons favored by either Quine or Davidson.

There are at least three quite formidable difficulties confronting Davidson's radical interpretation thesis, as far as external holism goes. One concerns coherentism itself, which Davidson has now relinquished, but that he somehow still invokes as the only articulated basis for his theory.[81] The second is the plain *obiter dictum* that claims that adopting the stance of radical interpretation is somehow necessary to any account of truth, which in effect makes extensionalism a constitutive condition of any acceptable theory of truth. The third is simply the benefit of common sense. Here I cannot do better than Fodor and Lepore, who call into question the plausibility of Davidson's conjecture about the central mass of our beliefs:

As a matter of fact, it's exactly where people's beliefs fail to make close contact with observables that we *don't* assume that what they believe is overwhelmingly likely to be true. We would, for example, boggle at a translation scheme that made most Greeks have false beliefs about whether they had hands; this surely is the point of Moore's reply to the sceptic. But we are perfectly willing to swallow a translation scheme that makes most of the Greeks have false beliefs about how far away the stars are and about whether matter is made of atoms.[82]

Precisely! But then there's nothing compelling that remains of Davidson's theory—on the matter of extensionalism. There is not even a sense that the project is really viable at all, except piecemeal and on all sorts of doubtful premises. (Though that alone hardly dislodges the need for a holism of some sort.)

VI

At a deeper level of reflection, we must remind ourselves that Sellars's eliminativism never addressed the question whether, in construing persons and minds (in fact, the entire familiar macroscopic world) as fictions or constructions of language, language might not itself be an ineliminable "part" of the same would-be fiction.[83] Extraordinary impasse. Nor can you find the question seriously broached in Daniel Dennett's eliminativist account of persons and minds, which, since Dennett is plainly influenced by Sellars,[84] might have been extended to the ordinary world. The question is indeed pointedly raised by Paul Churchland, another "Sellarsian," as it must be if eliminativism is to make any sense at all—although whether it *can* make sense is an essential part of the puzzle of realism itself—hence also of the theory of science. Churchland is distinctly sanguine here. Sellars is not, given that his scruple extends to the neurophysiology of the brain.

Dennett is convinced that he uses his own eliminativist policy in an empirically responsible way—as in rejecting the "Cartesian theater" and all awareness of "inner mental states."[85] But whether first-person reports and avowals might play an ineliminable role in public science, without implicating Cartesian dualism or disordering science itself, Dennett nowhere carefully considers. He is persuaded, of course, that Science (not any mere dogma) positively requires our dismissing the first-person stance altogether![86] But he nowhere satisfactorily addresses the effect of such a drastic surgery on the coherence of the resultant language or, indeed, on the price of losing viable data.

I do admit that a full-blown realist treatment of intentionality and mental states would put extensionalism at mortal risk. But there is no known argument that shows that science (or Science) *must*—or even could—take such an extreme form.[87] Certainly, Dennett nowhere supplies the argument. In any case, it would be odd to ignore the natural objections to Dennett's proposal.

If, furthermore, as both Sellars and Churchland maintain (though not Dennett), the entire "manifest image" of our ordinary world (Sellars)—alternatively, our "folk-theoretical" picture of reality (Churchland)—is only fictionally constructed in accord with natural-language categories,[88] we cannot then, if we mean to test eliminativism at all, help asking questions like these: (1) whether language is not itself an essential part of the same would-be construction; (2) how linguistic reports and claims of any kind can constitute a bona fide science without admitting the realist standing of human selves or human agents or subjects; and (3) what possibly could serve as a pertinent and viable basis for assessing the use of language and the work of science, or of dismissing or replacing such outmoded vestiges altogether? For example, there is no account, in Sellars's doctrine, of the realist status of "raw feels," on the strength of which (as it seems) the work of *both* the "manifest image" *and* the "scientific image" depends. The posit seems to be quite impossible to manage coherently, since the two conceptions that admit raw feels do so in absolutely opposed and exclusionary ways.[89]

Dennett proceeds piecemeal, largely by way of a deep animus against intentionality and whatever he takes to belong to the Cartesian theater; Sellars proceeds globally, rather than by detail, in the name of a privileged atomism that (on his own say-so) is invariant, accords with the exceptionless laws of nature, and yields a causally closed universe; and Churchland, agreeing with the spirit of all the foregoing, proceeds by replacing, on grounds he views as testable in principle, the entire folk-theoretic account of mental states and mental aptitudes (including linguistic and epistemic aptitudes) by computational programs neurophysiologically defined in strictly extensionalist terms.

There are, of course, many strong lines of objection against reductionist and eliminativist versions of realism. Eliminativism, as in Sellars, seems puzzlingly naive, in the plain sense that Sellars fails to explain—or even address—the realist conditions on which his own claims make sense or could be straightforwardly tested. That cannot be a matter of ordinary neglect. Recent self-styled Sellarsians like Robert Brandom and Richard Rorty simply dismiss or ignore (by a stage whisper) Sellars's eliminativist side and feature instead his "Kantianism" and/or his pragmatism.[90] But that too calls for a strenuous explanation, since, apart from the bare eliminativist issue, the intended reading simply reverses (without a by-your-leave) Sellars's obvious penchant for extensionalism.

In any case, these late readers are unwilling to test the viability of Sellars's scientism. When, for instance, Rorty summarizes the general trajectory of Sellars's important essay, "Empiricism and the Philosophy of Mind," he compares Sellars favorably with the Wittgenstein of the *Investigations* and straightforwardly concludes—summarizing Sellars's view—with the following: "In other words, knowledge is inseparable from a social practice— the practice of justifying one's assertions to one's fellow-humans. It is not presupposed by this practice, but comes into being along with it."[91]

This is not the Sellars Dennett and Churchland mean to improve—or improve on! Rorty offers a kind of Hegelianized Kantian, a theorist for whom a strict extensionalism would have been impossible. He poses a curious problem for himself and Brandom—*and* Dennett *and* Churchland. For if the world of "social practice" is itself unreal, there surely is no point to Rorty's and Brandom's resurrecting Sellars's account of language *or* Dennett's or Churchland's efforts to provide an extensionalist account of the world. There's a deep muddle there. I should add that Brandom is no eliminativist, but Rorty is equivocal.

There is also no holism in Sellars, Dennett, or Churchland on a realist reading of their respective programs. Fodor and Lepore barely mention Sellars. But, given their noticeably skewed sense of "holism," Sellars, Dennett, and Churchland all count as "holists." Rorty also makes a lot of Dennett's "holism," which he loosely associates with Quine's holism and which therefore serves to remind us of his own holism.[92] The difference and the linkage between the two uses of the term are worth comparing. Fodor and Lepore are particularly instructive here:

> Though [as they say] anatomism [that is, the thesis diametrically opposed to semantic "atomism"] isn't the only philosophical issue about semantic holism, it nevertheless suffices to distinguish two great traditions in the philosophy of language. The atomistic tradition proceeds from the likes of the British empiricists, via such of the pragmatists as Peirce and James. The *locus classicus* is the work of the Vienna Circle, but see also the Russell of *The Analysis of Mind*. The contemporary representatives of this tradition are mostly model theorists, behaviorists, and informational semanticists. Whereas people in this tradition think that the semantic properties of a symbol are determined solely by its relations to things in the nonlinguis-

tic world, people in the second tradition think that the semantic properties of a symbol are determined, at least in part, by its role in a language. Languages are, *inter alia, collections* of symbols; so, if what a symbol means is determined by its role in a language, the property of *being a symbol* is anatomic. This second tradition proceeds from the likes of the structuralists in linguistics and the Fregeans in philosophy. [Fodor and Lepore are not entirely sure about Frege himself.] Its contemporary representatives are legion. They include Quine, Davidson, Lewis, Dennett, Block, Devitt, Putnam, Rorty, and Sellars among philosophers; *almost* everybody in AI and cognitive psychology; and it may be that they include absolutely everybody who writes literary criticism in French.[93]

You might suppose that Fodor and Lepore mean to disjoin the "metaphysical" and the "semantic," but that would not be true. "Semantic holism," they declare at the outset of their book, "is a doctrine about *the metaphysically necessary conditions* for something to have meaning or content."[94] As they explain: "A property is anatomic just in case if anything has it, then at least one other thing does" (the property of being a sibling for instance); otherwise, it is "punctate" or "atomistic," that is, *not*—as with being a sibling—"*metaphysically dependent* upon someone else's being a sibling."[95]

To my mind, this yields a distinctly eccentric sense of metaphysical dependence, which may explain why it is entirely fair to say that Sellars, Dennett, and Churchland are not holists "in the realist sense," though they clearly are holists in Fodor and Lepore's sense. I daresay almost no one holds the "atomist" position nowadays—though apparently (or at least perhaps) Fodor does! Surely the British empiricists were completely wrong in not recognizing that (however understandable their mistake) language *is* a "social practice," is (in spite of theories like Chomsky's) largely a social construction of some kind (that may depend, in some measure, on innate competencies, not necessarily linguistic).[96] (Peirce is too simply described by Fodor and Lepore, because, of course, Peirce's theory of signs presupposes "Thirdness" in nature at large—at times, a shadowy mind in nature apart from human minds.) Once such corrections are granted, the meaning of a linguistic symbol *is* surely "determined, at least in part, by its role in a language." To tell the truth, I cannot imagine anyone's seriously denying this extraordinarily modest claim. (Though the evidence more than suggests that Fodor does!)

Nevertheless, whatever may be said on the matter, "semantic holism" can only be a "part" of the internal holism I've attributed to the Wittgenstein of the *Investigations*. The latter is not a specifically semantic doctrine at all. In that sense, Sellars, Dennett, and Churchland are all, as realists, anti-holists or atomists—a sense that is not initially keyed to the semantic at all, though it has consequences for semantic analysis.[97] Of course, Fodor's anti-holism and the anti-holism of Sellars, Churchland, and Dennett are, though they are doctrines of very different kinds, still notably similar in their zeal to eliminate every obstacle to a thoroughgoing extensionalism cast in materialist terms. In an obvious sense, they converge, therefore, as do Quine and Davidson as well (from the holist side), as partisans of opposed strains of what may be fairly said to be a generic form of scientism. That is precisely what Wittgenstein opposed among his own Tractarian efforts.

On Fodor and Lepore's view, "there is an argument (the crucial premise of which is the failure of the analytic/synthetic (a/s) distinction) which suggests that if a semantic property is anatomic, then it is also holistic."[98] The whole point of their book, *Holism*, is to *show* that "there is no very pressing reason to suppose that semantic properties are typically anatomic." I'm inclined to think that their conclusion is due in good part to their very odd definition of "anatomic." For surely the point of emphasis in semantic holism is that the semantic properties of a "linguistic symbol" depend to a significant degree on the structure of the sentence or the discourse or the portion of language or the inclusive language in which it occurs. *That* alone is hardly inconsistent with Fodor and Lepore's original definition of the "anatomic," according to which "the semantic properties of a symbol are determined, *at least in part*, by its role in a language." But, by the end of the book, they reach a more drastic conclusion: at that point, even the modest claim just mentioned is said to be in jeopardy. That is a most unpromising leap.

What Fodor and Lepore appear to mean is that semantics, viewed in some sense as an autonomous discipline (separable, say, from the implications of anything like Wittgenstein's *Lebensform*), *can* defeat or at least stalemate the thesis of "semantic holism" when that doctrine is itself viewed in terms of semantics narrowly construed. But that obviously leaves us with a conceptual dangler, namely, the deeper concern of the semantic holists to investigate "the metaphysically necessary conditions for something to *have* meaning or content." Here, the deeper divide concerns the holist "metaphysics" of culture itself, the very enculturation of human selves. It is here, precisely, that the deeper difference between Quine's and Wittgenstein's holisms makes itself felt, for, of course, the holism of Quine's attack on the analytic/synthetic distinction is intended to serve the interests of a deeper scientism. That, in effect, is what Fodor neglects. The eccentric distinction between the "two" holisms follows apace.

Fodor and Lepore conclude: "if semantic properties are typically anatomic and there is no a/s [analytic/synthetic] distinction, then meaning
holism is true"; further, that "if the reason why there are no pressing reasons
to suppose that semantic properties are typically anatomic is that, as a matter of fact, semantic properties are typically punctate, then conceptual role
semantics won't work and we desperately need an atomistic theory of meaning to replace it."[99] They are clearly drawn to the latter possibility. But they
suggest that to reach it, we must "invent a nonepistemic notion of conceptual role"; for, though Quine did *not* (as they emphasize) "refute" the
a/s distinction in the "Two Dogmas" paper, he *did* show that "it can't be re-
constructed in terms of *epistemic* categories."[100]

They themselves agree that "the argument from anatomism to holism itself depends on the premise that no principled a/s distinction can be
drawn."[101] But there's the Achilles' heel. For they do treat the semantic question "metaphysically," though they somehow obscure the fact; and if the
post-Kantian argument (preeminently, Hegel's) holds—against the Cartesians (against Fodor and Lepore themselves)—then *metaphysics and epistemology must be inseparable,* must infect the analysis of meaning, and then
their last hope fails. In that case, the semantic holists win! But they do so on
realist grounds that Fodor and Lepore never rightly consider. I should add,
for the sake of clarity, that, according to Fodor and Lepore's usage, "holistic" means no more than "being *very* anatomic": "Holistic properties are
properties such that, if anything has them, then *lots* of other things must
have them too"—being a natural number for instance.[102] So it matters very
little that they treat Dennett and Churchland as semantic holists, though it
does confirm that they themselves intend to be the last defenders of a thoroughly extensionalist account of language. They favor a scientism very close
to Chomsky's.

VII

It begins to dawn on us why, if an internal-holist reading of realism (*per*
post-Kantianism) promises to provide the most viable and convincing
premise on which to salvage realism from the pre-Kantian and Kantian *aporiai* (a realism suited to the sciences), the extensionalism favored in all scientistic programs cannot but be doomed. We can pay the argument out in
pieces if we wish: for instance, by analyzing, more or less separately, meaning, truth, reference, predication, contextual relevance, knowledge, confirmation, normativity, legitimation, linguistic competence, responsibility,
reality, mind, belief, intentionality, and similar topics; but they will all, fi-

nally, prove to be pieces of a single encompassing argument that neither eliminativism nor reductionism can smash through.

Those "atomists" who—like Sellars, Dennett, Churchland, the Wittgenstein of the *Tractatus,* the positivists, the Cartesians—eschew holism altogether (in spite of what Fodor and Lepore say) fall back to cognitive privilege or (what comes to the same thing) unavoidable truths about "metaphysics" apart from "epistemology." The external holists, preeminently Quine and Davidson, invoke a "principle of charity," which amounts to reclaiming a "privileged" premise that appears to be innocuous (but is not). The internal holists, preeminently the Wittgenstein of the *Investigations,* also, for instance, John Dewey (who developed the notion of an "indeterminate situation"[103]) reach their own premises by way of resolving what is already admitted to be a philosophical paradox, stalemate, regress, or muddle that needs to be managed without invoking privilege. In effect, they *earn* the right to advance their holistic resolutions.

The argument that is favored here yields to Hegel in accord with solutions sketched in the *Phenomenology* and *Encyclopedia* and signifies internal-holist constraints on all satisfactory analyses of the concepts enumerated a moment ago. That, for instance, is the point of remarking (as I have) that there seems to be no way of avoiding the judgment that reference (or denotation) and predication are insuperably intensional.

I would say that, in Dennett's and Churchland's theories, semantic analysis follows the extensionalist guidelines of what, in rather different ways, each takes to be the requirements of scientific realism. Fodor and Lepore have misled us here. For they have enlarged the apparent relevance of semantic holism in a way that obscures the supposed accessibility of the computationalist resources upon which Dennett and Churchland draw—which may even be construed (may have to be construed) as yielding an alternative kind of semantics.[104] (You must bear in mind that there is no satisfactory way of prioritizing semantics over metaphysics or epistemology, or vice versa.) In fact, computationalism is the most promising of the current analytic strategies, fitted to psychology and favored by recent realisms of an uncompromising extensionalist cast. I shall not hurry to stigmatize computationalism as a form of scientism, though I suspect that this is what it is. But I'll close this account by noting a number of difficulties or limiting constraints that bear on our assessment of both Dennett's and Churchland's conjectures, which, if not resolved, would justify the label. Certainly, there is no assured incoherence in the computationalist conception. Let that count as a reasonable measure of conceptual tolerance.

First, then, two difficulties for Dennett. There is, for one thing, a nagging *non sequitur* in Dennett's early essays that (as far as I can tell) has never been satisfactorily removed from his later papers that urge a computationalist analysis of mental or psychological states. It has a definite Sellarsian (eliminativist) cast. Dennett transcribes the psychologist's notion of "informational content" in terms preparatory to a computational (or AI) paraphrase in the following way:

> The *content* . . . of a particular vehicle of information, a particular
> information-bearing event or state, is and must be a function of its
> function in the [entire] system [say, the information of a particular
> neuronal discharge in the psychological life of a frog]. This is the
> sense of "information" utilized in our model (and in psychological
> models generally); so when I assert that, for instance, there is a
> transfer of information from some perceptual analysis area to M
> [a short-term memory store within the entire system], I endow that
> transfer event with content, and the content it has is to be under-
> stood as a function of the function within the whole system of that
> event.[105]

There are two constraints on information intended here: one, that, contrary to "information-theoretic" accounts (suited to computationalism), "information" is intensional—hence, needs to be suitably replaced by an extensionalist reduction or paraphrase; the other, that information is relationally defined by Dennett in terms of a sub-function of a function—hence, it cannot be directly replaced by any extensionalist substitute without an intervening justification.

These two qualifications define what Dennett calls a "homunculus," the site of a sub-functional function of some molar function assignable to a system as a whole (a functioning person, say, a human being who thinks and acts intelligently). What Dennett has in mind is that we can always introduce, top-down, sub-homuncular homunculi to subdivide the work of sub-personal homunculi until we reach a level of "stupid" functioning (restricted, say, to binary options for "atomic" functions) so that we may simply plug in, *bottom-up,* the events (say, neurophysiological discharges) described entirely in extensionalist terms that match the top-down strategy.[106] According to this argument, we can eliminate persons and minds, though Dennett does not quite address the implications for the rest of the macroscopic world (as Churchland attempts to do).

Nevertheless, the "bottom-up" strategy is extensionalist and atomic, and the "top-down" strategy is intensional and "holist" (or relational). The two analyses are simply incommensurable as they stand. You will have guessed, of course, that in the passage cited, the intensional complications at the molar (top-down) level of analysis are simply assumed to yield to the ultimate (bottom-up) replacement of homuncular (sub-functional) analysis, that is, an ultimate analysis assumed to fit the extensionalist model without difficulty.

To my knowledge, Dennett has never carried out an analysis of the psychological that shows convincingly how the computationalist replacement works empirically. I do not deny that it is a coherent idea, but then it would remain coherent even if it were false! (I think it is false. It rests on an unacknowledged incommensurability.)

The second difficulty is more serious: it is directed (by Dennett) against the supposed "irreducibility" of the intentional to the physical (in effect, the intensionalist to the extensionalist). So it allows "Brentano's Thesis—all mental phenomena are intentional" but treats it "as a *reductionist* thesis of sorts, parallel to [Alonzo] Church's Thesis . . . every 'effective' procedure in mathematics is recursive, that is, Turing-computable." Dennett acknowledges that "Church's Thesis is not provable, since it hinges on the intuitive and unformalizable notion of an effective procedure, but it is generally accepted."[107] Fine. The trouble, however, lies elsewhere.

Dennett slips here, holding that "the AI researcher . . . is confident that any design he can state *clearly* [his paraphrase of Church's Thesis or a corollary of it] can be mechanized . . . [is] expressible in a programming language at some level."[108] In that sense, if it is "clear," it is computable! The argument is a *non sequitur:* "clarity" need not be absent from what is inherently non-computational, and clarity alone does not yield "effective" computability. There is always a prior analysis required to show that a given process *is* inherently computational.[109] For instance, it might well be that a given process is *simulable* by computational means, without its being the case that the original process, however "clear," is itself computational. Actually, this is also the point of an essential objection against Churchland. Consider, for instance, that a telephone system may provide for a machine's voicing the names of all subscribers drawn from the printed names. It's reasonably clear that there is no algorithm by which the requisite utterances are actually generated; but it's equally obvious that a program may be progressively improved by which a would-be algorithm may be simulated.

Churchland's argument is more resilient, though it is also inconclusive. I think we cannot show, in principle, that an extensionalist reduction of intensional structures or features is physically impossible. But if it should turn out that every would-be extensionalist replacement or approximation is, as empirically introduced, more likely to be a simulation than a robust or re-alist analysis or adequate replacement of a given process, *or* an explanatory model generated and controlled by our own "folk-theoretical" science, then *any* argument of Churchland's sort will not succeed either eliminatively or reductively. There's no question that Churchland makes a convincing case for simulation and new explanatory models.[110] But it's not clear *what* Churchland *has* demonstrated when viewed in the light of what he believes he's demonstrated! He would not be content with any of the alternatives I've just offered him.

For instance, he says, provocatively, at the beginning of *A Neurocomputational Perspective,* "folk psychology [the conceptual scheme more or less in place through the entire history of Western civilization, though not con-fined to the West, of course] is, empirically, a radically inadequate account of our internal [or mental] activities, too confused and too defective to win survival through intertheoretic reduction. On this view, it will simply be dis-placed by a better theory of these activities."[111] But isn't the charge that this is so itself formulated in terms of our "folk psychology"? Or, if it is not, how should it be characterized? Churchland has himself mentioned (more re-cently) "the evident conflict between the eliminativist's apparent *belief* that FP [folk psychology] is false, and his simultaneous claim that there *are* no beliefs."[112]

I see no way of understanding these matters except to admit that Church-land's assertions, and similar assertions (by others) answering his, are meant to have *cognitive standing* of some kind; and if that is so, then, for one thing (as already remarked), we must acknowledge that epistemological and metaphysical concerns are conceptually inseparable—so that to claim (as Churchland does) that FP is false (about psychological reality) is to claim as well that an FP account of what it is to *know* whatever is true of that part of the world is also "too confused and too defective to win survival"; and, for another, Churchland nowhere explains *how* the anti-FP pronouncement (just cited) can ever get things right or get them right without FP entangle-ments! No matter how Churchland supposes he can elude the paradox, there seems to be a dilemma. Suppose (as I am inclined to believe) *our cognitive stance* is *not* a "theory" that can be replaced at will, even if we suppose (as I'll concede) that the FP theories we assume to be true may be as "confused" and "defective" as Churchland says they are (though not for his reasons). I take this to say nothing against the possible "evolution" and change of our "cognitive stance" or, indeed, the FP theories that we currently favor.

Nevertheless, I cannot see any coherent way in which Churchland could possibly propose a theory of perception or memory or inference or thinking, *or* a replacement of same, that could "correctly" characterize what we are now actually doing (in mental or psychological respects—*as* FP now understands things, mistakenly perhaps) *that is not itself under the executive control of the cognitive stance (and concepts) that FP paradigmatically characterizes as it does.* In this sense, FP may not itself be "an explanatory theory," in spite of its being the only source we have *for* generating and testing explanatory theories.[113] *That* is the sense in which FP *cannot* (in any essential sense) *be* no more than an empirical theory. There seems to be no manageable way to segregate the cognitive "site" that we call a person or self or mind and the originating interests, concepts, perspectives, enabling aptitudes—notably, language—by which that site *is* contingently formed as it is; and there is no way to characterize any evidentiary source apart from the distinctive work of would-be scientists themselves. In an interesting sense, I see this as a not-too-distant confirmation of Hegel's thesis, in the *Encyclopedia,* to the effect that there is no principled disjunction between the cognizing "I" *and* its concepts *and* the concepts by which, as it evolves, it understands its own competence *and* the objective world it comes to know.[114]

I see no evidence that Churchland has overcome his own *aporia,* and it's my view that he has misdescribed what he is actually championing. Whatever he offers seems to be a theory meant to improve on the theories *now* linked so intimately with what we understand our cognitive powers to be, that *we* cannot coherently separate what we may wish to reject or replace, without rendering profoundly problematic our understanding of "ourselves."

Under the circumstances everything that Churchland offers can be reclaimed under the terms of simulation, analogy, analysis, or explanation of our cognitive stance, reflexively considered, without actually replacing it in the radical manner Churchland believes is necessary but cannot yet show to be a coherent possibility. I say his replacements are not possible in the way he proposes; and where they are possible, they are not the proposals he claims to advance!

I don't deny our theory of one's cognitive powers is bound to change, but it cannot be eliminated in the blanket form Churchland favors. If, as I argue, the paradigm model of our mental and cognitive life *is* "linguaform," to use Churchland's pejorative term[115]—not necessarily *confined* for that reason to the "theories" we currently accept and may yet replace, as Churchland urges—then there *can't* be any escape from the FP stance by escaping any particular empirical theory, though there may yet be some unimagined evolution of thought that has actually been set in motion that will displace the current paradigm. For the time being, however, extensionalism and elimi-nativism cannot fail to be FP-sponsored proposals *themselves*. But then, they must make sense in FP terms, which is to say, they cannot count on being exceptionless or constrained by advantages gained from whatever "folk-the-oretic" accounts they exploit—which they also ultimately reject. They can-not ensure *a priori* or empirically the eventual success of their extreme forms of scientism. Nothing of these sorts seems to work.

Beyond the cleansing of the stables, I confess I begin to see the lineaments of a possible rapprochement among the principal lines of Eurocentric phi-losophy. The enabling discovery is this: the very precision, the rigorous power, of science and philosophy is the creature of the reflexive competence of human beings disposed to examine themselves and their ability to un-derstand their world; but that competence has proved unable (for very good reasons) to overcome its own informality by reductive or eliminative means.

Notes

INTRODUCTION

1. For a sustained discussion of this development, see Joseph Margolis, *Reinventing Pragmatism: American Philosophy at the End of the Twentieth Century* (Ithaca: Cornell University Press, 2002).

2. See, further, Michael Friedman, *Reconsidering Logical Positivism* (Cambridge: Cambridge University Press, 1999), particularly chaps. 7 and 9. What is telling about Friedman's account is that, at least up to the time of this publication, and despite his very strong preferences for Carnap over Quine, Friedman is not quite prepared to mount a full-scale challenge to Quine's discussion of the analytic/synthetic "dogma." I have, however, heard Friedman present a paper at the annual meeting of the American Philosophical Association (Eastern Division)—I think it must have been December 2001—"'Two Dogmas' and the Philosophy of Science," an excellent paper that challenges Quine's reliance on the adequacy of first-order logic without attention to the conceptual (and existential) requirements of a mathematized physics.

Friedman reads Carnap's defense of the "dogma" in terms of a "relativized" reinterpretation of Kant's synthetic *a priori,* which requires a careful sorting of two distinct meanings of the *a priori* in Kant: the "necessary and [the] unrevisable, [what is] fixed for all time . . . and [what is] 'constitutive of the concept of the object of knowledge.'" (I take the phrasing from Friedman's typescript, which Friedman shared on request.) I find the argument reasonable and immensely worthwhile. However, I don't think we have enough material to decide the issue between Quine and Carnap, and I am certainly not qualified to judge the conceptual needs of contemporary physics. The apparent "a priori" of the mathematics in terms of which physics is "mathematized" seems to mean no more than "analytic." My own intuition has it that Quine *is* right, seen from his semantic orientation, and that Carnap *is* right in his Kantian-like explication of the work of recent physics; also, that it *is* true that Quine neglects Carnap's sense of Carnap's problem and that it *is* true that Carnap does not bring that matter to bear on Quine's global challenge to the "dogma."

I don't think it is entirely clear whether admitting the constitutive invariance (in effect, the definition) of the concepts of physical *denotata* in terms of "invariant" mathematical axioms (said to be chosen for "pragmatic reasons") *is* incompatible with (or defeats or stalemates) the implications of Quine's holism. What is important to bear in mind is that Quine's holism *is* incompatible with admitting the synthetic *a priori* (in whatever sense it may be said to bear on the analytic/synthetic distinction)—for instance, as falling *outside* the scope of the proposed holism. I am not clear about what Friedman would say about that.

3. See, further, Alex Orenstein, *W. V. Quine* (Princeton: Princeton University Press, 2002), particularly pp. 67–71 and chap. 6. Quine appears to have resisted the separation of "the inscrutability of reference" and the "indeterminacy of translation," though he also seems to regard them as quite different problems rightly "solved" in different ways. As far as I understand the matter, both attitudes are tethered to Quine's notions of "stimulus meaning" and "radical translation" *and* (in that context) a reliance on the holism of "holophrastic sentences": that is,

given these notions (which I touch on more pointedly in chapter 4), *both* sorts of "indeterminacy" follow.

I confess I have never rightly understood what Quine means by "holophrastic sentences." They are certainly not merely "one-word sentences," as in responding to the question put by someone who has never seen snow before: "What is that?" pointing to the snow; whereupon you answer, "Snow." The problem of reference and the problem of predicative meaning are inseparable *if* you mean to speak of ordinary discourse, that is, *not* holophrastic sentences. But if you allow holophrastic sentences, it may well appear that you could separate the two sorts of indeterminacy. I do not believe that this is possible or in accord with Quine's purpose. Hence, though Orenstein pointedly suggests that Quine may have seen an advantage in considering the two sorts of indeterminacy "separately," I wonder whether he didn't also see the danger. I don't know what to make of Quine's fiddling with the difference, though it's clear enough that they are not "quite" the same. They *are* inseparable, however. See chapter 4, below.

4. See Richard Rorty, introduction to *The Linguistic Turn: Recent Essays in Philosophical Method* (Chicago: University of Chicago Press, 1967).

5. W. V. Quine, *Word and Object* (Cambridge: Harvard University Press, 1960), p. 221.

6. See Robert B. Brandom, *Articulating Reasons: An Introduction to Inferentialism* (Cambridge: Harvard University Press, 2000); and Richard Rorty, introduction to *Empiricism and the Philosophy of Mind*, by Wilfrid Sellars (Cambridge: Harvard University Press, 1997).

7. Wilfrid Sellars, "The Language of Theories," *Science, Perception and Reality* (London: Routledge and Kegan Paul, 1963), p. 126; italics in original.

8. See Richard Rorty, "Robert Brandom on Social Practices and Representations," in *Philosophical Papers*, vol. 3 (Cambridge: Cambridge University Press, 1998).

9. See Wilfrid Sellars, "Philosophy and the Scientific Image of Man," in *Science, Perception and Reality* (London: Routledge and Kegan Paul, 1963).

10. See Rudolf Carnap, "Psychology in Physical Language," trans. George Schick, in *Logical Positivism*, ed. A. J. Ayer (Glencoe: Free Press, 1959).

11. See Pierre Duhem, *The Aim and Structure of Physical Theory*, 2d ed., trans. Philip P. Wiener (New York: Atheneum, 1962).

12. Sellars, *Empiricism and the Philosophy of Mind*, sec. 20.

13. Quite recently, editing the final draft of my manuscript, I came across Frederick A. Olafson's *Naturalism and the Human Condition: Against Scientism* (London: Routledge, 2001). It approaches, in phenomenological and Heideggerean terms, objections to scientism not altogether unlike the objections I have in mind. But it is critical of the work of the natural sciences in a way that is very different from that favored here. Olafson's thesis is captured in the following pronouncement: "The main significance of the fact that we live in the world and not in nature [the 'nature' of the physical sciences] is that the destructive impact on our understanding of ourselves of the scientific thesis that we are denizens of nature is much reduced" (p. 108). I find myself in considerable sympathy with Olafson's criticism, which (I would say) may be "translated" and effectively applied against, for example, Quine, Dennett, and Churchland. The decisive difference—a large difference—between the traditions Olafson pits against one another (which cannot be rightly rendered by a mere contrast between analytic philosophy and phenomenology or Heideggerean phenomenology) concerns a choice between an adequate conception of "nature" and the theme of "transcendence" that Heidegger features. Olafson himself sees the contest in terms of Hegel and Heidegger, which is very well perceived. My own sense is that the Hegelian vision needs to be recovered in its slimmest terms and that the Heideggerean alternative does not really succeed. On Heidegger, see for instance, my "Martin Heidegger: A Pragmatist by Any Means," publication pending. In any event, pragmatism pretty well equates "nature" and "the world" (though not reductively); whereas Heideggereans do not equate the two. Their "world" becomes instead a rather mysterious space in which Being is encountered in a momentous but inexplicable way.

14. See Quine, *Word and Object*, sec. 49–50.

15. See, for instance, Noam Chomsky, *Knowledge of Language: Its Nature, Origin, and Use* (New York: Praeger, 1986). See also, however, Chomsky's *New Horizons in the Study of Language and Mind* (Cambridge: Cambridge University Press, 2000) and Jerry A. Fodor, *The Language of Thought* (New York: Thomas Y. Crowell, 1975).

16. Henry Plotkin, *Evolution in Mind: An Introduction to Evolutionary Psychology* (Cambridge: Harvard University Press, 1998), p. 88.

17. See W. V. Quine, "Epistemology Naturalized," in *Ontological Relativity and Other Essays* (New York: Columbia University Press, 1969); and Donald Davidson, "A Coherence Theory of Truth and Knowledge," in *Truth and Interpretation: Perspectives on the Philosophy of Donald Davidson*, ed. Ernest Lepore (Oxford: Basil Blackwell, 1986). See, further, Margolis, prologue to *Reinventing Pragmatism.*

18. See Richard Rorty, "Pragmatism, Davidson and Truth," in *Truth and Interpretation: Perspectives on the Philosophy of Donald Davidson.*

19. See Daniel C. Dennett, *Consciousness Explained* (Boston: Little, Brown, 1990); see also Richard Rorty, "Daniel Dennett on Intrinsicality," in *Philosophical Papers,* vol. 3 (Cambridge: Cambridge University Press, 1998).

20. I note here that Dennett's view is flatly incompatible with Donald Davidson's, for instance. Davidson clearly holds—and I agree but find his explication inadequate—that there is a public role for first-person reports and avowals of inner mental states—hence also a conceptual connection between first- and third-person discourse. See Donald Davidson, *Subjective, Intersubjective, Objective* (Oxford: Clarendon, 2001). Far more satisfactory are arguments associated with Wittgenstein's attack on private languages. A perspicuous line of reasoning akin to Wittgenstein's but seemingly independent may be found in P. F. Strawson, *Individuals: An Essay in Descriptive Metaphysics* (London: Methuen, 1959), pp. 103–115. As far as I know, Dennett does not discuss objections based on such considerations. But they are far more important for his purpose than the views he attacks (Thomas Nagel's, for instance). For a more general sense of fresh worries among the scientistically minded (but not more), see David Chalmers, *The Conscious Mind: In Search of a Fundamental Theory* (New York: Oxford University Press, 1996).

21. P. K. Feyerabend, "Materialism and the Mind-Body Problem," in *Philosophical Papers* (Cambridge: Cambridge University Press, 1981), 1:161, 166.

22. Peter Hylton, *Russell, Idealism and the Emergence of Analytic Philosophy* (Oxford: Clarendon, 1990), p. 105.

23. Ibid., p. 107. This, therefore, marks a source of Russell's philosophy very much slighted in D. F. Pears, *Bertrand Russell and the British Tradition in Philosophy* (London: Fontana Library, 1967).

24. Hylton, *Russell, Idealism and the Emergence of Analytic Philosophy,* p. 106.

25. See, for instance, John R. Shook, *Dewey's Empirical Theory of Knowledge and Reality* (Nashville: Vanderbilt University Press, 2000).

26. See, for instance, Tom Rockmore, *Cognition: An Introduction to Hegel's Phenomenology of Spirit* (Berkeley: University of California Press, 1997).

27. See Michael Devitt, *Realism and Truth,* 2d ed. (Princeton: Princeton University Press, 1990); Michael Dummett, *The Logical Basis of Metaphysics* (Cambridge: Harvard University Press, 1991); Davidson, "A Coherence Theory of Truth and Knowledge"; and John McDowell, *Mind and World* (Cambridge: Harvard University Press, 1994, 1996).

28. See Margolis, *Reinventing Pragmatism,* chaps. 3 and 4.

29. On Putnam's own view of his "internal" or "pragmatic realism," see Hilary Putnam, "Sense, Nonsense, and the Senses: An Inquiry into the Powers of the Human Mind," *Journal of Philosophy* 91 (1994); on the general treatment of realism in pragmatism and analytic philosophy, see Margolis, *Reinventing Pragmatism.*

30. See Thomas S. Kuhn, *The Structure of Scientific Revolutions,* 2d ed. enlarged (Chicago: University of Chicago Press, 1970); "Reflections on My Critics," in *Criticism and the Growth of Knowledge,* ed. Imre Lakatos and Alan Musgrave (Cambridge: Cambridge University Press,

1970); and Paul Feyerabend, *Against Method: Outline of an Anarchistic Theory of Knowledge* (London: Verso, 1975). See also Donald Davidson, "On the Very Idea of a Conceptual Scheme," in *Inquiries into Truth and Interpretation* (Oxford: Clarendon, 1984).

1. MATERIALISM BY LESS THAN ADEQUATE MEANS

1. Steven Pinker, *How the Mind Works* (New York: W. W. Norton, 1997), pp. 31, 33, 35, 36.

2. Ibid., pp. 34–35.

3. Ibid., p. 83.

4. Ibid., pp. 69–70.

5. See, for instance, Warren S. McCulloch, "Why the Mind Is in the Brain," in *Embodiments of Mind* (Cambridge: MIT Press, 1988).

6. See Herbert Feigl, *The "Mental" and the "Physical": The Essay and a Postscript* (Minneapolis: University of Minnesota Press, 1967); and Paul M. Churchland, *A Neurocomputational Perspective: The Nature of Mind and the Structure of Science* (Cambridge: MIT Press, 1989); and also by Churchland, *The Engine of Reason, The Seat of the Soul: A Philosophical Journey into the Brain* (Cambridge: MIT Press, 1995).

7. Daniel C. Dennett, *Darwin's Dangerous Idea: Evolution and the Meanings of Life* (New York: Simon and Schuster, 1995), pp. 368, 443. Clarification of "vast" appears on p. 109. Also see Roger Penrose, *The Emperor's New Mind: Concerning Computers, Minds, and the Laws of Physics* (Oxford: Oxford University Press, 1989).

8. See Richard Dawkins, *The Selfish Gene*, rev. ed. (Oxford: Oxford University Press, 1989), and *The Extended Phenotype: The Long Reach of the Gene*, rev. ed. (Oxford: Oxford University Press, 1999); also, François Jacob and Jacques Monod, "On the Regulation of Gene Activity," *Cold Spring Harbor Symposium on Quantitative Biology* 26 (1961). Compare Jacques Monod, *Chance and Necessity*, trans. Austryn Wainhouse (New York: Vintage, 1971); *The Concept of the Gene in Development and Evolution: Historical and Epistemological Perspectives*, ed. Peter Beurton, Raphael Falk, and Hans-Jörg Rheinberger (Cambridge: Cambridge University Press, 2000); and Evelyn Fox Keller, *The Century of the Gene* (Cambridge: Harvard University Press, 2000).

9. See, for instance, Philip Kitcher, *Vaulting Ambition* (Cambridge: MIT Press, 1985).

10. See Noam Chomsky, *New Horizons in the Study of Language and Mind* (Cambridge: Cambridge University Press, 2000), p. 163.

11. Dennett, *Darwin's Dangerous Idea*, pp. 59, 203.

12. See W. V. Quine, "Epistemology Naturalized," in *Ontological Relativity and Other Essays* (New York: Columbia University Press, 1969); and Dennett, *Darwin's Dangerous Idea*, pp. 384–400.

13. Chomsky, *New Horizons for the Study of Language and Mind*, p. 134.

14. See Daniel C. Dennett, chap. 4 in *Consciousness Explained* (Boston: Little, Brown, 1991).

15. Chomsky, *New Horizons in the Study of Language and Mind*, pp. 76, 134.

16. See E. O. Wilson, *Sociobiology: The New Synthesis* (Cambridge: Harvard University Press, 1975) and *On Human Nature* (Cambridge: Harvard University Press, 1978); and C. Lumsden and E. O. Wilson, *Genes, Mind, and Culture* (Cambridge: Harvard University Press, 1981). For a thorough assessment of sociobiology, see Kitcher, *Vaulting Ambition*.

17. See Lumsden and Wilson, *Genes, Mind, and Culture*, p. 27.

18. Chomsky, *New Horizons in the Study of Language and Mind*, p. 91.

19. Ibid., pp. 144–145.

20. See Richard Rorty, "Daniel Dennett on Intrinsicality," in *Philosophical Papers*, vol. 3 (Cambridge: Cambridge University Press, 1998). See, further, Joseph Margolis, *Reinventing Pragmatism: American Philosophy at the End of the Twentieth Century* (Ithaca: Cornell University Press, 2002), chap. 6.

21. Dennett, *Consciousness Explained*, pp. 70–72. The matter is indifferent with regard to the realism/anti-realism issue and to the quarrel between dualism and anti-dualism. See, for

instance, Arthur Fine, chap. 7 in *The Shaky Game: Einstein, Realism and the Quantum Theory* (Chicago: University of Chicago Press, 1986).

22. Chomsky, *New Horizons in the Study of Language and Mind*, p. 92. See, further, Thomas Nagel, "Searle: Why We are not Computers," in *Other Minds* (New York: Oxford University Press, 1995).

23. Chomsky, *New Horizons in the Study of Language and Mind*, p. 92.

24. Ibid., pp. 122–123.

25. See Noam Chomsky, *Aspects of the Theory of Syntax* (Cambridge: MIT Press, 1965).

26. Noam Chomsky, *Language and Responsibility*, trans. John Viertel (New York: Pantheon Books, 1977), p. 151.

27. Ibid., p. 153.

28. Peter Mühlhäusler, *Pidgin & Creole Linguistics* (Oxford: Basil Blackwell, 1986), pp. 39–41, 126–133. The general issues are treated in an explicitly reductionist way by Derek Bickerton. See Derek Bickerton, *Language & Species* (Chicago: University of Chicago Press, 1992); and *Language and Human Behavior* (Seattle: University of Washington Press, 1995). Here is Bickerton's view: "we cannot flatter ourselves that language was a discovery born of our own superior skills. On the contrary, it is a feature of our species biology written into the genetic code.... True language had to wait in the animal sense on a further evolutionary accident, but one of a different kind: not a change in behavior, but rather a change in neural organization that caused us to slot meaningful symbols into formal structure and to do so quite automatically, without any conscious effort in either production or comprehension," *Language & Species*, p. 256. As far as I can see, Bickerton offers no interesting defense at all for this conclusion.

There is plenty of reason to be suspicious of linguists' easy generalizations. No one, to my knowledge, has ever made a convincing case that, say, Chinese has the same deep grammatical structure (however generously construed) as the Indo-European languages. The alien nature of Chinese was already a worry to linguistic universalism in the late eighteenth century. There is, as far as I know, no more fair-minded and cautious reflection on the entire matter than that offered in Wilhelm von Humboldt, *Linguistic Variability and Intellectual Development*, trans. George C. Buck and Frithjof A. Raven (Philadelphia: University of Pennsylvania Press, 1971). See, particularly, chaps. 19, 21. Certainly Humboldt's account is the beginning of any balanced judgment on the matter.

29. Chomsky, *New Horizons in the Study of Language and Mind*, p. 118.

30. Ibid., pp. 33–34.

31. Neil Smith, foreword to *New Horizons in the Study of Language and Mind*, p. xiii.

32. Lumsden and Wilson, *Genes, Minds, and Culture*, pp. 99, 349, 357–358. See also Kitcher, *Vaulting Ambition*, pp. 331–350.

33. Dawkins, *The Selfish Gene*, pp. 191, 193–194, 200.

34. Henry Plotkin, *Evolution in Mind: An Introduction to Evolutionary Psychology* (Cambridge: Harvard University Press, 1998), p. 89. The reference to culture appears at p. 222.

35. See Dennett, chap. 5 in *Consciousness Explained*.

36. See Franz Brentano, *Psychology from an Empirical Standpoint*, ed. Linda L. McAlister, trans. Antos C. Rancurello, D. B. Terrell, and Linda L. McAlister (New York: Humanities Press, 1973).

37. Chomsky, *New Horizons in the Study of Language and Mind*, pp. 8, 10.

38. Ibid., p. 8.

2. INCOMMENSURABILITY MODESTLY RECOVERED

1. This is not to deny that, with the appearance of Thomas S. Kuhn's *The Structure of Scientific Revolutions* (Chicago: University of Chicago Press, 1962; revised and enlarged in 1970), the incommensurability issue (better: incommunsurabilism) was hotly debated. The discussion of Kuhn's thesis was something of an embarrassment, since what it exposed was the

perennial philosophical impulse to protect the flank of one's own theory, seemingly put at risk if one admitted Kuhn's thesis. I won't attempt to provide a history of the controversy here. I have still to lay out the quarrel as I see it—as well as its resolution; and I have not even begun to identify the principal players in the contest. But I can recommend the very helpful discussion in Bjorn T. Ramberg, chap. 9 in *Donald Davidson's Philosophy of Language: An Introduction* (Oxford: Basil Blackwell, 1989). Ramberg collects and analyzes very neatly an important and generous sample of the responses to Kuhn (and Paul Feyerabend). I agree with most of what Ramberg says, though not, as you will discover, his own suggestion that "incommensurability is a diachronic relation, not a synchronic one; it is not [he says] a relation between structures, but a symptom of structural change" (p. 131). I think that's only part of the story.

2. Hilary Putnam, "Wittgenstein on Reference and Relativism," in *Renewing Philosophy* (Cambridge: Harvard University Press, 1992), p. 177; compare Hilary Putnam, "Two Conceptions of Rationality," in *Reason, Truth and History* (Cambridge: Cambridge University Press, 1981).

3. See Myles Burnyeat, "Protagoras and Self-Refutation in Plato's Theaetetus," *Philosophical Review* 85 (1976), punctuation streamlined.

4. See Peter Winch, *The Idea of a Social Science* (London: Routledge and Kegan Paul, 1958).

5. See Leopold von Ranke, *The Theory and Practice of History*, ed. Georg G. Iggers and Konrad von Moltke, trans. Wilma A. Iggers and Konrad von Moltke (New York: Irvington, 1983).

6. See Joseph Margolis, *The Truth about Relativism* (Oxford: Basil Blackwell, 1991).

7. I discuss Putnam's account in greater detail in my *Reinventing Pragmatism: American Philosophy at the End of the Century* (Ithaca: Cornell University Press, 2002).

8. Putnam, *Reason, Truth and History*, p. 216.

9. Donald Davidson, "On the Very Idea of a Conceptual Scheme," in *Inquiries into Truth and Interpretation* (Oxford: Clarendon, 1984).

10. Putnam, "Wittgenstein on Reference and Relativism," p. 176.

11. Hilary Putnam, *The Many Faces of Realism* (LaSalle: Open Court, 1987), pp. 17–18.

12. Putnam, "Irrealism and Deconstruction," p. 120.

13. See W. V. Quine, *Pursuit of Truth*, rev. ed. (Cambridge: Harvard University Press, 1992), pp. 1–18.

14. See Putnam, lecture 2 in *The Many Faces of Realism*.

15. See Hilary Putnam, *The Threefold Cord: Mind, Body, and World* (New York: Columbia University Press, 1999).

16. See Davidson, "On the Very Idea of a Conceptual Scheme," and Putnam, "Two Conceptions of Rationality."

17. See Michael Dummett, *Truth and Other Enigmas* (Cambridge: Harvard University Press, 1978).

18. Michael Devitt, *Realism and Truth*, 2d ed. (Princeton: Princeton University Press, 1996).

19. See, for instance, Jaegwon Kim, *Philosophy of Mind* (Boulder: Westview Press, 1996), p. 10.

20. See Davidson, "On the Very Idea of a Conceptual Scheme," pp. 185–189. Compare Ian Hacking, "Language, Truth and Reason," in *Rationality and Relativism*, ed. Martin Hollis and Steven Lukes (Cambridge: MIT Press, 1982).

21. See Richard J. Bernstein, *Beyond Objectivism and Relativism: Science, Hermeneutics, and Praxis* (Philadelphia: University of Pennsylvania Press, 1983), and Hilary Putnam, "Two Philosophical Perspectives," in *Reason, Truth and History*.

22. Davidson, "On the Very Idea of a Conceptual Scheme," p. 190.

23. Ibid., p. 190.

24. See chap. 4 below. The idea of linking (or comparing) incommensurability with intranslatability already appears in Karl R. Popper, "Normal Science and Its Dangers," in *Criticism and the Growth of Knowledge*, ed. Imre Lakatos and Alan Musgrave (Cambridge: Cambridge University Press, 1970). Ramberg is particularly forceful on the issue; his remarks

center on the thought "that we cannot make sense of the idea of intranslatable languages," as he states in *Donald Davidson's Philosophy of Language*, p. 120. Of course he's right. He also finds "odd" (his term) Davidson's attributing to Kuhn "the idea that incommensurability implies intranslatability," pp. 125–126. He cites Kuhn's own remarks (as early as 1969) to show that this goes absolutely contrary to Kuhn's explicit views. Davidson's paper, "On the Very Idea," was published in 1974. For a sense of the reception of Kuhn's theory (itself admittedly contested), see Steve Fuller, *Thomas Kuhn: A Philosophical History for Our Times* (Chicago: University of Chicago Press, 2000).

25. Quine actually addresses Davidson's paper. See W. V. Quine, "On the Very Idea of a Third Dogma," in *Theories and Things* (Cambridge: Harvard University Press, 1981). What Quine makes clear is that, insofar as Davidson had Quine in mind as an advocate of the "third dogma," he misread him. When Quine distinguishes between "scheme" (read: "language") and "content," he means to treat the disjunction not in terms of a theory of truth but in terms of a theory of evidence—hence, as not even a "dogma" but a way of making scientific method "empirical" instead of being "a quest for internal coherence" (p. 39). It needs to be said as well that Quine agrees with Davidson's rejection of incommensurability (in the context of Kuhn's claims) though (of course) not for Davidson's reasons (see p. 42).

26. There is no conceivable way in which Quine's "indeterminacy" thesis could have excluded incommensurable parsings; hence, since the indeterminacy of translation is bound up with Quine's holism (and the use of "holophrastic sentences"), there is no way in which Quine could have escaped admitting some form of incommensurabilism. That he takes the perfunctory stand he does against (one supposes) Kuhnian incommensurabilism, in "On the Very Idea of a Third Dogma," suggests that there is more to the indeterminacy issue than meets the eye (or meets Quine's "surface irritations").

27. See Kuhn, *The Structure of Scientific Revolutions*, sec. 10. See also Peter Galison, chap. 1 in *Image and Logic: A Material Culture of Microphysics* (Chicago: University of Chicago Press, 1997).

28. I have relied here on the research of Melissa Bowerman, part of which I have now seen in published form. A brief but convenient summary appears in Melissa Bowerman, "Learning a Semantic System: What Role Do Cognitive Predispositions Play?" in *Language Acquisition: Core Readings*, ed. Paul Bloom (Cambridge: MIT Press, 1996), pp. 337–346.

29. See Noam Chomsky, *New Horizons in the Study of Language and Mind* (Cambridge: Cambridge University Press, 2000); see also chap. 1 above.

30. Bowerman, "Learning a Semantic System," pp. 339–343.

31. See Ludwig Wittgenstein, *On Certainty*, ed. G. E. M. Anscombe and G. H. von Wright, trans. Denis Paul and G. E. M. Anscombe (Oxford: Basil Blackwell, 1969). I take this drift toward historicism to be part of the essential upshot of Wittgenstein's later philosophy.

32. Robert Brandom's recent "inferentialism" is premised on a strong disjunction between sensory experience and enlanguaged belief or judgment, though it is also opposed (in favoring Wilfrid Sellars's well-known attack on empiricism) to the idea of the empirically "given." See Robert B. Brandom, introduction and chap. 1 in *Articulating Reasons: An Introduction to Inferentialism* (Cambridge: Harvard University Press, 2000). You must also bear in mind that any such formula is profoundly anti-Darwinian.

The argument—in Brandom, also in Richard Rorty—confuses or conflates the sense of brute "sensation" or "sensory experience" with what is constitutive of what is usually meant by "sensory perception." Where sensation and perception are distinguished in the requisite way, "sensation" designates a theoretically posited ingredient in perception: it is then never reported or reportable. The notion that sensory perception involves concepts is perfectly straightforward, even among languageless animals such as pigeons trained to discriminate geometric forms. On the strength of the human paradigm, we regard the pertinent (learned) pecking behavior of the trained pigeon as manifesting conceptual competence of some kind (however diminished). Concepts themselves are not empirically discerned, unless in a "theory-laden" way. See Richard Rorty, "The Very Idea of Human Answerability to the World: John McDowell's Version of Empiricism," in *Philosophical Papers*, vol. 3 (Cambridge: Cambridge University Press, 1998).

33. See Quine, "The Very Idea of a Third Dogma." Quine makes it quite clear that when he speaks of "surface irritation" (in perceptual contexts), there is—by the time he writes *Word and Object*—no "overtone of sensory quality": "I wrote explicitly [he says] of the triggering of sensory receptors," p. 40. Now, I must be frank to say that this strikes me as incompatible with what I've just reported Quine as holding regarding the "third dogma." I think it is a deep—Cartesian-like—mistake that could never justify redeeming what Quine says in favor of holophrastic sentences. Compare Gareth Evans, *The Varieties of Reference*, ed. John Mc-Dowell (Oxford: Clarendon, 1982), for instance, the tension between what is said on pp. 123 and 277.

34. See Eleanor Rosch, "Principles of Categorization," in *Cognition and Categorization*, ed. Eleanor Rosch and Barbara B. Lloyd (Hillsdale: Lawrence Erlbaum, 1978).

35. See W. V. Quine, *Word and Object* (Cambridge: MIT Press, 1960), sec. 15–16.

36. Jerry Fodor springs to mind as a "reluctant" Platonist of the innatist sort. See Jerry A. Fodor, *The Language of Thought* (New York: Thomas Y. Crowell, 1975). See also Jerrold J. Katz, *The Philosophy of Language* (New York: Harper and Row, 1966); and, for a sense of Chomsky's doubts about Fodor's thesis, see chap. 2 in Noam Chomsky, *On Nature and Language*, ed. Adriana Belletti and Luigi Rizzi (Cambridge: Cambridge University Press, 2002).

37. See Donald Davidson, "A Coherence Theory of Truth and Knowledge," in *Truth and Interpretation: Perspectives on the Philosophy of Donald Davidson*, ed. Ernest Lepore (Oxford: Basil Blackwell, 1986).

38. Paul Feyerabend, "Explanation, Reduction, and Empiricism," in *Scientific Explanation, Space and Time*, vol. 3 of Minnesota Studies in the Philosophy of Science, ed. Herbert Feigl and Grover Maxwell (Minneapolis: University of Minnesota Press, 1962), p. 82.

39. Davidson, "On the Very Idea of a Conceptual Scheme," pp. 188–189.

40. Ibid., p. 188.

41. Feyerabend, "Explanation, Reduction, and Empiricism," p. 89.

42. See note 3 above.

43. See chap. 3 below.

44. For the relevant background regarding Davidson's response to Kuhn and Feyerabend, see Donald Davidson, "The Structure and Content of Truth," *Journal of Philosophy* 87 (1990). This comprises Davidson's Dewey Lectures. See also Davidson, "A Coherence Theory of Truth and Knowledge" and Richard Rorty, "Pragmatism, Davidson and Truth," in the same volume.

45. Compare Pierre Duhem, *The Aim and Structure of Physical Theory*, trans. Philip P. Wiener (New York: Atheneum, 1962).

46. Thomas S. Kuhn, "Reflections on My Critics," in *Criticism and the Growth of Knowledge*, ed. Imre Lakatos and Alan Musgrave (Cambridge: Cambridge University Press, 1970), pp. 266–267.

47. Davidson, "The Very Idea of a Conceptual Scheme," p. 190.

48. Kuhn, "Reflections on My Critics," p. 266.

49. Ibid., p. 268.

50. Ibid., pp. 269–271.

51. Davidson, "On the Very Idea of a Conceptual Scheme," pp. 184, 189–190.

52. See Quine, "On the Very Idea of a Third Dogma."

53. See Benjamin Lee Whorf, "Language, Mind and Reality," in *Language, Thought, and Reality: Selected Writings of Benjamin Lee Whorf*, ed. John B. Carroll (Cambridge: MIT Press, 1956). See also W. V. Quine, "Two Dogmas of Empiricism." See also *From a Logical Point of View* (Cambridge: Harvard University Press, 1953).

54. Both Kuhn and Feyerabend would be unwilling to accept these simplifications. See Thomas S. Kuhn, "Commensurability, Comparability, Communicability" and "Reflections on My Critics," in *The Road Since Structure: Philosophical Essays, 1970–1973, with an Autobio-*

graphical Interview, ed. James Conant and John Haugeland (Chicago: University of Chicago Press, 2000). See also Imre Lakatos and Paul Feyerabend, *For and Against Method,* ed. Matteo Matterlini (Chicago: University of Chicago Press, 1999).

55. Ronald N. Giere, *Explaining Science: A Cognitive Approach* (Chicago: University of Chicago Press, 1988), pp. 36–37.

56. Ibid., p. 37.

57. There is an excellent appreciation of the matter in Alasdair MacIntyre, *Whose Justice? Which Rationality?* (Notre Dame: University of Notre Dame Press, 1988). Unfortunately, MacIntyre solves the problem by a piece of conceptual machinery that violates the very condition he himself invokes in explaining its seriousness.

58. Davidson, "On the Very Idea of a Conceptual Scheme," p. 183.

59. Ibid., p. 184.

60. Ibid., p. 188.

61. Ibid., p. 198.

62. See Hilary Putnam, *Renewing Philosophy* (Cambridge: Harvard University Press, 1992).

63. See Hilary Putnam, lectures 2 and 3 in *The Many Faces of Realism* (La Salle: Open Court, 1987). It is an irony several times compounded that Rorty, identifying himself as a pragmatist, a Deweyan in fact (though he deforms Dewey along the lines of his well-known postmodernism), claims that "'pragmatism' might also be called 'left-wing Kuhnianism.'" By this he means to retire all second-order legitimative questions. But if, against his own account, postmodernism proved to be conceptually irresponsible (as I would argue, that is, if *Rorty's* doctrine could be shown to entail *some* need for legitimation, even if historicized or consensual rather than privileged or universalist or necessary), then Rorty would have committed himself to relativism and incommensurabilism—against both Putnam and Davidson. I believe that would make good sense and would bear on Dewey's doctrine as well as Rorty's. From my own point of view, the entire matter may be put in a single line: viz., that pragmatism is committed to the flux—not chaos but a space in which all would-be structures are contingent, constructed, historicized, and open to relativistic and incommensurabilist constraints. See Richard Rorty, "Science as Solidarity," in *The Rhetoric of the Human Sciences,* ed. John Nelson, Allan Megill, and Donald McCloskey (Madison: University of Wisconsin Press, 1986).

64. I offer this chapter to Johannes Kranz (of the University of Graz), to make amends, insufficiently I would say, for having broken off communication without explanation. Kranz worked with me for a brief interval, during 1999. Our topics included the incommensurability issue—on which I think we made considerable progress together. But sometime after Kranz left, I found it impossible to keep up with a deluge of correspondence from him and others and simply ended all correspondence until I could return to it at a normal pace. I'm very sorry for that, but my silence went on too long to be able to explain it in any plausible way. I hope he will forgive me.

3. RESTORING THE BOND BETWEEN REALISM AND TRUTH

1. See Donald Davidson, "The Folly of Trying to Define Truth," *Journal of Philosophy* 43 (1996); reprinted in *Truth,* ed. Simon Blackburn and Keith Simmons (Oxford: Oxford University Press, 1999). Page references to Davidson's article are to this edition. But see note 3 to chapter 4, below. The use of terms like "deflationary" and "redundant" as distinct from "disquotational" are often misleading. Sometimes they are read as equivalent to "eliminable," in the sense that an analysis of "true" contributes nothing at all to the theory of meaning. But I don't think that is the case in either Alfred Tarski's theory or, I should say, in Frank Ramsey's: not in Tarski's, because of Tarski's commitment to extensionalist constraints; not in Ramsey's, because of Ramsey's pragmatist preferences. Davidson, I venture to say, is severely hobbled, because he treats "true" in strictly semantic terms, does not come to terms completely with Tarski's intention (as I explain), and is explicitly opposed to the pragmatist theory of truth. See F. P. Ramsey, "Facts and Propositions," in *The Foundations of Mathematics,* ed. R. B. Braithwaite (Paterson: Littlefield, Adams, 1960).

I take the occasion to note that the pragmatist account of truth cannot be plausibly regarded as a criterial account, as James often supposes in his embarrassing attempts to reconcile science and religion. James's characterization may still stand, though it must be read as an informal description of the generic function of any particular theory of truth, in virtue of which truth is seen to have an explanatory role precisely because of its *not* having any criterial standing. The explanatory role of truth rests with the kinds of reasons we provide for relying on one policy or another regarding the ascription of truth-values. All competing such accounts are explanatory in the pragmatist sense: viz., that "truth is one species of good." "The true [James says] is the name of whatever proves itself to be good in the way of belief, and good, too, for definite, assignable reasons." What counts here is simply that "true" answers to human interests, has a normative function relative to belief about the world when read in terms of our interests, practical in that sense, not open to any fixed criteria of validation in terms of a relationship between human cognizers and cognized world, subject to change and divergence in terms of changing interests, conjectures, history, experience, and the like, and not otherwise assignable any explanatory function. Such an account of truth is extremely modest: its best shot is that truth-values are assigned on constructivist grounds (and not otherwise). Hence, in explaining what "makes" beliefs and assertions true, we fall back to explaining why we choose this rather than that policy of confirmation and disconfirmation applied to the claims in question. See William James, "What Pragmatism Means," in *Pragmatism: A New Name for Some Old Ways of Thinking* (New York: Longmans Green, 1907). The reasonableness of viewing matters thus shows how unnecessary Davidson's excessive caution is.

2. See Paul Horwich, "The Minimalist Conception of Truth," in *Truth*. This is a slightly revised version of the postscript to Paul Horwich, *Truth*, 2d ed. (Oxford: Oxford University Press, 1998). References are to the Blackburn and Simmons edition cited above.

3. See Richard Rorty, "Pragmatism, Davidson and Truth," in *Truth* (Oxford: Oxford University Press, 1999), which appeared originally in *Truth and Interpretation: Perspectives on the Philosophy of Donald Davidson,* ed. Ernest Lepore (Oxford: Basil Blackwell, 1986). References to Rorty's article are to the Lepore edition. Also see Richard Rorty, "Is Truth a Goal of Inquiry? Donald Davidson versus Crispin Wright," in *Philosophical Papers*, vol. 3 (Cambridge: Cambridge University Press, 1998).

4. See G. W. F. Hegel, *Phenomenology of Spirit*, trans. A. V. Miller (Oxford: Oxford University Press, 1977); also [G. W. F. Hegel,] *Hegel's Philosophy of Mind; Being Part Three of the Encyclopedia of the Philosophical Sciences (1830),* trans. William Wallace, *together with the Zusätze in Boumann's text (1845),* trans. A. V. Miller (Oxford: Clarendon, 1971).

5. The most sustained recent attempt to construe the acquisition of linguistic competence *from* the aggregated assent of individual agents *not yet enlanguaged*—in effect, by way of an original contract or convention—appears in Margaret Gilbert, *On Social Facts* (London: Routledge and Kegan Paul, 1989). (The sketch is noticeably crude.) I'm bound to say that it completely fails to examine the nature of *collective* attributes, which seem to me to be distinctive of the cultural world and to provide the essential clue to the emergent, irreducible nature of language, culture, and history. I don't believe an adequate account of language—hence, an adequate account of what is entailed in the epistemological role of "true"—can be given without an analysis of the *gemeinschaftlich* (collective and communal) and *gesellschaftlich* (aggregative and cooperative) aspects of human society. I take these to be indissolubly co-functioning features of every process of culturally significant societal life, which, to be sure, may be weighted in different ways in one society or another. They are fully present but largely implicit in Hegel's account of *Geist* (and history). A first pass at an analysis—but only barely—may be glimpsed in the classic study by Ferdinand Tönnies, *Community and Civil Society*, ed. Jose Harris, trans. Jose Harris and Margaret Hollis (Cambridge: Cambridge University Press, 2001). To put the point diagnostically, I would say that the linkage between the two is hardly present in more than a "formal" sense in Wittgenstein's *Investigations* and is all but absent from McDowell's *Mind and World*, that is, in two important accounts opposed to modern Carte-

sianism. For a sense of recent readings of Hegel's theory of the relationship between human agents and society, see Charles Taylor, "Hegel and the Philosophy of Action" and A. S. Walton, "Hegel: Individual Agency and Social Context," both in *Hegel's Philosophy of Action,* ed. Lawrence S. Stepelevich and David Lamb (Atlantic Highlands: Humanities, 1983).

6. The latter term is Horwich's and is used in a strict and delimited sense. See Horwich, "The Minimalist Conception of Truth," p. 239.

7. Ludwig Wittgenstein, *Tractatus Logico-Philosphicus,* trans. D. F. Pears and B. F. McGuinness, rev. ed. (London: Routledge and Kegan Paul, 1972).

8. Ludwig Wittgenstein, *Notebooks 1914–1916,* ed. G. H. von Wright and G. E. M. Anscombe, trans. G. E. M. Anscombe, 2d ed. (Oxford: Basil Blackwell, 1961), p. 9e (6 October 1914).

9. Max Black, *A Companion to Wittgenstein's 'Tractatus'* (Ithaca: Cornell University Press, 1964), p. 78.

10. Wittgenstein, *Notebooks 1914–1916,* "Notes on Logic" (Appendix 1), p. 94. Wittgenstein actually explains his point more forcefully in "Notes Dictated to G. E. Moore in Norway" (April 1914), included as Appendix 2 in the *Notebooks.* There he says: "That a proposition has a relation (in wide sense) to Reality, other than that of *Bedeutung,* is shown by the fact that you can understand it when you don't know the *Bedeutung,* i.e. don't know whether it is true or false. Let us express this by saying 'it has *sense*' (*Sinn*)," p. 111. I take this to be an important challenge.

11. Aristotle, *Metaphysics* Gamma, 1011b, trans. W. D. Ross, in *The Complete Works of Aristotle,* ed. Jonathan Barnes, vol. 2 (Princeton: Princeton University Press, 1984).

12. John McDowell, *Mind and World* (Cambridge: Harvard University Press, 1994, 1996), pp. xi–xii.

13. For an analysis of Dewey's theory, see Joseph Margolis, chaps. 3 and 4 in *Reinventing Pragmatism: American Philosophy at the End of the Twentieth Century* (Ithaca: Cornell University Press, 2002).

14. Richard Rorty, "The Very Idea of Human Answerability to the World: John McDowell's Version of Empiricism," in *Philosophical Papers,* 3:145.

15. Rorty, "Pragmatism, Davidson and Truth," p. 335.

16. I take the liberty here of drawing attention to the important fact that Wittgenstein's use of "zeigt" is akin to, but also utterly unlike, the use of "aletheia" in Heidegger's account of truth—notably associated with Heidegger's analysis of a change in Plato's theory of truth. *Aletheia,* in Heidegger, is completely non-propositional and never systematically or explicitly linked with the propositional use of "true." (Which is Wittgenstein's intention regarding "zeigt.") I would say that Heidegger's use is merely "formal" on the "metaphysical" side, in a sense analogous to the sense in which McDowell's use of "correctly" is entirely formal on the "epistemological" side. An adequate theory of truth must overcome what is formal in "zeigt" and "aletheia" in a way that is at once semantic, epistemological, and metaphysical. I cannot see how, frankly, that can be accomplished in our post-Kantian world in any way that fails to come to terms with Hegel's instruction. That, precisely, is what I find rewarding in Dewey's rather modest proposal. For an illuminating analysis of Heidegger's account of truth, which demonstrates (inadvertently) the compensating one-sidedness of recent continental philosophy (occupied with the question of truth), see Robert Bernasconi, *The Question of Language in Heidegger's History of Being* (Atlantic Highlands: Humanities Press International, 1985). I have examined Heidegger's nearly impenetrable account of *aletheia* in an article whose publication is pending, titled "Heidegger on Truth and Being."

17. W. V. Quine, *Philosophy of Logic* (Englewood Cliffs: Prentice-Hall, 1970), p. 12. This qualifies the sense in which Quine is said (often enough) to subscribe to a deflationary theory of truth. Quine does admit a "deflationary" use of "true" (in effect, the disquotational use); but he is not a deflationist because he is not a mere disquotationalist. I believe this amounts to a reasonable reading of Gary Ebb's strong essay, "Truth and Trans-theoretical Terms," in *Hilary Putnam: Pragmatism and Realism,* ed. James Conant and Urszula M. Żegleń (London: Rout-

ledge, 2002), which Putnam endorses. See below, chap. 4, note 22. The issue ultimately bears on the meaning of Quine's "indeterminacy of translation" thesis and Putnam's pluralist reading of realism.

18. Quine seems to have gradually changed his mind about how to regard his notion of "the indeterminacy of translation," in terms of what the right linkage is between the indeterminacy (or "inscrutability") of reference and the indeterminacy of meaning. I admit the importance of the difference, though I take the two issues to be finally inseparable. Alex Orenstein has apparently elicited concessions along these lines from Quine himself. See his chap. 6 in *W. V. Quine* (Princeton: Princeton University Press, 2002). I don't believe any adjustments here (on Quine's part) affect my discussion of the problem. But perhaps I'm mistaken. See, further, chapter 4, below. I venture to suggest that, despite large differences in orientation, Quine was concerned to elucidate the fuller meaning of "true" in just the sense I mark in Wittgenstein and Heidegger, which of course is already Plato's concern.

19. See Rorty, "Pragmatism, Davidson and Truth."

20. Rorty, "The Very Idea of Human Answerability to the World: John McDowell's Version of Empiricism," p. 139.

21. Ibid., p. 147.

22. Wilfrid Sellars, "The Language of Theories," in *Science, Perception and Reality* (London: Routledge and Kegan Paul, 1963), p. 126.

23. Rorty, "The Very Idea of Human Answerability to the World: McDowell's Version of Empiricism," p. 144.

24. Donald Davidson, "A Coherence Theory of Truth and Knowledge," in *Truth and Interpretation: Perspectives on the Philosophy of Donald Davidson* (Oxford: Basil Blackwell, 1986), p. 308.

25. Davidson, "A Coherence Theory of Truth and Knowledge," p. 308.

26. Davidson, "The Folly of Trying to Define Truth," pp. 312–314.

27. See Alfred Tarski, "The Concept of Truth in Formalized Languages," in *Logic, Semantics, Metamathematics,* ed. John Corcoran, trans. J. H. Woodger, 2d ed.(Indianapolis: Hackett, 1983), as well as the postscript.

28. See Donald Davidson, "Afterthoughts, 1987," appended to a reprinting of "A Coherence Theory of Truth and Knowledge," in *Reading Rorty: Critical Responses to Philosophy and the Mirror of Nature (and Beyond)*, ed. Alan R. Malachowski (Oxford: Blackwell, 1990), p. 135.

29. Davidson, "Afterthoughts, 1987," p. 135.

30. Davidson, "The Folly of Trying to Define Truth," p. 319.

31. This is Horwich's formulation. See Horwich, "The Minimalist Conception of Truth," pp. 249–250.

32. Horwich goes to great lengths to show how, if "propositions" are admitted, one can formulate a coherent account of understanding propositions that does not invoke the concept of truth. See Horwich, "The Minimalist Conception of Truth," pp. 247–250.

33. See Anil Gupta, "A Critique of Deflationism," in *Truth* (Oxford: Oxford University Press, 1999), p. 282; see also Hilary Putnam, "On Truth," in *Words and Life,* ed. James Conant (Cambridge: Harvard University Press, 1994).

34. Davidson, "The Folly of Trying to Define Truth," p. 309.

35. See Donald Davidson, "Mental Events," *Essays on Actions and Events* (Oxford: Clarendon, 1980).

36. See Davidson, "A Coherence Theory of Truth and Knowledge," pp. 309–310.

37. See Rorty, "Pragmatism, Davidson and Truth."

38. Davidson, "A Coherence Theory of Truth and Knowledge," p. 311.

39. Ibid., p. 312.

40. See Rorty, "Pragmatism, Davidson and Truth."

41. See Gupta, "A Critique of Deflationism," p. 282.

42. See Hilary Putnam, "Realism and Reason," in *Meaning and the Moral Sciences* (London: Routledge and Kegan Paul, 1978).

43. Hegel, introduction to *Phenomenology of Spirit,* sec. 85.

44. Donald Davidson, "Epistemology and Truth," in *Subjective, Intersubjective, Objective* (Oxford: Clarendon, 2001), p. 188.

4. THE UNRAVELING OF SCIENTISM

1. The best impression (regarding the early reception of Wittgenstein) of the mixture of guarded respect, admiration, openness, and confusion at having to compare the *Tractatus* and the *Investigations* can be gathered from the excellent near-contemporary account (1957) given by John Passmore in his indispensable *A Hundred Years of Philosophy* (London: Duckworth, 1957). Passmore's review is scattered over several chapters. But he remarks, in a footnote to his discussion of the *Tractatus:* "What follows must be read as an interim report. Important Wittgenstein manuscripts, which can be expected to throw considerable light on the *Tracta-tus,* are now being prepared for publication" (p. 351n). When he turns, in chapter 18, to bring us up to date on the reception of the *Investigations* (1953), the principal impression is that Wittgenstein did indeed move his contemporaries (particularly in England and particularly at Oxford) to turn their inquiries in a "therapeutic" direction ("relieving" us of conceptual disorders due to the practice of philosophy itself) and to uniting their steady academic exercises with the study of the roots of such work in the analysis of the practice of natural-language discourse.

Thus, Passmore reports Gilbert Ryle's "conversion [around 1931]—although, he [Ryle] said, a reluctant one—to the view that the task of philosophy is 'the detection of the sources in linguistic idioms of recurrent misconstructions and absurd theories'," p. 440. This is not to say that Ryle was a Wittgensteinian or that Wittgenstein was an "ordinary-language" philosopher. But it begins to focus the sense in which, after Wittgenstein returned to Cambridge, in 1929, after a period of "silence" following the publication of the *Tractatus,* other currents converged with Wittgenstein's dissatisfaction with the *Tractatus* (and Russellian "logical atomism")—not very distant from Wittgenstein's having come to think that "philosophers . . . had made the mistake of trying to model their activities on those of science—as, indeed, the very phrase 'logical atomism' suggests," p. 426.

Passmore then collects a considerable number of influential British philosophers who may (for all he can guess at the moment of writing) eclipse Wittgenstein himself and lead philosophy in another direction. Among these, he discusses John Wisdom, Gilbert Ryle, J. L. Austin, P. F. Strawson, and Friedrich Waismann. The impression given is that we cannot say what strong direction philosophy will take or whether Wittgenstein will remain an important figure. You must remember that, at the time of Passmore's writing, Quine had not yet published *Word and Object* (1960) and the American wave of "analytic philosophy" had not yet achieved its characteristic form. The salient topic is obviously that of the viability of the scientisms of the day.

2. This may seem to force a comparison between Wittgenstein's *Kehre* and Martin Heidegger's announced *Kehre* in moving from *Sein und Zeit* (1927) to what the "Letter on Humanism" (1946) ushered in. But the contrast between Wittgenstein and Heidegger does play a very large role—not entirely subterranean, of course—in the appraisal of the entire trajectory of twentieth-century Eurocentric philosophy. Both have been claimed as the single most important genius of twentieth-century philosophy.

3. I take the occasion to note that F. P. Ramsey, who seems to have influenced Wittgenstein profoundly in the formulation of both the revised German and English rendering of the *Tractatus,* leading to the *Investigations,* also provides an important clue to a radically different account of meaning and truth (from the line of reflection that accords with Wittgenstein's thinking in both the *Tractatus* and *Investigations*): namely, a fairly explicit version of a pragmatist theory of meaning (*a fortiori,* truth) seemingly strongly influenced by his (Ramsey's) reading of Charles Sanders Peirce's "The Fixation of Belief" and "How to Make Our Ideas Clear," though more immediately by his appreciation of Bertrand Russell's "pragmatism" (Ramsey's term). The details and the persuasiveness of Ramsey's thought on these issues are

made admirably clear in Nils-Eric Sahlin, *The Philosophy of F. P. Ramsey* (Cambridge: Cambridge University Press, 1990); see especially chap. 2. Sahlin provides further details in his "'He is no good for my work'[:] On the Philosophical Relations between Ramsey and Wittgenstein," *Poznań Studies in the Philosophy of the Sciences and the Humanities* 51 (1997).

The strategic intuition seems to be this: the theory of meaning cannot be confined in purely semantic or linguistic terms, is grounded rather in practical life—hence, should be construed in terms of beliefs (and their proper analysis). Ramsey therefore sought an account of belief that did not presuppose the concept of truth (*The Philosophy of F. P. Ramsey*, p. 56). This begins to show why what is now called the disquotational theory of truth needs to be carefully distinguished from the so-called redundancy theory. Ramsey's point is *not* that "true" is never more than semantically redundant but that the key to a correct account of truth is not primarily semantic at all but pragmatist, that is, developed along the lines of how an agent is poised to act on his pertinent beliefs (in Peirce's sense). One sees here how utterly different Ramsey's reasoning is from, say, Donald Davidson's somewhat self-baffling reflections. To favor Ramsey is, I think, to set Davidson's views completely aside (particularly his rejection of James's problematic continuation of Peirce's line of thought). But what is interesting in the present context is the importance of a *pragmatist* challenge to both the *Tractatus* and the *Investigations*, where the *Investigations* is misleadingly taken to be "pragmatist" by, say, Richard Rorty. See, chapter 3, above. The principal essay of Ramsey's to consider is "Facts and Propositions," in *Philosophical Papers*, ed. D. H. Mellor (Cambridge: Cambridge University Press, 1990). I do agree, however—more than merely concede—that Wittgenstein's *Investigations* is not confined to the semantic; though Ramsey, of course, had the advantage of actually speaking with Wittgenstein about the matter.

4. Richard Rorty, introduction to *Empiricism and the Philosophy of Mind*, by Wilfrid Sellars (Cambridge: Harvard University Press, 1997), p. 1.

5. Richard Rorty, introduction to *The Linguistic Turn: Recent Essays in Philosophical Method* (Chicago: University of Chicago Press, 1967).

6. Rorty, introduction to *Empiricism and the Philosophy of Mind*, pp. 1–2.

7. Ludwig Wittgenstein, *Tractatus Logico-Philosophicus*, trans. by D. F. Pears and B. F. McGuiness, 2d ed. (London: Routledge and Kegan Paul, 1972), 6.45.

8. See Robert B. Brandom, *Making It Explicit: Reasoning, Representing, and Discursive Commitment* (Cambridge: Harvard University Press, 1994); and Rorty, introduction to *Empiricism and the Philosophy of Mind*. See also Richard Rorty, "Robert Brandom on Social Practices and Representations," in *Philosophical Papers*, vol. 3 (Cambridge: Cambridge University Press, 1998).

9. I am aware that, in speaking of extensionalism (or "extensionality") as loosely as I do, readers may wish for a more pointed account of what the concept includes and excludes. I don't believe there is any simple or straightforward answer to such a request. For example, Quine would emphasize the elimination of "intensional" contexts. See, for pertinent details, Alex Orenstein, chap. 7 in *W. V. Quine* (Princeton: Princeton University Press, 2002). By contrast, Carnap, because of his view of the nature of mathematics in the context of physics, would not be willing to restrict an answer to the question of extensionalism to anything like Quine's adherence to first-order logic. This clearly bears on Quine and Carnap's disagreement regarding analyticity. See note 2 in my introduction to this book, First Word. I hope it will be sufficient to say, first, that the notion is flexible in terms of its own extension and that, second, it permits, where pertinent, any of the obvious intentions of figures like Russell, Frege, Wittgenstein, Carnap, and Quine (and lesser figures, for that matter, who, like Dennett and Churchland, have some form of extreme reductionism or eliminativism in mind). Of course, standard constraints like the substitutivity of identicals will always be included; but apart from such constraints, different, even opposed, conceptions of logic ought to be consulted (for instance, logicist and intuitionistic conceptions).

10. W. V. Quine, *Word and Object* (Cambridge: MIT Press, 1960), sec. 56.

11. See W. V. Quine, "Two Dogmas of Empiricism," in *From a Logical Point of View* (Cambridge: Harvard University Press, 1953).

12. See First Word, note 3, above.

13. Quine reports Davidson as trying to dissuade him on the matter of the "stimulus," in his own (Davidson's) behalf. See W. V. Quine, *Pursuit of Truth,* rev. ed. (Cambridge: Harvard University Press, 1992), pp. 41, 42, 44; but he resisted, he says, because of epistemological concerns. See also Thomas S. Kuhn, *The Structure of Scientific Revolutions,* 2d ed. enlarged (Chicago: University of Chicago Press, 1970); and "Second Thoughts on Paradigms," in *The Essential Tension: Selected Studies in Scientific Tradition and Change* (Chicago: University of Chicago Press, 1977), pp. 308–309.

14. Quine, *Pursuit of Truth,* pp. 2–3.

15. Ibid., chap. 3 and p. 41. On the expression "fact of the matter," see W. V. Quine, *Theories and Things* (Cambridge: Harvard University Press, 1981), p. 23.

16. W. V. Quine, "Reply to Jules Vuillemin," in *The Philosophy of W. V. Quine,* ed. Lewis Edwin Hahn and Paul Arthur Schilpp (La Salle: Open Court, 1986), p. 620. See, also, Quine's reply to an overstatement on the issue by Rorty, in his "Let Me Accentuate the Positive," in *Reading Rorty: Critical Responses to Philosophy and the Mirror of Nature (and Beyond),* ed. Alan R. Malachowski (Oxford: Blackwell, 1990), p. 117. See, also, Kuhn's friendly concern about Quine's epistemic intentions regarding "stimulations": Thomas S. Kuhn, "Reflections on My Critics," in *Criticism and the Growth of Knowledge,* ed. Imre Lakatos and Alan Musgrave (Cambridge: Cambridge University Press, 1970), pp. 266–269.

17. See Donald Davidson, "On the Very Idea of a Conceptual Scheme," in *Inquiries into Truth and Interpretation* (Oxford: Clarendon, 1984); also, "A Coherence Theory of Truth and Knowledge," in *Truth and Interpretation: Perspectives on the Philosophy of Donald Davidson.*

18. See chap. 2 above.

19. See Donald Davidson, *Subjective, Intersubjective, Objective* (Oxford: Clarendon, 2001), in particular, the papers of the first section of the book, under the head Subjective.

20. Quine, "Reply to Jules Vuillemin," p. 622.

21. Ibid., p. 620.

22. See, further, W. V. Quine, "Reply to Hilary Putnam," in *The Philosophy of W. V. Quine;* and Hilary Putnam, "Meaning Holism," in the same volume.

Quite recently, Putnam has added some extremely telling observations about Quine's theory in a short response, "Comments on Gary Ebb's paper," in *Hilary Putnam: Pragmatism and Realism,* ed. James Conant and Urszula M. Żegleń (London: Routledge, 2002). I take the liberty of citing his comments here. First, with regard to Quine's notion of "radical translation," Putnam notes that "the behaviorist story makes no real sense of practices of agreement and disagreement" (p. 186). Second, with regard to the "indeterminacy of translation" and, accordingly, with regard to the "inscrutability of reference" (on nearly any reading), he remarks, quite correctly, that "Quine is an eliminativist with respect to reference" (p. 186). And, third, with regard to "holophrastic sentences," Putnam maintains that, at least up to the first edition of *The Philosophy of W. V. Quine,* ed. Lewis Hahn and Arthur Schilpp (La Salle: Open Court, 1988), Quine "thought that observation sentences had determinate meaning *holophrastically.* Thus 'gavagai' has the same holophrastic meaning as 'A rabbit [is] over there'. It is only the reference of the parts that is indeterminate. But as wholes, the two sentences are, so to speak, *equivalent*" (p. 186). This appears to be inconsistent with the indeterminacy thesis and signifies a potentially serious confusion on Quine's part. Subsequently, he notes, "Quine admitted an indeterminacy affecting even the holophrastic meaning of observation sentences" (p. 187). See W. V. Quine, "In Praise of Observation Sentences with Appendix on Neural Intake," *Journal of Philosophy* 90 (1993); mentioned by Putnam.

I agree with Putnam's findings; but I cannot see how, if those findings stand, anything can be salvaged from Quine's account of "radical translation" and the "indeterminacy of translation." The idea that holophrastic sentences, taken pair-wise could be equivalent, though when taken singly, could be indeterminate, strikes me as incoherent. Accordingly, I must add that it is also hard to see how Putnam could have confined his own pluralism (the pluralist feature of his realism) in the referential way he does; he surely must have been aware of the difficulty of fixing reference, and so would have realized that the "indeterminacy" of reference would have exposed the limited range of his defense of his own realism in a way not altogether unrelated to Quine's difficulty (though cast in entirely different terms). Frankly, I think Putnam would not have been able to outflank or neutralize the threat of relativism and incommensurabilism in the relaxed way he believes he has. See chap. 2, above.

23. See Quine, *Word and Object,* sec. 15–16.

24. Ibid., p. 28.

25. Ibid., pp. 28–29.

26. Ibid., pp. 32–33.

27. Quine, *Word and Object,* p. 92. See, further, W. V. Quine, *The Roots of Reference* (La Salle: Open Court, 1974).

28. See Otto Neurath, "Protocol Sentences," trans. George Schick, in *Logical Positivism,* ed. A. J. Ayer (Glencoe: Free Press, 1959).

29. Compare Pierre Duhem, *The Aim and Structure of Physical Theory,* trans. Philip P. Wiener (New York: Atheneum, 1962); and W. V. Quine, "Two Dogmas of Empiricism," in *From a Logical Point of View* (Cambridge: Harvard University Press, 1953) and *Word and Object.*

30. See Davidson, "A Coherence Theory of Truth and Knowledge" and "On the Very Idea of a Conceptual Scheme."

31. See Wilfrid Sellars, *Science, Perception and Reality* (London: Routledge and Kegan Paul, 1963).

32. See Wilfrid Sellars, "Empiricism and the Philosophy of Mind," in *Science, Perception and Reality* (London: Routledge and Kegan Paul, 1963), also published as a separate monograph.

33. See, for instance, Richard Rorty, "The Very Idea of Human Answerability to the World: John McDowell's Version of Empiricism," in *Philosophical Papers,* vol. 3 (Cambridge: Cambridge University Press, 1998). In a very recent remark, McDowell supports a line of objection, effectively against Rorty's comment, that accords with my own reading of Rorty. See John McDowell, "Responses," in *Reading McDowell on Mind and World,* ed. Nicholas H. Smith (London: Routledge, 2002), p. 275: "answerability to the world and answerability to each other have to be understood together"—this is directed against Brandom. See also Joseph Margolis, chap. 2 in *Reinventing Pragmatism: American Philosophy at the End of the Twentieth Century* (Ithaca: Cornell University Press, 2002).

34. See Quine, *From a Logical Point of View.*

35. For an account of the entire episode, see my *Reinventing Pragmatism.*

36. The most careful recent discussion of the "Duhem/Quine thesis" appears in Jules Vuillemin, "On Duhem's and Quine's Theses," in *The Philosophy of W. V. Quine,* ed. Lewis Edwin Hahn and Paul Arthur Schilpp (La Salle: Open Court, 1986). Quine seems quite respectful of Vuillemin's account.

37. For one of the best-known discussions of Quine's (and Davidson's) holisms, see Jerry Fodor and Ernest Lepore, chaps. 2 and 3 in *Holism: A Shopper's Guide* (Oxford: Blackwell, 1992). I have not yet pursued, here, Fodor and Lepore's treatment of either one for at least two reasons: first, because they restrict their own account to the analysis of the analytic/synthetic question (in the "Two Dogmas" paper)—they say nothing further about *Word and Object* or *Pursuit of Truth;* and, second, because their formulations ignore the strong likelihood that, on an external holist commitment, epistemological, metaphysical, and semantic questions would have to be treated constructively.

Fodor and Lepore address and oppose semantic holism, primarily. But what Quine grasped (which they ignore) was the need to fall back to a ramified holism that would unite semantic, epistemological, and metaphysical considerations coherently and constructively. They collect the internal difficulties of one and another version of *semantic* holism, but they never examine the resources of the constructivist (constructive realist) option, which (for example) does not really appear in the "Two Dogmas" paper, though it does in *Word and Object*. They champion the thesis that "semantic properties are typically punctate," that is, not holistic (p. 206); and they suppose that their survey shows that the punctate thesis may well be valid. But they neglect to examine the matter in the space in which Quine's arguments (and those of others) *might be epistemologically required*. What they say, therefore, is largely irrelevant to the grander issues holism raises. See, for instance, Quine's treatment of "ontological relativity," in W. V. Quine, *Ontological Relativity and Other Essays* (New York: Columbia University Press, 1969), for example regarding "charity," p. 46. Nevertheless, I return to Fodor and Lepore's views toward the end of this account.

38. See Quine, *Word and Object*, p. 27.

39. Ibid.

40. Ibid., p. 53.

41. See Kuhn, *The Structure of Scientific Revolutions*, sec. 10.

42. See, for instance, Donald Davidson, "Afterthoughts, 1987," appended to the reprinting of "A Coherence Theory of Truth and Knowledge," in *Reading Rorty: Critical Responses to Philosophy and the Mirror of Nature (and Beyond)*, ed. Alan R. Malachowski (Oxford: Blackwell, 1990).

43. I may perhaps add here that sometime after the first annual University of Western Ontario Philosophy Colloquium, in 1966, at which Quine was to be the featured speaker (he was caught in a snow storm in Buffalo and couldn't complete his flight), he was kind enough to start up a small correspondence with me on the basis of a few papers I had written on *Word and Object*. I had in fact given them to Davidson (who also attended the conference), on Davidson's invitation. I have no idea whether Quine actually received those papers—they were fledgling efforts—but I suppose he must have. There were three exchanges and the correspondence broke off abruptly (I never learned the reason) when, in my last letter, I pressed the idea that word and sentence were correlative distinctions with regard to natural language and that one-word sentences did not affect the matter. The idea was that the holism of *Word and Object* risked incoherence. Quine never relented; in fact, he stiffened his commitment in *Pursuit of Truth*. But I cannot see that he ever answered the objection, and it still seems fatal to me.

44. Quine, *Pursuit of Truth*, p. 5.

45. Ibid., pp. 2, 6, 7.

46. W. V. Quine, "Empirical Content," in *Theories and Things* (Cambridge: Harvard University Press, 1981), p. 26.

47. Quine, *Pursuit of Truth*, p. 7.

48. Ibid., p. 8.

49. Ibid.

50. See Quine, *Word and Object*, sec. 15–16.

51. Ibid., p. 31, for instance.

52. See Quine, *Pursuit of Truth*, pp. 37–38.

53. Ibid. In *Word and Object* (p. 28), Quine says, speaking of "radical translation": "I shall imagine that all help of interpreters is excluded." Compare Quine, "Ontological Relativity," especially pp. 26–27. Quine misleads us, I'm afraid, about the sense of the line he cites from Dewey: "Meaning . . . is not a psychic existence; it is primarily a property of behavior." The line appears in John Dewey, *Experience and Nature* (New York: Dover, 1958), p. 179. It's quite remarkable that, on the same page, Dewey also uses the term "stimulus" in an altogether different sense from Quine's: "the stimulus [in a situation involving a certain A and B—A asks B to bring him a flower—a situation that clearly resembles the sort of cases Quine treats in terms of radical translation] is [Dewey says] B's anticipatory share in the consummation of a transaction in which both [A and B] participate." The sense of the context provided on pp. 178–180 makes it quite clear that Dewey means to link first-person avowals with observable behavior but not to reduce the first in behaviorist terms or to eliminate first-person dis-

course in favor of third-person discourse. I find it additionally intriguing that Dennett, who acknowledges his having been influenced by Quine, published *Content and Consciousness* in 1969. Dennett of course professes to believe (in *Consciousness Explained,* for instance) that Science somehow requires that we abandon first-person discourse. I pick up the thread of this idea later in the present chapter.

54. Quine, *Word and Object,* p. 3.

55. Ibid., p. 35.

56. It is worth comparing Daniel Dennett's philosophical prejudice against admitting first-person avowals of one's own experience, in the name of Science. See Daniel C. Dennett, chap. 4 in *Consciousness Explained* (Boston: Little, Brown, 1991).

But that cannot be more than the opportunistic part of the story—the lesser part, the part that depends on conceding the effective force of Quine's account, or of another like it. The evidence now assembled, however, demonstrates as well as possible, that Quine nowhere succeeds in capturing the high ground for his own large scientist program. Once you see how much attention Quine pays to the problem of *demarcating* the extensionally "safe" domain within which all the important issues are supposed to yield to a favorable resolution—in effect, the demarcation between "internal" and "external" questions—you cannot fail to see the obvious sense in which Davidson's entire game is devoted to defining the canonical boundaries with greater caution than Quine shows—but without any firmer arguments!

Still, to admit the reasonableness of reading both Quine and Davidson in this tendentious way is to see at once the deeper sense in which Quine's own project remains fixed at the same point at which, even more disastrously, Carnap attempted to demarcate, quite late in his career, a principled division between what he explicitly calls "internal questions" and "external questions." There is no conceivable way, I submit, of recovering Carnap's distinction coherently: "internal questions" prove to be completely aimless and arbitrary, detached from "external questions"; "external questions" prove to be completely pointless and meaningless, detached from "internal questions"; and the integration of the two proves to be illicit and inadmissible, on Carnap's theory! In a very real sense, therefore, there is a perfectly straightforward line of descent, that runs from Carnap to Quine to Davidson, that confirms the fixity of the single most influential version of scientism that the entire twentieth century can boast, that, nevertheless, never succeeds in defining its own pale of legitimacy coherently. To my mind, the entire exercise may be more than plausibly read as a weak recapitulation of the *agon* that runs from Descartes to Kant—that is finally put to rest (in its broadest terms) by Hegel. We have come full circle. See, further, Rudolf Carnap, "Empiricism, Semantics, and Ontology," in *Meaning and Necessity,* 2d ed. enlarged; and Wolfgang Stegmüller, "Ontology and Analyticity," in *Collected Papers on Epistemology, Philosophy of Science and History of Philosophy,* vol. 1 (Dordrecht: D. Reidel, 1977), especially pp. 220–223. Stegmüller draws on a notably early paper of Quine's, "On Carnap's View on Ontology" (1951), in *The Ways of Paradox and Other Essays* (New York: Random House, 1966). Predictably, Quine repudiates Carnap's distinction between internal and external questions—in "Ontological Relativity."

57. Quine, *Word and Object,* p. 83.

58. Quine, *Pursuit of Truth,* p. 62.

59. See, for instance, Donald Davidson, "Radical Interpretation," in *Inquiries into Truth and Interpretation* (Oxford: Clarendon, 1984).

60. See Donald Davidson, "Mental Events," in *Essays on Actions and Events* (Oxford: Clarendon, 1984).

61. Quine, *Pursuit of Truth,* p. 1.

62. See, for instance, Quine's notorious attempt to treat proper names as predicates, *Word and Object,* sec. 37–38.

63. See Newton Garver, chap. 15 in *This Complicated Form of Life: Essays on Wittgenstein* (La Salle: Open Court, 1994).

64. Ludwig Wittgenstein, *Philosophical Investigations,* trans. G. E. M. Anscombe (New

York: Macmillan, 1953), sec. 241, 242, 481. Wittgenstein italicizes only *sagen* (say) and *Sprache* (language). I have italicized the rest of the thought for easy reference.

65. For a sense of the most prominent dispute—predictably, a dispute about skepticism—occasioned by Wittgenstein's view of "rules" in the context of language games and the *Lebensform*, see Saul A. Kripke, *Wittgenstein on Rules and Private Language: An Elementary Exposition* (Oxford: Basil Blackwell, 1982); and G. P. Baker and P. M. S. Hacker, *Skepticism, Rules and Language* (Oxford: Basil Blackwell, 1984).

66. See Carl G. Hempel, "Empiricist Criteria of Cognitive Significance: Problems and Changes" and "Postscript (1964) on Cognitive Significance," in *Aspects of Scientific Explanation and Other Essays in the Philosophy of Science* (New York: Free Press, 1965). For a specimen of an entirely different but extremely telling sort—one regarding an extensionalist and materialist account of real "possibility," ultimately based (let it be noted) on the atomism of Wittgenstein's *Tractatus*—see D. M. Armstrong, "The Nature of Possibility," *Canadian Journal of Philosophy* 16 (1986). Armstrong's account actually fails to consider the implications of there not being any atomic facts to rely on, hence no "combinatorial" (that is, extensional) strategy to invoke in defining possibility relative to actuality, and no reason to suppose that emergence even in physical and biological terms could be managed combinatorily. Wittgenstein saw the difficulties of his own (Tractarian) model when F. P. Ramsey identified the insuperable puzzle of the color problem. But of course if the notion of real possibility cannot be convincingly managed along extensionalist lines, then that would be another nail in scientism's coffin.

67. Davidson, "Radical Interpretation," pp. 129–130.

68. Donald Davidson, "Reply to Foster," in *Inquiries into Truth and Interpretation* (Oxford: Clarendon, 1984), p. 176.

69. See, for instance, Jaegwon Kim, *Supervenience and Mind: Selected Philosophical Essays* (Cambridge: Cambridge University Press, 1993). Kim's view, which is not Davidson's, is actually more ramified and betrays, by its detail, the difficulty of confirming it in any of its probable forms. Notably, of course, supervenientism depends on the assumption of the causal closure of physical nature. But if (as Davidson admits) intentional phenomena can play a causal role, or, further, if, according to Davidson's argument, there can be no psychophysical laws, *or* if Davidson's "anomalous monism" is either incoherent or profoundly problematic as to its coherence, then (1) the closure of the physical world cannot be demonstrated, (2) supervenience cannot be demonstrated or taken for granted, and (3) extensionalism must remain problematic.

70. See Alfred Tarski, "The Concept of Truth in Formalized Languages," and postscript, in *Logic, Semantics, Metamathematics,* ed. by John Corcoran, trans. J. H. Woodger, 2d ed. (Indianapolis: Hackett, 1983). Corcoran once told me (private communication) that Tarski was rather pained by Davidson's application of his theory to natural languages—that is, along the lines of the remark just cited, which amounts to a complete reversal of Tarski's opinion.

71. Fodor and Lepore, *Holism,* pp. 102–103.

72. Compare, for instance, Jerry A. Fodor, *A Theory of Content and Other Essays* (Cambridge: MIT Press, 1990), and *Concepts: Where Cognitive Science Went Wrong* (Oxford: Clarendon, 1998).

73. See Davidson, "Radical Interpretation," pp. 128–130.

74. See Davidson, "A Coherence Theory of Truth and Knowledge," p. 309; compare pp. 311–313.

75. Davidson, "Radical Interpretation," p. 135.

76. Ibid., p. 130.

77. See ibid., p. 138; and Fodor and Lepore, *Holism,* pp. 60–61.

78. Davidson, "Radical Interpretation," p. 139.

79. Ibid., p. 137; "A Coherence Theory of Truth and Knowledge," p. 308.

80. Fodor and Lepore, *Holism,* p. 59.

81. See Davidson, "Afterthoughts, 1987."

82. *Holism,* p. 101.

83. See Wilfrid Sellars, "The Language of Theories." Interestingly, Rorty ignores the question, though he is obviously aware of it. See Rorty, introduction to *Empiricism and the Philosophy of Mind,* by Wilfrid Sellars. For an opposed view, see Hilary Putnam, *The Many Faces of Realism* (La Salle: Open Court, 1987), Lecture I.

84. See Dennett, chap. 4 in *Consciousness Explained;* and *Content and Consciousness* (London: Routledge and Kegan Paul, 1969), pp. 189–190.

85. See Dennett, chap. 5 in *Consciousness Explained.*

86. Ibid., chap. 4.

87. See Wilfred Sellars, "Philosophy and the Scientific Image of Man," in *Science, Perception and Reality* (London: Routledge and Kegan Paul, 1963); and Paul M. Churchland, *A Neurocomputational Perspective: The Nature of Mind and the Structure of Science* (Cambridge: MIT Press, 1989), pp. 17–22.

88. Compare Nancy Cartwright, *How the Laws of Physics Lie* (Oxford: Clarendon, 1983); and Bas C. van Fraassen, *Laws and Symmetry* (Oxford: Clarendon, 1989).

89. See Sellars, "Philosophy and the Scientific Image of Man"; also, for an illuminating reflection on Sellars's text, Hilary Putnam, *The Many Faces of Realism* (La Salle: Open Court, 1987), Lecture I.

90. See Brandom, *Making It Explicit;* and *Articulating Reasons* (Cambridge: Harvard University Press, 2000); and Rorty, "Robert Brandom on Social Practices and Representations"; and introduction to *Empiricism and the Philosophy of Mind.*

91. Rorty, "Introduction," p. 4.

92. See Richard Rorty, "Daniel Dennett on Intrinsicality," in *Philosophical Papers,* vol. 3 (Cambridge: Cambridge University Press, 1998); also, the discussion of Rorty and Dennett in Margolis, chap. 2 in *Reinventing Pragmatism.*

93. *Holism,* p. 7.

94. Ibid., p. 1. Italics in original.

95. Ibid. Italics in original.

96. See my chapter 1, above. A plausible line of speculation is sketched, informally, in Jerome Bruner, *Child's Talk: Learning to Use Language* (New York: W. W. Norton, 1983), chap. 2.

97. One begins to see that Rorty invokes holism chiefly as a device by which to preclude the need for any metaphysics or epistemology. I was struck by this fact, reflecting on the noticeably insistent way in which Rorty treats Dennett as a "holist"—close to the "holism" Rorty assigns to Davidson. See Richard Rorty, "Daniel Dennett on Intrinsicality," in *Philosophical Papers,* vol. 3. Here, Rorty is discussing Dennett's views in *Consciousness Explained.* I resolved to see whether the attribution was justified at all. It was not! There is only one use of "holism" indexed in Dennett's book and that has absolutely no bearing on Rorty's interpretation. The fact is, Dennett is (on his own say-so) an old-fashioned realist and materialist and believes his argument is strengthened by straightforward empirical evidence. Rorty attempts to color the reading of Dennett's philosophy of mind so as to accord with his own "postmodernist" tolerance of materialism, that is, on less than philosophical grounds.

I think it not unreasonable to construe Rorty's use of "holist" as a device for deflecting attention from the fact that Dennett, like Davidson, vindicates extensionalism in a straightforward way and that, on his own advice, Dennett need no longer bother.

98. *Holism,* p. 8.

99. Ibid., p. 206.

100. Ibid., p. 207.

101. Ibid., p. 23.

102. Ibid., p. 2.

103. See John Dewey, *Logic: The Theory of Inquiry* (New York: Henry Holt, 1938).

104. Churchland has met their objection (in this sense) in a very strong and convincing way. See Paul M. Churchland, "Conceptual Similarity across Sensory and Neural Diversity:

The Fodor-Lepore Challenge Answered," in Paul M. Churchland and Patricia S. Churchland, *On the Contrary: Critical Essays, 1987–1997* (Cambridge: MIT Press, 1998).

105. Daniel C. Dennett, "Toward a Cognitive Theory of Consciousness," in *Brainstorms: Philosophical Essays on Mind and Psychology* (Montgomery: Bradford Books, 1978), p. 163.

106. See Daniel C. Dennett, "Artificial Intelligence in Philosophy and Psychology," in *Brainstorms;* and Dennett, *Content and Consciousness*, pp. 189–190, which reads very much like Sellars's eliminativism.

107. Daniel C. Dennett, introduction in *Brainstorms*, p. xviii.

108. Daniel C. Dennett, "Why the Law of Effect Will Not Go Away," in *Brainstorms*, pp. 82–83.

109. See, particularly, J. C. Webb, "Gödel's Theorem and Church's Thesis," in *Language, Logic, and Method*, ed. Robert S. Cohen and Marx W. Wartofsky (Dordrecht: D. Reidel, 1983). Dennett relies on Webb's analysis, but Webb instructively demurs.

110. See Paul M. Churchland, *The Engine of Reason, the Seat of the Soul: A Philosophical Journey into the Brain* (Cambridge: MIT Press, 1995); also, "Conceptual Similarity across Sensory and Neural Diversity."

111. Churchland, *A Neurocomputational Perspective*, p. 6.

112. Paul M. Churchland, "Folk Psychology," in Paul M. Churchland and Patricia S. Churchland, *On the Contrary: Critical Essays, 1987–1997* (Cambridge: MIT Press, 1998), p. 9.

113. See P. H. Strawson, "Persons," in *Concepts, Theories, and the Mind-Body Problem*, ed. H. Feigl, M. Scriven, and G. Maxwell, Minnesota Studies in the Philosophy of Science, vol. 2 (Minneapolis: University of Minnesota Press, 1958); mentioned by Churchland. See also the very lively account in Stephen P. Stich, *Deconstructing the Mind* (New York: Oxford University Press, 1996), chap. 1.

114. See [G. W. F. Hegel,] *Hegel's Philosophy of Mind: Being Part Three of the Encyclopedia of the Philosophical Sciences (1930)*, trans. William Wallace, *together with the Zusätze in Boumann's text (1845)*, trans. A. V. Miller (Oxford: Clarendon, 1971).

115. See Churchland, "Folk Psychology," p. 12. For a more favorable account, see Joseph Margolis, *Historical Thought, Constructed World: A Conceptual Primer for the Turn of the Century* (Berkeley: University of California Press, 1995).

Index

Chomskyan caveats on, 27–28, 30–31
computational view of (Pinker), 19–21
Darwinian reduction of, 20, 22, 24–27
"folk" account of, 23–24
and Idealism, 11–14
Monod, Jacques, 25
Moore, G. E., 11, 12
Mühlhäusler, Peter, 34–35

Nagel, Ernest, 67
Nagel, Thomas, 8, 30, 31
"Natural-Computation" (Pinker), 21
naturalism, 7, 78
Chomsky on, 28–29
as "naturalizing" (Quine, Davidson), 7–8, 27
pragmatist view of, 7
Neurath, Otto, 123, 131
Nietzsche, Friedrich, 13, 14, 102

objectivism, 53–54, 58
"observation sentences" (Quine), 113, 121–123, 126
and Carnap, 132
and extensionalism, 130–131
among infants, 124–125
and "observation," 126, 127
"primitive," 128
and *Protokollsätze*, 122
Olafson, Frederick, 154

Peirce, C. S., 3, 14, 50, 87, 144
Penrose, Roger, 24–25
Pinker, Steven, 6–7, 19, 21, 25, 29, 39
Platonic Forms (Platonism), 61, 63, 86
Plotkin, Henry, 39–40
pluralism (Putnam), 45–48, 53, 62
and "cultural relativity," 46–48
and realism, 46
vs. relativism and objectivism, 46
Poincaré, Henri, 4
Popper, Karl, 4
pragmatism, 1, 2, 5, 7, 8, 12, 76, 106, 121
prepositions, 60
Protagoras (Protagorean), 43, 46, 66, 91
Protokollsätze, 111, 122
Pythagorean theorem, 42, 55–56, 59

Quine, W. V. (Quinean), 2–5, 17, 27, 28, 30, 31–32, 47, 57–58, 61–62, 67, 69–70, 86, 94, 105–141, 145–146
on Carnap, 119, 132
and Davidson, 120–124, 135–137
Darwinian theme in, 133
and Dewey, 169
and Duhem, 113
external holism in, 107–124, 130, 133
Friedman on, 153
and "holophrastic sentences," 47, 57, 58, 110–113, 118–119, 121–122, 127–132

and "indeterminacy of translation," 47, 57–58, 62, 106, 108–118, 119, 125, 159
and "inscrutability of reference," 132–133
internal holism in, 107, 117–119, 125
on "observation sentences" ("observation"), 126–132
Orenstein on, 153–154
and positivism, 3, 107–108, 111, 119, 122
as pragmatist, 4, 131
Pursuit of Truth, 47, 125, 127–129
Putnam on, 167–168
on "radical translation," 114–117, 121, 127, 132–133
and scientism, 5–8, 119, 120, 170
and Sellars, 5
on "stimulus meaning" ("stimulation"), 124–133
"Two Dogmas," 2, 16, 106, 107, 117, 119, 120, 146
and Wittgenstein, 135
Word and Object, 3, 5, 47, 107, 118, 131–132

Ranke, Leopold von, 44
realism, 11, chap. 3, 146
reductionism:
and ampliative materialism (Chomsky), 38, 40
and Brentano's distinction, 39–40
defined as reductive materialism, 38–39
Reichenbach, Hans, 4, 17
relativism:
Burnyeat on, 66
and coherence, 65
incommensurabilism a form of, 43
and rationality, 44
and realism, 46
as relationalism, 43, 66
as solipsism (Putnam), 43–44, 45, 52
Theaetetus on, 43, 66
and truth (truth-values), 44
Rorty, Richard, 1–8, 31, 77–78, 81, 86, 87–91, 94, 97–98, 106–107, 120, 121, 142–143, 161
Russell, Bertrand, 1, 3, 11, 12, 82, 105, 106, 107

Schelling, Friedrich von, 12, 14, 50
"scientific image" (Sellars), 6
scientific method (science), 28, 31
and first- and third-person discourse, 28
scientism, chap. 4
and analytic philosophy, 16–17
as Cartesianism, 11
characterized, 6–7
Searle, John, 8, 30
Sellars, Wilfrid (Sellarsian), 4–6, 9, 90, 92, 106–107, 118, 119, 135
"Empiricism and the Philosophy of Mind," 5, 6, 106
Sellarsian "pragmatists," 4–5

sensory "stimulation" (Quine), 109, 111, 113, 115
  and "assent," 110
  contrasted with *Protokollsätze,* 111
  evidentiary role of, 110–111
  and Kuhn and Davidson, 110
  not perceptual, 109
  See also holism; "observation sentences"
    (Quine); Quine, W. V.: on "radical trans-
    lation"
skepticism, 78
Skinner, B. F. (Skinnerian), 28, 32
Smith, Neil, 37
Strawson, P. F., 3
supervenience (supervenientism), 51–52, 136

Tarski, Alfred, 77, 83, 91–96, 101–102, 123, 136–
  139
Theaetetus (Plato), 43, 46, 66, 91–92
"true":
  and *adaequatio,* 78, 82
  Aristotle on, 82, 86
  as constructivist (Hegel), 79–80
  as correspondentist, 84, 87
  as deflationary (Rorty), 77, 79, 83, 86, 89
  as disquotational (Tarski), 77, 79, 83, 86, 89
  Dummett on meaning and, 103
  as epistemic, 87
  as holist, 83–86, 95, 101
  James on, 87
  as indefinable (Davidson), 93, 96

made (James), 81, 86
McDowell on, 84–86, 87–88
as minimalist (Horwich), 79, 93
as normative (McDowell), 89, 96
Quine on, 86
as realist (Wittgenstein), 80–82, 85, 88–89,
  94
and relation to meaning (Davidson), 98–99,
  101–102
as semantic only, 77, 79, 84, 86, 89
Tarski on, 91–92, 94
Wittgenstein on, 80–84
truth, chap. 3
  pragmatist theory of, 161–162
  Ramsey on, 165–166
  Wittgenstein and Heidegger on, 163

Vienna Circle (positivism), 17

Wilson, E. O., 29, 37
Winch, Peter, 44
Wittgenstein, Ludwig (Wittgensteinian), 1, 6,
  45, 61, 80–84, 86, 102, 105–107, 118, 134–
  135, 140, 145, 147
  and internal holism, 107, 118, 134–135
  Notebooks, 81–82
  Passmore on, 165
  Philosophical Investigations, 16, 105–107, 118,
    124, 134
  Tractatus, 80–81, 105–107